Both boys were sitting up, staring at each other from their separate beds. John gasped. "You mean to say— good heavens, you are telling me you don't know?"

"Know what?" Jesus demanded.

"But you must know!" John said. He came, almost angrily, to perch beside his cousin on the couch. He sat there, staring into the tormented face. "You were born with the knowledge. You are the one who must save us."

"I am but twelve years old!"

"We will soon be men. We are men already in the sight of God. And we both have a thing to do. But I am nothing compared to you," John said bluntly. "I will simply go ahead to prepare the way. When the time comes I will tell the people who you are."

John sprang up abruptly and plunged to the window. All his bright bravado had vanished. His shoulders were hunched together, bowed, as if under some intolerable burden; he seemed very young and defenseless as he stood there, gazing out into the night.

Jesus waited, shaken. It was hard to breathe, such fear, such sudden terrible fear for his cousin clutched his heart.

John finally turned to face him, but it was a moment before he could bring himself to say the words: *You are the Messiah.*

THREE FROM GALILEE

THREE FROM GALILEE
The Young Man from Nazareth

Marjorie Holmes

BANTAM BOOKS
TORONTO · NEW YORK · LONDON · SYDNEY · AUCKLAND

THREE FROM GALILEE

*A Bantam Book / published by arrangement with
Harper & Row, Publishers, Inc.*

PRINTING HISTORY

*Harper & Row edition published September 1985
Bantam edition / December 1986*

*Bantam Books are published by Bantam Books, Inc. Its trade-
mark, consisting of the words "Bantam Books" and the por-
trayal of a rooster, is Registered in U.S. Patent and Trademark
Office and in other countries. Marca Registrada. Bantam
Books, Inc., 666 Fifth Avenue, New York, New York 10103.*

PRINTED IN THE UNITED STATES OF AMERICA

KR   0 9 8 7 6 5 4 3 2 1

To my wonderful husband, Dr. George Schmieler, whose patience, confidence and encouragement spurred me on at times when the task seemed impossible, and whose keen insight and suggestions were a genuine contribution to this book.

Acknowledgment

I want to acknowledge the invaluable help of Dr. Roy Blizzard, former instructor in Hebrew, Biblical History and Archaeology at the University of Texas. Dr. Blizzard studied at the Hebrew University in Jerusalem, has worked on archaeological excavations throughout Israel, speaks fluent Hebrew and is the author of *Let Judah Go Up First* and coauthor of *Understanding the Difficult Words of Jesus*. It has been my privilege to accompany him on several historic and archaeological seminars in Israel. He is one of the few Americans licensed to guide in Israel. Dr. Blizzard has been my constant consultant for accuracy in writing this book. If there are any errors, they are not his, but mine.

Author's Note

This book is a novel, a work of fiction. I do not pretend to claim that this is the way things actually happened; only that, given the facts of Jesus' life and times as we know them, this is the way they *could* have happened.

It was written humbly, with great reverence and love and conviction. I can only pray that most people, Jews and Christians alike, will read it as a believable and dramatic retelling of the story we all know so much (and so little) about.

As John, Jesus' favorite apostle, wrote in concluding his own account of his Master's remarkable life: *And there were many other things which Jesus did, which, if they should be written down, every one, I suppose that the world itself could not contain the books that should be written* (John 21:25).

BOOK ONE

Boyhood

Chapter 1

*H*annah had been restless all night. Her husband, Joachim, beside her on the pallet, heard the dry rustling protest of the straw tick repeatedly as she threshed about, felt her small bony hand groping for his. A habit she didn't even know she had, but one that always moved him strangely. She had been so young when he first brought her to his bed—scarcely twelve—and so frightened. But in sleep, at least, so trusting.

As he had clasped that tiny claw long ago and so many times since, he clasped it now, stroking it, trying to soothe her.

"Mary!" she cried out plaintively. "*Mary.*"

"Hush," he muttered, though his own heart broke. "It's all right, Hannah, my little one, she's—the Lord is with them."

If his wife heard, she gave no sign. With a little jerk, the hand was withdrawn. She turned her back and began to breathe deeply. Now it was her husband who lay troubled, staring into the darkness.

Where were they? It had been weeks since a messenger from the caravan had brought them Joseph's letter. Their obvious poverty smote Mary's father. For it was written, not even on papyrus but on a shard of pottery, this letter saying Mary and Joseph were leaving Egypt at last. "Jerusalem should be safe now. I'll surely find work there." Mary and the child were well, Joseph added.

Hannah had wept wildly. "But when are they coming *home?*" she demanded of Joachim. "When will I ever see my grandchild?"

3

"Now, now, they will write again," he told her.

But this silence. This strange silence. Mentally Joachim lay tracing their journey. They would come along the coastal plain, the *Derech Hayam*, Way of the Sea. He hoped they had joined a caravan. He thought of robbers—and of that devil Herod. For the news of Herod's death, which had brought such great rejoicing, was only to be followed by a cruel blow: another monster was mounting the throne, Herod's son, Archelaus. This news evidently hadn't reached Joseph before they departed.

No, now, stop it. Worries loomed larger in the darkness, multiplied, did no good. Joachim kicked off the coverlet, creaked heavily to the doorway, then turned and trudged back to tuck it about the small figure hunched against the wall.

A lamp burned in the niche beside the cupboard where a bag of goat's milk hung. Joachim reached for the bag, tempted, but sternly put it back that he might first whisper his waking prayer of thanks to God "for having returned to me my soul, which was in your keeping." It had special significance for him this day as he prayed fervently as well for his daughter's safe return. Joachim then drank deeply of the milk, its cool raw strength a solace to his dry throat. He wiped his grizzled mouth and stood staring out the window, a big blunt country man still in his nightshift. His hair, once bushy and red as a torch, had thinned and faded, but the curly mat on his chest was still vivid.

He gazed out the window, grateful for morning.

Birds were beginning to chirp. In the gently graying light he could see the mountains, the fields, and nearby the outlines of the sheepfold, the cistern—and the shed where the ox was kept. The place where the whole strange business had begun. His shed! An ancient tumbledown shed. For it was there, Mary had told them, incredibly, in that very shed, that an angel had appeared before her, bearing news so profound it would change her life forever—and for that matter, their lives as well. A story it took almost superhuman faith to believe. But he had believed. And in time, even Hannah. . . . *His* shed, Joachim sometimes realized, in awe and wonderment.

Later, he and Hannah had learned that the heavenly child itself was born in a cave. Among the beasts! They were bewildered. Nothing they had experienced heretofore had shocked them quite so much.

The sodden earth smelled sweet. A cock's crowing drilled the silence; other cocks began to answer from neighboring hills, a raucous, faintly comical chorus that lifted his spirits. Soon it would be time to get into the fields; things were less threatening by daylight, and work helped.

Joachim turned, startled by the patter of footsteps. "Hannah!"

Her thin flyaway hair was already skewered atop her head. Unlike him, she was fully dressed. "Our daughter will be home on this day," she announced. Her tone was firm, almost flat, but her deep-set eyes were excited. "Before nightfall."

"Hannah, don't," her husband pleaded.

"But they're coming, they're on their way," she insisted. "I know it, something tells me! I knew it the minute I heard the cock crow. *Mary*, it kept shouting, *Mary!*"

Reluctantly, Joachim laughed. He would never understand her. "It said nothing of the kind to me."

"I'll need more wood for the fire. And food—more milk. Joachim, you *didn't* drink that whole skin?" she scolded. "Well, no matter, Esau can get more. And meat— Joachim, don't work in the fields today, it's too wet—slaughter a lamb."

"A lamb!" he protested. "That's extravagant. We can't spare a lamb right now."

"Well, then, a kid. Surely we can have meat for our daughter's homecoming."

"Hannah, stop." He caught her wrist, firm with his intense little wife when he had to be. "You must not count on this. I can't let you be hurt."

"Never you mind about that," she said defiantly, almost gaily. Twisting away, she began breaking sticks across her knee. "For once, just once, believe me—the way you were always so quick to believe Mary," she could not resist adding.

Instantly she regretted her words. Poor Joachim,

standing there in his nightshift, looking so stricken. Loving their firstborn no more than she did—no, that would be impossible, for Mary was her pride, her passion—but in a way that sometimes maddened Hannah, for it somehow shut her out. Also, it was most unusual, this relationship between her husband and their daughter. Didn't good Jewish men thank the Lord every day "that thou has not made me a woman" and generally prefer their male children? It was almost unseemly, the way Joachim acted. But then they were so alike, those two—both dreamers, even Joachim, beneath his gruff exterior. They'd had their little games and songs and secrets from the time Mary was a tiny girl. To Hannah's dismay, even when Mary was older it was her father she more often turned to. Hannah felt baffled and forsaken even as she remembered.

But this was no time to rekindle old coals. Not when she and Joachim had drawn so close in their mutual concern. Not when her own conviction was so strong.

Impetuously, she flung her wiry arms around him. She had to stand on tiptoe to reach his broad chest. "I know, I know, I'm not as devout as you; I would never claim God spoke to me, not even in a dream. But *something* has told me. We must get ready, for they will be here this day."

Sighing, Joachim stomped back to their chamber. But a strange sensation was rising up within him to match her mood. Such folly, he warned himself. Exasperation, an almost constant companion, warred with his love for Hannah. His helpless abiding tenderness. Hannah, so tiny, dry, and caustic, who had little imagination and so was often impatient with those who had. Yet who could be so stubborn about her own ideas. And so devastated when proven wrong. To resist her, however, was fruitless misery. And there was always the chance, he consoled himself—in this case the sweet possibility—that she might be right.

The children had roused and began to appear. They were overjoyed at the news. Only Esau, their eldest, who was blind and crippled, seemed puzzled, realizing that actually there had been no word. Nonetheless, they flew to do their mother's bidding. And by midafternoon when Salome, married now and expecting a child herself, came trudging up the hill, the house was scrubbed and shining. Hannah had flung the doors wide. Fresh palm branches were strewn on the floor. The sun was bright once again, drying the glistening puddles. Even Esau had hobbled into the fields and plucked an armload of wild lilies. Salome helped her mother plunge them into water and set them about, a sweet explosion of scarlet and gold and blue that filled the humble rooms.

Outside, she spoke quietly to her father. "Why is our mother so sure?"

He shook his head, grinned faintly. "I am the last person to explain the ways of your mother. She even wanted me to slaughter a lamb."

"A lamb!" Salome exclaimed. "In the middle of the week? Not even on a feast day?"

"I know, I know, but your sister—after all she's been through—" Joachim shuddered, unable to speak of it further, the thing that haunted him and made his wife cry out so often in the night: the butchery of all those babies in Bethlehem. How Mary, Joseph, and the child had had to flee for their very lives. "When she does return it will be a feast day indeed! As for now, to appease your mother I at least took some large fat ducks to be properly killed."

"And if she's disappointed?"

His big rough hand went to his brow. "She'll suffer, we'll all suffer. She'll have one of her headaches, I fear. But wait, let's not expect the worst. Your husband will come up for supper. I'll open a fresh wine jug; we'll celebrate anyway. And who knows?" Slowly, deliberately, he turned his whole body, searching the road that led into the village, his eyes anxious, willing the sight into existence.

Except for a boy herding his goats, the road was vacant. Joachim could hear the bleating of the animals, along with the voices of his family from the yard, where a fire was already kindled under the spit. To his dismay, Hannah insisted on preparing the ducks early. Joseph, she said, liked his fowl well done. . . . And suddenly another scene came flooding back, another night of commotion and anticipation at the cooking of a duck: The night Mary had overridden their objections and invited her beloved to eat with them. A time when Hannah had disapproved of Joseph so violently the very thought of his joining them had sent her to her bed.

"I'd better go help," Salome said. She stood a moment regarding her father—a tall, pensive girl, already motherly at fourteen. She carried the baby in her plumpish, dimpled body with an air of both humility and pride. There was a serenity about Salome that went strangely with her youth. She was very fair, with her lovely skin and large velvety eyes, but plainer, even so, than Mary. She was resigned to the fact she would never be as dear to Joachim as his first daughter. "Try not to worry, Father." She pressed his arm. "I do hope Mary comes soon."

The sun was getting lower beyond the olive grove. In the blue distance, Mount Tabor was drawing on its cloaks of mauve and purple. Matthew, ten, already in from herding the sheep, was perched on the fold, counting them carefully with his rod as they entered. Joachim could hear their gentle blatting; he answered his second son's wave.

It was later than Joachim had thought; the other animals must be fed.

He headed for the stable, slow-footed, determined to prolong his chores, dreading what awaited his return. He crouched through the low door, began forking hay. The place smelled musty from the rains, strong of animal hides and dust and the tang of the rustling hay. The fragrance of roasting fowl began to drift inside. Joachim sensed the increased activity, and when he heard voices shouting his heart lurched foolishly. But striding to peer out, he saw it was only the children welcoming Salome's husband, Ephraim.

Joachim could hear him laughing. Ephraim was a big fair fellow, young and exuberant; he had bright friendly eyes and a way of making everyone feel better. Joachim was suddenly relieved and fortified. Bracing himself, he went forth to meet his son-in-law.

But he could scarcely bear to look at Hannah, who could no longer postpone the meal. Curtly she ordered the children to carry the smoking meat indoors. The ducks lay, crisp and brown and succulent, bigger than Joachim remembered and almost painfully festive. Grimly Hannah was putting last-minute touches to the low table. He could see, as she handed him towels for the washing, that she was fighting back tears. But when he reached out a hand to comfort her, she twisted aside.

"We will put a portion aside for them. The day is not yet over!"

Then, as the men and boys sat down upon the cushions, as Joachim lifted his hands for the blessing, a little cry escaped his wife. She flung down her serving tool and ran for the door. Here she emitted another cry, a sound of such triumph and rejoicing it was almost like an animal in pain.

Joachim arose, incredulous. The others sprang up too, pushed past him. By the time he reached the door, all the family were flying down the hill, Hannah in the lead, arms outspread.

Joachim did not follow. He couldn't; something held him, some sweet yet awful paralysis that would only allow him to support himself here at the sill, his big arms braced. She was home at last, their darling, *his* darling; she was safe. Enough just to savor this knowing. It must be enough, for his legs felt weak. And there was something more: Let Hannah have this first precious moment with them.

For he remembered how he had had to restrain her that bitterly cold morning when the young people had set off from Nazareth for Bethlehem, Mary big with child, but so pathetically small herself as Joseph led the donkey. He remembered the fog, the cold, the dark looming mountains, and how Hannah, in her desperation, would have run after them, crying out so late—too late—the words it had taken her so long to utter: "I believe, oh, Mary, I believe!" No, let her be first to embrace the three who were approaching.

Sternly, Joachim tried to compose his working face. His eyes were wet; he could scarcely see them: they were like figures in a dream—Joseph, once again cheerfully leading the donkey, and Mary, now bouncing along beside it, waving and smiling even as she supported the child who proudly rode its back. My grandchild! Joachim realized, shaken. My first grandson.

* * *

Hannah carried the child excitedly inside: a beautiful boy, a little past two years old. His small brown sandaled feet dangled, his arms clung tightly around her neck. He had an explosion of blue-black curls and huge sweet shining eyes. Like his parents, he was deeply tanned from the desert sun.

"We all look like Bedouins," Mary said, during the laughing and hugging and crying. Her teeth flashed white in her strangely dusky face. It was very becoming. She was even more beautiful than her family remembered. "And we're so unkempt, but there was no place to stop without spending the night."

Mary was gazing around the room, this room of her childhood she had dreamed of so long. Its spicy fragrance of fire and food, the flowers, the familiar chests and cupboards—how could they be so much the same? As if she had never been away. And the people, these dear faces and voices—the same, the same, and yet even in these few years, so changed. For a startled minute they seemed to her almost strangers. Esau had shot up taller than she was. Little Salome, big with child. Worry had darkened the circles beneath her mother's hollow eyes. Joachim's bushy hair had thinned; his broad shoulders were no longer so erect. . . . It hurt, it hurt to notice. In a burst of tenderness, Mary ran to embrace them both again. "And we were *so* anxious to get home!"

But she too was different now: a mother, a woman who had traveled far; she sensed that her family was a little in awe of her. She and Joseph were indeed weary and travel-stained, however. Hannah, refusing to set the child down, ordered her other daughters to fill the basins, a task Salome had already begun.

"And you must be hungry. We'll reheat the supper. Fortunately, there's plenty. I *knew* you were coming!" her mother triumphed. "Didn't I, Joachim? Didn't I foretell their return this very day?" She kept kissing the little boy, who was gazing about, bewildered. But when his father appeared in the doorway, he struggled and held out his arms.

Joseph, with the help of Esau and Matthew, had been unloading and watering the donkey. He was taller than

Joachim remembered, even more handsome, and certainly more mature. His bearing, always graceful and self-assured, had a new authority about it as he entered the room to embrace them. His shoulders seemed broader to the arms Joachim flung gratefully about him. Those still-radiant sea-gray eyes—there was something newly sober about them, too. Truly he had proved himself as a man; he had seen their daughter through a strange ordeal, even terrible danger, and brought her safely home. Their Mary and—her child.

Joachim turned to fill his gaze with the little boy, who was crying, striving to reach his father. "Now, now," Joseph soothed, kissing Hannah as she reluctantly gave him over. "He's just tired."

"And hungry," Hannah declared. "We must feed him. Grandmother must feed her little one at once." She flew about, deriding her own neglect, ordering Judith, her eight-year-old, to help clear away the food and warm it. "But don't touch the milk. I myself will pour it for this precious baby."

Already Hannah had staked her claim to this, her first grandchild.

Salome, who would soon be in labor herself, felt only a brief pang as she trudged about doing her mother's bidding. Salome had never envied her sister, who was so beautiful, always so poised and sparkling, drawing everyone to her. Salome's own nature was shy, a bit submissive; she found it hard to meet people's eyes. But she had a way of looking up suddenly, with a quick little smile that charmed them.

She had worshiped Mary since childhood, been inconsolable when they were apart. And the mystery of Mary's conceiving had only intensified her devotion. Salome had been so young when it was first discovered that Mary was with child . . . and not yet married! Her distraught parents, how they had tried to spare her. Salome hadn't understood their story, only that the whole family must rally in loving defense of Mary, who could do no wrong. Of all the children, Salome had been the most worried about the three so far away from home. But now here they were, warm, real, alive! She could hardly contain her relief and delight.

What did it matter that though her mother's fierce little heart loved fully, it had such a special place for the few on whom it fastened? Let Hannah rejoice in this child, as both parents had rejoiced in Mary above all others. God must have his reasons.

Washed, changed, and fed, the little boy was soon toddling about the floor. His young aunts and uncles adored him, vied for his attention. Matthew was chasing Judith in a game of hide and seek which made the baby shriek with laughter. Esau cheered from the darkness.

"Except for a couple of Egyptian children, he's had no one to play with," Mary told Salome as they washed the dishes. "And to think he'll soon have someone else," she marveled. "You, my little sister, married!" She hugged the warm sweet bulk beside her, in which a new heart beat. "How wonderful that the Lord has blessed your womb."

"It's been a great comfort to our mother." Salome looked up with that quick, half-shy little smile. "She will attend me, of course. Oh, Mary," she said intensely, "you will never know how much she missed you. We sometimes feared for her health."

They both regarded Hannah, who was searching the cupboard for a ball of yarn and some clay rattles that Esau's skilled fingers had fashioned for his nephew's homecoming. Usually the youngsters were not allowed to play in the small crowded house, but tonight was exceptional. It was still too wet for the family to visit on the roof; the men were gathered around the glowing fire, plying Joseph with questions about Egypt. Mary and Salome hung up their towels and sat watching as Hannah joined the children on the hard-packed clay floor, tossing the ball to the little newcomer, then scambling about to help him find it. The sisters smiled; it had been years since they had seen their mother so animated.

Joachim smiled too, turning to watch them. How the little boy responded, clapping his hands, hugging Hannah in return when she caught him fervently to her. Joachim's eyes were fixed in wonder on the child, puzzled, searching—for what? A curious sense of hope mingled with his vague unease.

"I love his name," Salome said. "Jesus. A fine old name, although never before used in our family. It's beautiful, it suits him. I'm glad you chose it." As Mary hesitated, Salome pressed her hand. "Was it terrible for you, Mary? Were you very frightened?"

"Yes, at first."

"And later, in Egypt?"

"Often there too," Mary acknowledged. "But Joseph comforted me." Her eyes sought him out, where he stood in earnest conversation with the men beside the embers. Even his shadow in silhouette against the whitewashed wall was fair—so fair that even now, weary as she was, and surrounded at last by those she had been so homesick for, she longed only to be near him. "Oh, Salome, no one will ever know how brave he was, how wise and strong, how hard he worked for us!" Mary sprang up, suddenly overcome with the wonder of it all: their incredible journey, their deliverance. "And God was with us," she added fervently. "It was he, even he, who sent us." She went to pick up her child. "It's late. We must take him home, Mother, and put him to bed."

"Home?" Hannah protested. "But you've only just arrived! And this is your home too. That house, the house you left, will be cold; it isn't ready."

"Father tells me he's taken care of it for us against our return. Joseph will build a fire—" She was suddenly unutterably tired. The vision of her own home, after the years of exile, was almost too sweet to believe.

At her signal Joseph stood up and came to claim the boy, holding him tenderly, his son. The others rose too, surrounding them, begging them to change their minds. There was plenty of room, they insisted. Plenty of pallets and covers. And they wanted to hear more about Bethlehem, the events that had driven them into Egypt, the village where the little family had lived, within sight of the Pyramids! In the first hours of reunion, of washing and eating and clearing up, there had been many questions and answers, a lively exchange of news. But they were eager to know more.

Joachim interceded. "No, now, let them go." He too

was exhausted, he realized. "God has brought them home. For now, let that be enough. We will have a lifetime to talk." He set about preparing the torches to light their way.

Mary's brothers held them high, leading the little procession down the steep old streets. The night was chill. A light rain had begun again, spattering the pomegranate and olive leaves. Their silver glistened in the tarry-smelling flames, and the air was sweet with blossoms. Mary ran a little ahead, face lifted, drinking it in, tugging at Joseph's hand, eager to see the house they had dreamed of so long. Her parents walked behind.

Hannah had insisted on coming too, throwing a shawl over her head, taking the child from Joseph, and carrying him wrapped snugly in a lamb's-wool blanket. Carefully she picked her way over the cobbles, clutching him to her breast. He was soon too heavy for her, however; when she stumbled, Joachim reached out his arms. "Let me have him."

Half fearfully, Joachim gathered Jesus close. It was the first time he had touched his grandson. Something had restrained him, as he had felt restrained at seeing the trio approaching—Mary and Joseph and the tiny stranger on the donkey—as before a mirage that might disappear. Now, as he felt the precious weight across his shoulder, the warm tender breath against his cheek, a great shout of joy arose in Joachim, a sense of some tremendous, almost absurd relief.

Why, he's just a little boy! he realized—although what he had expected he didn't quite know—a perfectly normal little boy who looks like Mary.

The evening flashed before him, scenes so merry and natural Joachim wanted to laugh: the chasing about of all the children, Hannah's getting down on the floor to play with them. Joachim was so shaken he had to press the child tighter. How long it had been since he had seen his wife in such a mood!

Chapter 2

———————◆———————

*I*t was spring now, truly spring—the second week of April,
for the doves had returned. Mary awoke one morning to the
sweet incessant music of their crooning. Looking out the
tiny slit of window, she saw them—some pied, some fawn-
colored, but most of them white as rain lilies—festooning
every tree in the garden, perched on walls and bushes, dipping their dainty heads to drink from the wet sparkling
grass.

A cry of delight escaped her. She ran to lift up her boy
and carry him to the window to see. And later, as they
walked to the well and home again, the birds were everywhere, fluttering and singing, clouds of them, as if little
living winged bouquets had dropped from heaven to welcome them home.

Not a sign of them was to be seen a few weeks before,
when Mary and Joseph had trudged their last weary mile
into Nazareth. Yet here they were, on schedule. You could
count on the doves; there was no deviation from their mi-
gration, not even by a day. As the prophet Jeremiah had
written, you could always "observe the time of their coming." Rejoicing, Mary set down her jug and ran after Jesus,
who was darting about, trying to catch them in his hands.
"Birds, birds!" he shouted, laughing as they darted off with
a silvery drumming of wings.

"Come, darling, we will see the birds when Mother
has finished her baking and we climb the hill."

Mary sang too as she opened the little bag of locust
flour she had brought all the way from Egypt, and mixed it
with spices and honey. Her heart, like the doves, had scarcely
15

left off its singing since her return. She felt akin to the doves, and grateful, as if God had sent these little messengers in welcome and reward, to observe the time of her own homecoming—and something more: to celebrate her life in its own new season.

For she realized now that she had been just a girl when she left, a very young girl, scared, confused, torn between her desperate love for Joseph and the awesome responsibility the Lord God himself had seen fit to put upon her body. No, more than her body—her very soul. But she had returned a woman. She had become a woman in that stable, in their ordeals on the desert, in the want they had known in Egypt, in Joseph's arms. Toughened by suffering, uplifted by love, she had failed neither her God nor her husband.

She could go forth into the morning, head high, fearing nothing, a proud young wife and mother leading her beautiful son. The women at the well confirmed this; they threw their arms around her in welcome, made a place for her in the line. There was the creak of rope and buckets, the sloshing of water into their vessels, a merry chattering above the mooing and blatting of animals at the trough. They vied to be first to share the village news, the latest gossip. Her own seeming fall from grace no longer mattered; they lavished kisses and compliments on her child.

Even her cousin Deborah, who now had two little girls clinging to her skirts. "Mary, Mary, why are you always so favored?" Deborah wailed. Deborah had a catlike beauty, a lively, excessive quality that made her dear. Their mothers had never quite succeeded in making them rivals. "Isn't it enough that you snatch the handsomest man in Nazareth from the rest of us? Do you have to produce such a firstborn son?"

Mary hugged her, relishing the old exaggeration: caustic, playful, half envy, half genuine affection. "Nonsense. Your Aaron is a wonderful man, and your daughters couldn't be more fair."

Smiling as she remembered, Mary put the cakes onto the coals. They were made from a recipe given her by a Bedouin woman. How kind and hospitable those dusky, jet-eyed people. Several times they had offered shelter in their long black tents: once from a sandstorm, again on bitter cold nights when jackals howled and there was nowhere else to turn. Mary had winced to see the women and children eagerly pulling off the heads and wings of the locusts, creatures that at home only spelled disaster, then drying the brittle bodies in the sun to be beaten into flour. But the little locust cakes were delicious.

She would carry some to Salome. Her sister had given birth two days before. Only a daughter, to everyone's disappointment. Nonetheless, there would be a celebration feast. Oh, there was so much to celebrate, and the doves proclaimed it! She would take Jesus out among the birds again, as she had promised. They would climb the plateau that encircled the town, so she could show him his homeland. They would follow the back route, and on the way they would gather flowers.

The dew was still heavy in the grass; their sandals were quickly soaked. But even this seemed wonderful after the brutal heat of Egypt. Sometimes Mary's throat still went parched and dry, and she would gulp whole pitchers of precious water. Her skin had lightened somewhat, but its sense of burning remained; she felt burned to the bone, seared by some fierce yet sacred fire, perhaps necessary to her own cleansing and reshaping. That must have been what God willed for her—and for Joseph. But even as the Lord had led their forefathers, he had brought them up out of Egypt! They had returned to Nazareth and to Galilee, the very flower of Israel. Their Promised Land. Pray heaven they would never have to leave it again.

Two hawks dipped above them, and higher in the sky black specks of vultures hung motionless, as if held by invisible threads. Something cold and nameless brushed Mary's heart. She rejected it violently. No, no, the threat was past, and she would not even think of the future. For now let it be sufficient, this bright sweet release into the cool breezes of the mountains, the jeweled wetness beneath her feet. On impulse, Mary fell to her knees and, like the birds, plunged her face into the moist clover. And Jesus, watching, did the same. What a mimic he was. Already he had little ways like his father, Joseph. Some people, eagerly scanning his face, even thought he resembled Joseph. Another miracle? No matter; it was enough that the two loved each other so much. The little boy could scarcely wait for his father's step at the door in the evening; he would fly into Joseph's arms. They would wrestle and play until Mary must make them stop. Joseph was already teaching him songs and psalms and whole passages from the Torah. In time, as was proper for Jewish fathers, he would teach this son his own trade in the carpenter shop.

Mary and her boy climbed on, clouds of doves whirring up about them at every step. The red-winged blackbirds had come back too, and finches and canaries, yellow as the vivid golden karkom and daffodils that paved the rolling hills. Butterflies dipped above the fragrant blossoms, and the steady hum of bees was background for the crooning chorus of the doves. But it was the doves that gave them most delight, spurting up in pairs, flirting their outspread tails.

The child's short legs tired; Mary lifted him to her shoulders. He liked to ride there, straddling her neck, clutching her forehead, surveying the world. And what a world it was from here! Below them, in the hollow, lay Nazareth, looking like a toy village of winding streets and shops. Its small, whitewashed stone-and-plaster houses clung to the surrounding hillsides. Other hills undulated as far as the eye could see, peering over each other's shoulders, then pitching into the Plain of Esdraelon or the valleys of the Jordan, or soaring to magnificent heights.

A brisk breeze that always blew in from the mountains tousled the boy's hair and twisted Mary's skirts as she pointed them out: "Over there in the distance, beyond those blue ridges—that's Mount Carmel. And closer, to the east—look, my darling, there is Mount Tabor. The psalmists have likened its rounded form to the breast of a beautiful woman. And that peak farther north is Mount Hattin. Though we can't see it from here, neither of them is far from the Sea of Galilee. There are many fish in its waters; sometime your father and I will take you there."

She had set down her basket. She kept turning,

breathing deeply of the cold bright air. "And look, to the right, where the sheep are grazing. Those are your grandfather's fields, where I used to play. Your grandfather Joachim would sometimes let me ride the ox—" she laughed—"to my mother's distress. His house is hidden by the trees, but we can see the beauty of the mountains from there too."

What joy to drink all this in once more! Nothing she and Joseph had seen in their travels could compare—except, perhaps, looking down from the Mount of Olives on the sacred Temple in Jerusalem. Certainly not the Pyramids, those huge moldy tombs stabbing the sky, or the Sphinx, secret and ominous, crouched on its paws: ugly monuments to long-dead kings, with only the lonely burning desert stretching endlessly toward the horizon. Mary shuddered. But today, oh how God had blessed her, for here she stood presenting this beautiful panorama to her son. Did he understand? No matter, for this was his home. He would grow up here; soon, too soon, he would be running about by himself, exploring these heights and fields and forests without her. Already his little limbs seemed to be stretching out, as if reviving in the mists and dews of Galilee, like a parched plant after rain.

Mary gripped his legs harder, pressed her lips against his knee. Then she set him down and gazed into his big excited eyes. For the doves had flocked here too; they were basking on the sunny rocks, walking in their little bobbing way among the flowers. As before, Jesus scampered among them, hands outstretched.

The sun was bright; the air was sweet with the perfume of hyacinths—whole hillsides were painted with their blue, as if someone had dumped on them buckets of sky. Scarlet poppies bloomed among them, like scattered drops of blood. Knee-high daffodils swayed in the wind. Mary knelt to gather some for her basket. When she looked up she saw that Jesus had somehow managed to capture a dove. He was squatted on the path, stroking it, talking softly to it. Then he saw, to her dismay, the open snare trap in the grasses behind it. Many people set these traps, wanting the birds for food or sacrifice. The poor thing must have been caught, and Jesus had released it: a female, Mary sensed, ready for nesting. Another bird, which could only be its mate, hovered frantically overhead.

Cradling the white treasure carefully in his hands, Jesus brought it to Mary to admire. "See, it likes me, it didn't like the net!"

"Yes, sweetheart, let it go, it wants to fly. It wants to lay its eggs." As she spoke, the male fluttered to their feet and began a ploy of limping off, dragging one wing.

"Here, bird, here!" Jesus shouted, running after the mate, trying to present his captive to him; but the female only flew to the child's shoulder and nestled there.

Jesus stood very still, frightened but awed. His black curls were wind-tossed. His tunic was very white in the sun. And as he stood so, the male dove returned, no longer alarmed, it seemed to Mary, and calmly perched on the other shoulder. A smile broke across the child's face. Cautiously reaching up, he cupped both feathered bundles and held them tenderly against his cheeks. Then he opened his hands. The birds fluttered an instant as if, it seemed to Mary, they were reluctant to leave; then they spurted upward, singing a song of love and joy.

The scene was as sudden and brief as the clouds that sometimes appear over the mountains and vanish almost before the eyes can comprehend. Nor was it so very strange, Mary told herself. It could happen to any little boy. Why then must her heart pound so? Why this sense of some trembling elation, mingled with an anguish she could not explain? It was one of many things she must ponder in her heart.

"Come, now," she said, and ran and caught him fiercely to her. "We must be on our way."

They found her father's house alive with women and children about to picnic on the grass. New babies always brought them swarming, long before the official celebration. Salome was the center of attention, holding her red-faced swaddled daughter as proudly as if she had been a son. Only her mother-in-law sat a little apart, a fat, rather disgruntled woman, looking unimpressed.

Hannah bustled about seeing to the food, in her glory. She loved eating outdoors where there was room to spread out, and the birds and grasshoppers and even the buzzing flies added to the liveliness. Also, this spontaneous gathering represented a triumph. Over the objections of Salome's in-laws, Hannah had insisted her daughter come home to be delivered. After all, if she the mother was to act as midwife, *she* was the one to be convenienced.

"Ah, but there was a battle," Hannah had informed Mary mischievously earlier. "To keep the peace I was forced to relent. But I knew the Lord would not let me down. As you know, your sister never fails to spend a part of each day with me." Hannah let this sink in as she vigorously stirred the pot. "Thus it was that she was here with me when the pains struck. Here she was, and here she will stay until the time of her purification."

The gibe was not lost on Mary. Salome was indeed a more dutiful daughter, she knew regretfully. Salome had not fallen desperately in love and insisted on having her way, but obediently accepted their choice of the tinner Ephraim. Evidently it had proved a happy match, except for his mother and sisters, who seemed to quarrel a great deal. Was it perhaps to escape them that Salome fled their company each day to be with her mother? Yes, surely, in part, for Salome was quiet and peace-loving. But Mary sensed that Salome clung to her parents not only to comfort herself but also to try to compensate for the suffering her sister had caused them.

Mary's heart went out to all of them as she remembered her own rebellion, and the shame that, however innocently, she had brought upon Hannah and Joachim: the pregnancy they could not, dare not even attempt to explain. The truth would only have made them laughingstocks in the village.

For Hannah, to whom pride meant so much, this was devastating. And then the cruel shock of realizing that she was not even to be present at the birth of her first grandchild! No wonder Hannah was so determined to have it her way when it came to Salome's baby. . . . And then the long separation. Nearly three years! Mary could not bear to think of her parents' pain—she thrust it aside, it would have shattered her if she let it. No, no, she could not even imagine how she and Joseph would feel if they had to be separated so long from their child.

In an access of love, Mary went to embrace Hannah, who was directing Judith to pass more cheese and dried fruit among the circle of guests, seated on cushions around the new mother. "I brought some cakes for the celebration," Mary said eagerly, "but why wait? I baked some little locust cakes."

"*Locusts?*" Hannah shuddered. "Vile noisy pests that devour the corn. I would sooner eat pork than have such a thing pass my mouth."

"They are very nourishing, Mother, when dried and ground into flour," Mary insisted. "And the bread and cakes they make are very good, especially the sweetened cakes."

"No, no, throw them out, throw them to the dogs."

Mary flushed, trying not to be hurt. How quickly her mother had fallen into her old sharp habits—even now, Mary thought, bewildered, though she loves me with a passion—as if to punish me for things neither of us can understand. In Mary's homesick dreaming, she had almost forgotten.

"I will do nothing of the kind," Mary said lightly. She kissed Hannah's cheek to allay the words' effect. "Come, Judith," she called. "Help me, we will carry them to Salome to decide."

Some of the women had overheard. They took up the merits and demerits of locust cookery, with Salome's mother-in-law surprisingly its most ardent advocate. Rousing from a kind of disapproving torpor, the woman began to talk, while greedily devouring the cakes. It seemed that for years her family had harvested the descending hordes, carried them home in baskets. On and on she went in her boring, authoritative voice. Locusts needn't just be pounded into flour, she claimed; they were delicious pickled or fried in olive oil.

Hannah was disgusted. *Heathens*, she thought. Smithies, pounding those creatures—and their pans. Inconsistently, though she and Joachim had picked Ephraim out, they felt superior to his family. Almost as they had felt superior toward the family of Joseph ben Jacob. It was not a matter of money, for Joachim had but a few sheep, a single ass, and an ox. Also, his oldest son was both blind and lame. But his two other sons were vigorous and all three daughters beautiful. There was a kind of lofty self-assurance about Joachim, burly farmer that he was; he understood the Law, his word was respected, he carried weight in the synagogue. While the sheer zest and spunk of his wife's personality made them a team to be reckoned with.

Hannah was not easily bested. In the midst of the flattering remarks about the cakes she ran to catch up Jesus, who was rolling around on the grass with several other children. "My grandson!" she announced, strutting around to show him off. "Did you ever see a child so beautiful? And you should hear him, he's already reciting the psalms!"

Embarrassed, Mary crouched by Salome, who was nursing her baby. Its head was like a silken shell, warm and fragile. Mary stroked it, filled with yearning. "I'm sorry," she said. "It is just our mother's way. She is really very proud of your darling Naomi."

Salome laughed softly and pressed her hand. "There is no need for us to explain our mother to each other, Mary. We each love our children, and we love each other. That's all that matters."

Mary felt better, once more elated—and hungry, she realized. She followed Hannah into the house, where a small struggle ensued over who would feed the child. Mary gave in. Hannah had missed so much already, and she was so much older, she would have fewer years to enjoy him. Suddenly the fact of her mother's mortality smote her: the lines so deeply etched on the gaunt little face, the wispy hair even thinner; a pathetic but vaguely comical pink bald spot showed through. And her hands were so wrinkled; the hands that were spooning soup into Jesus' mouth were even shaking slightly, Mary noticed.

It was the hands that did it. Mary threw her arms about both of them where they sat beside the oven and wept, using the diminutives of her childhood. "Oh, Mama, Mama, forgive me! I will try to be a better daughter to you.

I too will come to see you every day. I will have more babies for you to deliver and for my father to hold upon his knees."

Tears she'd forgotten how to cry ran down her cheeks. Some dry, searing, frozen thing had locked them back or burned them from her. The savage heat by day, the nights of brutal cold. And terror, sheer terror, during the time of their flight and hiding, for soldiers had followed them well beyond the border; she would never forget the sound of the horses' hooves or the thresh of sabers beating the bushes. Sometimes she fancied she could even smell again that chill, wild, leathery odor of men and beasts.

She had not cried then, for Joseph was with her, and God was with her, and to cry would have been weak and unworthy. A breach of faith. "How brave you are," Joseph said many times. But it was not bravery that sustained her; it was something else. Something stronger, fierce and strange and curiously free, and in its own way curiously pleasing. For she was a different person out there so far from home; she was a girl no more.

But here, now, in this room, with her mother's warm, tart-sweet little body against her . . . her mother's scent, even her sharp-sweet tongue . . . Mary dissolved.

"What's this?" Hannah drew back. "Now, now, hush, child, you have made me spill the soup!" But her own eyes filled, fastening avidly on Mary.

Jesus wormed down from her lap while the two held each other, rocking to and fro, weeping. They wept for all the mothers and daughters since Eve. They wept for the awful misunderstandings, the separations and reunions. They wept for love.

"You didn't *write*," Hannah moaned softly. "You could have made Joseph write more often. We nearly went crazy, we were so worried. We nearly went out of our minds!"

"Mother, Mother, you don't know what it was *like!*" Mary cried. She gripped the bony arms, almost shaking Hannah in her frenzy, as if Hannah were now the child. "Traveling through the desert with a baby so young. It was a very hard journey; we could have died! If it hadn't been for the Bedouins who took us in—"

"Why didn't God protect you? Why, why, if he were truly the one who chose you to bear his Son?"

"If?" Mary gasped. "Mother, don't tell me you harbor doubts even now?"

"No, no, forgive me. I am only an ignorant woman, not as familiar with the Scriptures as your father. There is so much I don't understand."

"Nor do I," Mary said. "I only know this: we suffered. And we will no doubt suffer again. God's purpose is beyond my comprehension. I only know that he brought us safely through. He will never abandon us—or his Son."

She wiped her eyes.

"Someday I will tell you all about it. How hard Joseph worked when we finally settled in Giza. He was a brick builder, he made bricks with his bare hands. We were terribly poor, and his back was nearly broken from his labors. There were no runners, at least none we could trust to bring you word. Remember, we Israelites are still looked on with suspicion by many Egyptians to this day, at least in most places—"

It was hopeless to convey, at least right now. Jesus had escaped, they realized; they must find him. They were neglecting their guests and Salome.

"Yes, yes, forgive me." Hannah hugged Mary more tightly. Then, feeling slightly guilty, yet united in a wonderful new way, they went back into the yard.

By midafternoon the other women had gathered up their children and departed. Mary lingered, holding her sister's sleeping baby gently against her heart. She too should be off. It was a long walk, and she must start the evening meal. Also, she had to drop in on Joseph's mother, Timna. But duty held her. To leave Hannah for Timna right now seemed a kind of betrayal. Here too the doves mourned, bees droned above the flower almond and oleander trees. Hannah drowsed on the grass at her feet, Jesus in the crook of one arm. Mary was reluctant to break the spell.

Presently she was aware of the soft plod of hooves as

Joachim led the ox up the path. Jesus sat up quickly, wriggled free, and ran to meet them. And shouting a greeting, Joachim scooped him up and placed him on the shaggy creature's back.

Mary, half asleep herself, sprang up, thrust the baby back on Salome, and ran after them, protesting. "No, no, set him down!" Hannah too scrambled frantically to her feet. But the boy was ecstatically clutching the beast's fur.

"See, see!" he shouted, eyes shining. "See me ride the ox!"

Joachim led them past the women again, round and round the yard. He was smiling faintly, but determined, asserting his own claim at last to the child. "You know I won't let him fall," he declared, half amused by their outcries, yet scornful. "Let him enjoy the ride. As you used to, Mary," he reminded.

"I was much older!" Mary wailed. She and Hannah were clutching each other, hearts pounding, in league against him.

"You were a girl. This is a man child."

Resolutely, Joachim prodded the beast, and slowly it began to trot, carrying the boy on toward the shed. Joachim trotted beside it, supporting Jesus with one hand. A foolish sense of release was flooding him. As if Yahweh himself were finally freeing him to enjoy Mary's boy. Something had held him back, a reluctance, half awe, half the feeling that he *should* feel something more . . . a restraint at odds with his own puzzled observations. How could it be? This little one who ate, slept, laughed, had to be protected, sometimes even had to be scolded . . . *this*, the Holy Child? The deliverer of Israel? . . . *The very Son of God*.

Over and over Joachim wrestled with it, unknown to anyone, least of all his daughter or his wife. Yet what had he expected? A winged cherub? A prophet, a priest? A grown *man*? He was stricken with the absurdity of his own imaginings.

Suddenly all this was ended. The incident of the ox brought Jesus and his grandfather close. The child could hardly wait to reach the little farm on the edge of town, where, as he grew older, he would run into the fields to seek Joachim out.

Joachim would pause in his plowing or reaping and smile to see the lithe figure bounding toward him up the hill. There developed a subtle rivalry between him and Hannah for the youngster's affections. When Jesus was very small, Hannah had the edge; she had time to rock him and play with him and ply him with sweets. He was especially fond of her fig cakes. Once he stuffed himself and was sick.

"Mother, you must stop spoiling him, you and Father," Mary pleaded.

Hannah turned from the basin where she was wringing out a cloth soaked in water and vinegar, her favorite remedy for everything. "You know this child cannot be spoiled," she said surprisingly. "No one on earth could accomplish such a thing."

"You've succeeded in making him sick!"

Hannah bit her lip, contrite. "Forgive me, so I have." Humbled, but clucking softly to him, Hannah bent to place the cool cloth upon her grandson's brow.

Actually, Mary felt a tender tolerance for her parents' foolish contending. Praise heaven it was not so with her and Joseph. And it had never been so with Joseph's parents, despite his father Jacob's over-fondness for the wineskins. Their rooms adjoining the carpenter shop had been a place of much laughter and singing, blessed with his mother's gentle presence—Timna so patient with her husband's weakness, for Jacob was amiable and loving whatever his state.

Timna still lived there; it was a joy to have her so close. Timna too adored Jesus, but her love did not devour and demand. Her son's house was just up the cobbled alley, above a cave where Joseph kept lumber and some of his tools. The little boy came running into Timna's quarters almost every day, radiant and lively, wanting to bestow his latest treasure—a flower, a beetle, a sparkling pebble—before darting back through the drapery to join his father in the shop.

Mary came too, usually bringing Timna jugs of water and things from the marketplace.

"Mary!"

"Mother Timna!"

They would embrace as eagerly as if they had been apart a long time. Then they would set about their work, grinding, weaving, sewing together, visiting in the way they had during those last precious months of waiting for the baby, before the trip to Bethlehem. There had been a mysterious rapport between them ever since Joseph first brought Mary home. White-haired, heavy-breasted Timna, poised and gracious but so warm, unperturbed by the fact that Mary's pregnancy made it impossible even to have a wedding feast. She only seemed to love her son and his chosen bride the more.

Now this devotion between them was intensified by the fact of the child, whom Timna was always to believe her own blood. He was the very image of Joseph, Timna was convinced, though she would not dream of contradicting Hannah, who was always pointing out how much Jesus favored the family of Joachim. Timna must reject the uncomfortable feeling they gave her sometimes, as if they had some prior claim. Or, since the homecoming of these three, as if they were privy to some secret knowledge concerning the child. Timna was miffed and half amused. But no, it was just their way, she reminded herself. The happiness of Joseph's little family, that was the main thing, and that she and Mary were so dear to each other.

One day when Jesus was nearly four, the two women could hear Joseph and the boy beyond the drapery, roughhousing again, throwing sawdust, rolling in the shavings. Mary's foot paused on the treadle. She tilted her head, smiling. How alike their laughter sounded. Their voices were also much alike already. "Those two! I probably should stop them."

"Let them play," Timna said. "Childhood is so brief, my Jacob always said. The burdens of manhood come all too soon. It's good for both of them."

Presently there was the sound of sawing. Timna went to pull back the drapery, then beckoned to Mary. Jesus was perched on the work table, holding a board for his father. The little saw and mallet Joseph had fashioned for him lay nearby. A shaft of sunlight from the open door gave the small tools a silvery brilliance and shone bright on the two faces, bent soberly now to their task. Mary caught her breath at how comely they were, working away in the afternoon sunlight, chatting, singing, or looking up to answer the greetings which people called in from the street.

How peaceful her life was, how joyful. She could feel God's blessings raining down warm in the sunlight; she could almost gather them in her fingers, out of this glittering shaft with the dust motes dancing. A lane of light that did not stop with Joseph and Jesus but flooded Timna, making a nimbus of her thick white hair. . . . To have such a mother-in-law—they were like Naomi and Ruth, they sometimes told each other—to have such a house only a few steps up the hill. The fine strong house Joseph had built for her with such feverish ardor during the time of their betrothal. They had had so little time to enjoy it between her return from Aunt Elizabeth's in Jerusalem and the shocking order from Herod that had driven them out on their wanderings.

But now, to live there at last, to have her own little house to keep. To be able to carry its water, tend its garden, clean it, cook in its oven, light its lamps, adorn it with flowers. To make it snug and happy for these two wonderful men God had given her. And to witness every day how much Joseph loved this son, who was not of his loins but was so proudly of his heart.

Even as they stood there marveling, Joseph looked up from his saw. He was whistling. He reached over to tousle the boy's black curls. "Jesus is a big help," he boasted. "See how fast he's learning."

His gray eyes, sweet with their secret, held Mary's.

For the long months of sacrifice and denial were over. The One who had entrusted them with this sacred life was a God of love. It was not his way to punish those who had served him so well and already suffered so much. To have doomed them to raise his child, to live together, yet forbidden to love each other, would have been impossible for the very author and giver of life, and their home unnatural for his son. Joseph was now her true husband, as God had ordered the men of Israel to be. And Mary was his true wife.

Mary had never been so happy. She was almost dizzy with it, so that the room swayed slightly, she had to grip the door. Timna looked at her, concerned. "My dear, are you unwell?"

"No, oh, dear Mother Timna, no, although I do have a joyous thing to tell you!"

Chapter 3

 ━━━━━━━━◆━━━━━━━━

They named the baby Joseph, after his father.

Joseph barred the shop from customers, all that day of Mary's labor, but worked savagely at his bench. Hannah had ruled that he must not be with her. A part of him was outraged; had he not seen her daughter safely through that unforgettable night so far from home when no midwife was to be found? If he was worthy then, he told himself, if God himself had deemed him worthy, why now exact the ancient taboo? Yet Joseph also felt spared. He wondered if he would be equal to seeing Mary go through such agony again.

At last, toward evening, Timna appeared to summon him. Hannah, disheveled but beaming, had just placed the swaddled newborn into Mary's arms.

And there she lay, his heart's darling, cradling their son. *His* son. His blood mingled at last with Mary's, a male of his own flesh lying there hot and red and sweet with life, sucking life from her breast.

Mary said it first, even before he reached her pallet. "Our son, Joseph. Oh, my beloved, I have given you a son!"

Joseph was too moved to speak. He kissed Mary over and over, her hair, her eyes, her cheeks. He kissed the baby's moist black head. Eyes wet, he arose to embrace his mother, who'd kept Hannah company during the long vigil. Hannah, busily scrubbing up, felt his hands around her tiny waist. To her sputtering astonishment, he picked her up and whirled her around like a child.

"No, no, no, you will disturb them! Be off to get Jesus and to tell Joachim."

The marketplace was emptying, shopkeepers pulling

down their awnings, people hurrying home. Joseph strode through them, radiant, announcing his joyful news. "A son, a son!" they exclaimed, clapping him on the back and passing it along to others. "Mary has given Joseph ben Jacob another son."

Another? He hurried on, in a dazzled confusion, for it was true and yet not true. No matter, let it be; all that mattered now was that Mary was truly his wife. God had not robbed him, as it had seemed in that shocked and desperate time when Mary first told him she was with child. When, sick unto death, he had heard his own voice crying, "*Whose?*" And she must tell him, try to make him realize—

No, no, that agony was over. And no child would ever be more dear to him than the one he had delivered with his own hands that night of her travail in Bethlehem. But surely the Lord who was raining so many blessings on them lately would understand his high heart today.

Joseph paused, in his climb up the hill, and lifted his eyes to the sunset bannering the sky. Gratefulness flooded him. He sensed, as Mary did, that these were to be their happiest years. Reunited with her family—even Hannah loved him now. Her little disputes with Joseph, as with Joachim, only seemed to enhance her fondness for him. The shop prospering. If he and Mary were favored with other children he would build an addition to their house—his brothers would help as they had before. . . . No, now he was going too fast! Heaven forgive my eagerness.

Joseph stood for a moment, shaken. That little boy he could see in the distance, tagging after Matthew, who was leading the sheep in from pasture. . . . A rosy haze bathed them. He could hear the tinkling bells, the bleating and, as the sheep drew nearer, the drumming of their hooves. He saw Matthew give the crook over to Jesus, as they disappeared in a veil of pink dust behind the fold. . . .

Your Son, God, whom you entrusted to *me* as well as Mary! The enormity and wonder of this smote him afresh, a sudden startling realization of the responsibility he still bore. It is not hard to serve God, he thought, when the Lord himself directs you, speaks to you in dreams. . . . Four times, he remembered, to his amazement, this had happened: first, when the angel told him he should not fear to take Mary as his wife; then, that he should take Mary and the child and flee with them into Egypt; again, that they should "go into Israel, for they are dead who sought the young child's life"; and, finally, that they should not return to Judea but turn back to Galilee.

Each time Joseph had responded, moved forward by commands and events beyond his power either to question or understand, propelled too by the danger and drama involving Mary.

But what of now, when the danger and drama were past? When the voice of God no longer roused him from dreams? Joseph sometimes lay expectant, listening, hoping for some word of direction; he heard only the mice nibbling in the rafters, the cry of an owl, the soft music of his beloved's breathing against his cheek. What of now? Now when things were well with him, and his own son slept at Mary's breast?

For the first time he felt inadequate, almost afraid. But this he knew, and he said it aloud: "Jesus will never have cause to feel unwanted. He will always be the firstborn of my household."

Matthew had lifted Jesus up to perch on the gates of the sheepfold; the child was holding the crook over them as they tried to crowd through. "See, Father, see!" he shouted as Joseph approached. "I am counting the sheep!"

"Yes, my son." Joseph ran to hold him. "But come, I have wonderful news. You have a brother!"

Jesus was elated. The coming of each baby thereafter became for him a special gift. As the eldest, he was first at his mother's bedside, first to kiss her and wipe her brow and lift up the swaddled miracle for the others to admire. "See what our mother has given us!" he would announce; then, at a signal from Joseph, the baby's name. A rich harvest of children, for again and again the Lord blessed Mary's womb. After Joseph came Ann, then James, Simon, Judas, and finally another girl, Leah.

Mary could scarcely believe her good fortune, for it was soon after the birth of Joseph that she realized she was

pregnant again. The new baby, Ann, was in her arms and
little Joseph barely two when Jesus started to school. Mary
stood in the doorway with them that first day as Jesus and
his father set off hand in hand. It was a bright autumn morning, cool and crisp, with birds singing. She wanted to cry for
love and pride in them, over the pain of missing Jesus already, a longing to call them back. How handsome they
both looked, the light falling on their new white tunics as
they strode along. The fairest in Nazareth; and Jesus would
surely be the brightest in the class. Then she caught herself—she sounded like Hannah!

The boy was bouncing with eagerness, proudly carrying his little bag of bread and cheese. His black curls
bobbed jauntily under his round velvet cap. But at the last
minute before they rounded the corner to the synagogue,
he hung back, turned almost forlornly, and gave them a
wistful wave.

Eyes wet, but smiling and calling encouragement,
Mary uncurled the baby's tiny fingers to wave back. Then
she stooped and gathered up her second boy, holding his
sturdy little body close. Her arms and her heart ached with
the precious weight of her children. "God go with him!" she
cried softly. And again she remembered her mother standing thus, eyes hungering after departing sons. A wave of
tenderness swept her.

I've been neglecting her, Mary thought. I will take my
mending and my little ones and go up to share this day with
her. Suddenly it seemed almost too much, this happiness.

Truly my cup runneth over!

Sometimes at such moments Mary felt almost guilty.
For there was suffering in the land, suffering and unrest.
There was no escaping it: The men spoke of it endlessly; it
hovered over her little family like a menacing cloud. For
Archelaus, ethnarch of Judea, had proved as terrible a des-
pot as his father, Herod—deposing the high priests, demanding even more staggering taxes to build more lavish
palaces, slaughtering the Jews who cried out against him—
three thousand in a single massacre of pilgrims to the Passover shortly after she and Joseph had returned to Galilee.

And his brother Antipas, tetrarch of Galilee, who ruled over Nazareth, was not much better.

Mary would never forget the people's tragic and futile rebellions. The first Passover there had been rumors of possible uprisings in Jerusalem. Filled with a dread premonition, Mary had begged Joseph not to go with her father and brothers for the annual celebration.

"My darling, you know I must go," he told her. "It's the Law. And would that you might go with me." He kissed her and picked up Jesus, hugged him against his chest. "As you will, when our boy is older." He caressed her with his eyes. "In any case, you are in no condition to travel."

He was right. Mary was carrying their child. Yet she was desperate with fear during the long week of waiting; and when at last she ran to the door to meet him, it was a grim and shaken husband that plunged into her arms. The crowds of pilgrims that swarmed the Temple had been in an angry mood, he told her, some of them threatening the soldiers sent to restrain them. "A few hotheads began to throw stones, and others began to shove. There was bloodshed, Mary." Shuddering, Joseph looked up from where he was fiercely scrubbing his hands. "They sent reinforcements. On horseback! Through the courts, up the sacred steps. Riding people down, using their swords. We escaped, but it was horrible." His usually calm young face had gone gray. Mary ran to embrace him; she had never seen Joseph like this. It was a moment before he could go on. "And now they are crucifying! The crosses—we saw the crosses lining all the roads."

A few weeks later Joseph brought home word that rebels had actually seized control of the Holy City. Nazareth, focal point of the caravan routes, received news almost daily. Zealots and self-appointed saviors were proclaiming their rule throughout the land. Roman legions were on the march to suppress them, savaging whole villages as they went. In Sepphoris, the capital, only four miles away, a man named Judas, whose father had been put to death by Herod, had gained a following and was claiming the crown.

Madness, sheer madness, Joseph and Joachim agreed,

while Mary listened, helpless. The time was not yet ripe for sedition; it could only mean punishment for everyone.

One night they were roused from sleep by the blatting of the ram's horn from the synagogue. By day the blowing of the shofar meant exciting news or signaled the start of the Sabbath. But at night those two bone-chilling blasts over and over could only mean danger. Joseph sprang up and ran to the window, where an eerie brightness was raining into the room. They were aware of the smell of smoke, and suddenly, of the heavy pounding at the door.

"Hide the child," Joseph ordered. He rushed to his couch to gather him up. "Take Jesus out the back way, into the cave!"

Mary obeyed, heart racing. In a few moments Joseph came for them, however. It was only Joachim, gruff, breathless, urging them to get dressed and come home with him. "The Romans are burning Sepphoris. That man has gotten too powerful; they're burning it to the ground. The troops will be marching this way." Matthew had already gone for Salome and her family. Everyone would be safer on the little home farm.

Lamps were being lit, a few people were running in the streets. There was the acrid smell of wood burning, even a few cinders falling, for Sepphoris was so close. Yellow flames tongued the sky. Mary would never forget their tortured dancing.

At Joachim's the whole family had gathered on the moonlit hill to watch in horrified fascination. The grass was wet beneath their feet; a sweet earthy scent blew in from the mountains. Silvery olive trees cast shadows. The men strode about expressing their outrage or simply stood mute, shaking their heads. Throats dry with excitement, curiosity and alarm, the women huddled together, ghostlike in their cloaks or shawls, children at their knees or in their arms.

Both Jesus and Salome's baby, Naomi, were wide awake, bright-eyed, pointing to the skies. The mothers wondered how much of this they would remember.

It was the last major rebellion; more severe restrictions were imposed. After that things were actually better, people realized, or at least easier to endure. Squelched, punished, humiliated by these heathens—pagans whom God did not even deign to speak to—the proud Jews bided their time. He would come, the faithful argued, their deliverer would come; and not just some upstart from the provinces, but a ruler able to overthrow any earthly Caesar and establish God's kingdom on earth. . . . Such times of ordeal and stress—were they not exactly what the prophets had said would precede his coming? Why then should they curse such trials, or even protest and bemoan them so much? Were they not a sign?

These fierce laments and feverish predictions: Mary had heard them since childhood. Yes, and her mother before her—all Jewish women for generations—like some dark wild background music for the simple drama of their lives. But now sometimes Mary's heart stood still to hear them, and she wanted to fling her hands over her ears. Her secret lay heavy but sweet within her, like a precious jewel with which she longed to comfort them. But mostly she tried not to listen. Soon, all too soon, God's will would be revealed.

For now let this be the time of happiness, the time of loving and begetting, her husband's arms around her in the night and all her children safe.

For Jesus, school was at first a shock. The synagogue, always noisy and crowded on the Sabbath, seemed strangely empty, echoing to the boys' voices and that of the schoolmaster rabbi sitting on the platform before them, austere and at first frightening, his dark bearded face peering at them from under his draped, tasseled prayer shawl.

The boys sat in a semicircle on the hard bare floor. At one end of the room stood the curtained chest containing the sacred scrolls. Small ruby lamps burned before it like alert red eyes, giving off an acrid smell of oil and incense and slightly filming the air. There was the fragrance of the cedar benches along the walls, the smell of well-scrubbed boys and morning; beyond the open slits of windows birds sang, carts rattled by. The boys sat trapped and anxious yet excited, as the master slowly unrolled the scroll.

Now it was beginning. Soon he would discover how

much or how little they already knew. "We always start with Leviticus," he said. "The third book of the Torah. A very important book, for it teaches us the essence of our religion. Can anyone tell us what that is?

"You shall be holy, for I, the Lord your God am holy!" several voices responded eagerly. "You shall love your neighbor as yourself!"

"Yes, yes, good—and what else?"

Jesus was leaning forward, shy, hopeful, anxious to do well, yet trembling, filled with a nameless fear and dread. He strove to answer—about the rules for being healthy and clean—but his voice could not be heard above the babble. "Sacrifice!" the others were saying. "It teaches us about sacrifice."

"Yes. The first half of Leviticus deals with sacrifice, which has always been an important part of worship among all races of men." The teacher paused, searching them with his stern but kindly eyes. "But for Jews what kind of sacrifice? Human sacrifice like those pagans who worship Molech and other false gods?"

"No, never!" the boys murmured in horror.

"That's right, *never*. And what do we offer up to die in our place? That's right—animals, the finest of our flocks, the beasts and birds. They are our substitute."

The man came down from the platform, folded his arms, and began to lecture as he paced, thoughtfully, gracefully, in measured tread, the four tassels on his shawl corners dancing. "Now the creatures acceptable for sacrifice are five: the bullock or ox, the sheep or lamb, the goat, the pigeon, and the turtledove. And these creatures must be without blemish: pure, like you, little children, so that the sacrifices are pure. . . . And the kinds of offerings are these: the burnt offering, which expresses our surrender to whatever God wills for us; the peace offering, to express our gratitude for his mercies and blessings; the sin offering, to show our sorrow at having broken his laws and our desire to be forgiven and united with him again."

Reb Solomon halted, fixing them with those expectant, gravely searching eyes. "Do you understand?"

The other boys nodded. Jesus looked miserably out the window, throat dry, heart racing.

"Well now, we will start. To learn these truths we will go directly to the sacred book and repeat the passages aloud, over and over, that they may be written forever on your hearts. Follow me as I recite for you the first passages wherein the Lord gives to Moses the manner of the sacrifice.

"And the Lord called unto Moses. . . . Speak unto the children of Israel. . . . If any man of you bring an offering unto the Lord, you shall bring your offering of the cattle, even of the herd and of the flock. . . ."

In unison the boys began to chant, to follow as their fathers had taught them; but soon some were rushing ahead, others falling behind, and the master must stop them and start over. He was very patient. He pronounced all the words carefully, beating time. His big bushy face had a mole beside his nose. Jesus watched him transfixed, trying to hide his mounting alarm. He could hear him, but he couldn't seem to make out the words, let alone say them. His tongue felt frozen.

He had cringed before these words even when Joseph spoke them, shuddered even then, safe in the crook of his father's arm: the pictures they evoked too horrible to comprehend—yet distant and unreal, like some of his grandfather's tales. But now—today! Here in the big echoing synagogue on this first day, booming from this huge man who was like a great if gentle beast himself, rhythmically padding, the boy was lost, confused, frightened, unable to join this bewildering chant of blood and fire.

"And he shall put his hand upon the head of the burnt offering . . . make atonement. . . . And he shall kill . . . and flay . . . and cut it into its pieces . . . and shall put fire upon the altar. . . . And the priests . . . lay the parts, the head, and the fat. . . . But its innards and its legs . . . wash in water; and the priest shall burn all. . . ."

Jesus hunched into himself, swallowed, covered his mouth. Something was whimpering deep inside. Don't let me be sick, it pleaded, don't let anybody see!

"And if his offering be of the flocks, namely, of the sheep, or of the goats. . . ." The sheep! The pet lamb that tagged him about. The goats so playful, with their leaf-shaped ears and golden eyes. The big patient thick-muscled ox plowing the fields, with him riding on its back sometimes. And the pigeons, the doves—the pure white doves!

"And the priest shall bring it unto the altar, and wring off its head, and burn it on the altar; and the blood thereof shall be wrung out at the side . . . and he shall pluck away its crop with its feathers and cast it. . . ."

Jesus writhed, made a small choked sound, for it was as if the strangling hands were on his own throat—he could feel them. He was burning, drowning in a sea of blood and flame, fighting like some poor doomed thing to survive. Yet a wild and desperate protest filled him at the same time: Why should these innocent creatures die for *him*? No, no, he couldn't bear it, he loved them; if something must be slain, he would rather die for them!

To his horror Jesus realized the room had fallen silent. The rabbi, seeing the boy's white face, had halted. "Jesus," he asked, concerned, "why don't you join in? Don't you feel well?"

Jesus was staring in awful fascination at the rabbi's hands. Those hands, so big and harmless as they gestured, were growing larger . . . larger . . . approaching . . . reaching out . . . they had become a priest's hands about to be laid upon him for the sacrifice!

"Would you like to be excused?" the man asked kindly.

Jesus shrank further into himself, wanting to cry. No, no—he tried to frame the words, but only a mournful bleat came from him, like that of a lamb; he was going to throw up if he didn't escape! . . .

He went home shamed and stricken. "They laughed at me!" he told his parents. "I have disgraced you."

Mary was nursing her baby, she could not go to him; but Joseph rushed to him, protesting, and held him. "You could never disgrace us," he said.

"It's the animal sacrifice," Joseph told Mary later. "We talked about it at length. You know how much he loves every living thing. I hope I made it clear that God's laws are always for our own good. He will participate tomorrow, he promised. And it will be easier later when they deal with holiness. Holiness, cleanliness, right living. He will have no trouble with that part of the book." Joseph hesitated, puzzled. "Jesus knows all the passages already; he would have recited the whole book for me, if I wanted. In fact, the whole Torah!"

"But I didn't think you had studied the whole Torah."

"We haven't," said Joseph.

His father was right. Jesus soon redeemed himself. He could even keep pace with the older students, although he strove to hold back, dreading the scorn that comes with envy. His head swam with the mystery of his own knowledge; it was as if everything he studied he already knew and yet he must experience in ways he did not understand.

Genesis was almost too familiar, he knew the story of creation too well, it was as if he was there, a part of it, drowning in the blankness, the darkness when the earth was without form and void. He must bring some order out of it! His face went pale with striving. Once again the words froze in his throat.

"Come, Jesus," said the master. "Speak up! I will allow you to lead us; speak up, recite."

Once again Jesus ducked his head, huddled into himself, dumb, though the wonderful words sang on and on in his mind: *And God said, Let there be light; and there was light. And God saw the light, that it was good: and God divided the light from the darkness.* . . . Freely and sweetly Jesus saw and heard and swam in the light . . . yet he shrank there, frozen in fear and darkness.

Puzzled and stubborn, the rabbi tried repeatedly all day. He was not a harsh man, merely determined. "This is ridiculous. You are not stupid, and your father has taught you well. What will your father think?"

Jesus gazed up at the rabbi, suddenly no longer afraid. "My father loves me," he said simply. "My father understands."

One afternoon the rabbi stopped in Joseph's shop. Jesus had run off into the hills, as he often did, to be with his grandfather.

"I have come to discuss your son," the rabbi said, uncomfortably. His tone was half complimentary, half concerned. "A very bright boy, yes, very bright, but in some ways I find him disturbing."

Joseph put down his plane, planted a foot on the bench, and eyed the man levelly. He had a sensation of threat, almost as on that night when he stood guard at the door of that Bethlehem stable, wanting to bar the sages from intruding on his little family. Rabbi Ezra was no sage; he was actually a burly tentmaker, and stripped of his scholarly garb, not even very imposing. Yet Joseph felt defensive.

"In what ways, Rabbi?" he asked courteously.

"Your son's imagination goes well beyond his years."

"God gives different children different gifts."

"But when an imagination is so vivid as to upset him, how can we be sure it is of God, friend Joseph, and not—forgive me—of the devil?"

Joseph laughed shortly. "This gift, I assure you, Rabbi, is not of the devil."

"I meant no offense," said the rabbi. "It's just that parents don't always realize. You must realize you have a very special son."

Thoughtfully, Joseph stroked the board he was planing. How smooth it was to his rough fingers, tawny and shining, a length of pine. Across his consciousness drifted an almost sensual memory of the table he had made as a betrothal gift for Mary: a beautiful thing. How he loved her. Finally he lifted his eyes, his composure belying the tangled pain and pride in his breast. "His mother and I realize," Joseph told him.

"In time," said the rabbi, now anxious to make amends, "Jesus should be sent to study with a really fine teacher in Jerusalem. One of the scribes, a scholar like Hillel, for example. Someone who can give him far more than I can. As you know, I am just a poor tentmaker."

"And as you know, I am just a poor carpenter," Joseph said, smiling. "But, God willing." He stood up and held out his hand. "Thank you for coming, Rabbi. If it is God's will, we will find the means to send him. People like us can only put their trust in God."

Suddenly, on common impulse, the men embraced.

Joseph told Mary of the encounter that night as they sat on the rooftop, after the children were in bed. They discussed it a long time, wondering. . . .

For Jesus, learning to write, however, was new and exciting. He loved the smell of the smooth wax-covered tablet and the feel of his sharp-pointed stylus forming the letters of the Hebrew alphabet; then, a little later, writing the lessons with pen and ink on parchment. His grandfather had bought him a little copper inkstand; it was a wonderful thing with a case attached for the small reed pens; he could stick it slantwise in his girdle in the manner of scribes or merchants and strut about without the ink's spilling.

His mother would make up his ink of lampblack, gum and water, putting a few palm fronds in the stand to keep the ink from drying. She loved to do this for him, and at night after his afternoon spent in the shop running in the fields, it pleased her to see him crouched on a cushion at the table, copying the Scriptures, his fine-boned olive face so earnest in the lamplight, his fingers carefully forming the letters with the thick black ink that she had made. She would come to stand over him and watch, pierced with a queer delight in the acrid tang of the ink, the scratch of the pen on the white papyrus. Papyrus was growing more plentiful and cheap; Joseph bought a quantity from a peddler.

Mary moved nearer one night, entranced by the shape of the black letters upon the creamy white. There was a mystery about them that spoke suddenly and terribly to her soul, these letters forming words. Words had enchanted her since childhood, perched on her father's knee, learning the Scriptures by rote as he spoke them to her. She soon knew the Torah as well as her brothers. But Joachim had refused to teach her to read and write.

"A woman has no need of such things," he declared, as he tousled her hair. "There are scribes for writing, and it is not the custom that women should read; why should they when they have husbands to do it for them?"

Now, strangely, a great word hunger roused up within her. Her son with his words—she must know what they were saying. It seemed critical, vital, like a command she must heed.

"Would that I too could read and write," she heard herself saying.

Jesus looked up, eyes bright. "I will teach you!"

Joseph, who was rolling up his own scrolls to be put into the cupboard, laughed and came to put his arm around her. "Your mother is busy with her babies," he said. "She has no time for such things."

"I am not too busy for anything so important," Mary insisted. "I want to learn, I must learn!" She turned on him, unlike herself, stubborn and angry, close to tears. "Why do men deny us something so harmless that could be so dear to us?"

Joseph was shocked. He felt bewildered and ashamed. "Mary. My dearest! You know I would never deny you anything within my power to give. Only tell me, why do you want this so much?"

"Some day our son will be a great teacher himself," Mary said. "When that day comes he may go away from us. If so, I pray he will write to us. I want to be able to read his words for myself. I want to be able to write him!"

Jesus reached up to take her hand. Drawing his mother down beside him on the cushion, he placed the pen in her trembling fingers. "Hold it thus, not too tight," he said. "Now make the stroke, carefully, carefully."

Joseph stood watching as she scratched away, forming the alphabet. Jesus smiled proudly up at his father. "She will make a fine student, Father. Our mother is wise as well as beautiful." For a moment he sat adoring her with his huge dark eyes. "Thank you for choosing her for us."

The bond between Jesus and his grandfather deepened. Joachim found himself watching for that little white tunic and curly head to appear in the distance and come bounding to him over the hills, begging to push the plow or swing the scythe. Joachim would lift him onto the ox and let him ride, as he once had Mary. It still amused and satisfied him that the women would scold him if they knew. Occasionally Joachim would leave his labors and trudge the whole afternoon with his grandson to find the sheep.

Hand in hand, or with the boy racing ahead, they would scramble over rock fences, push through thickets and brambles, cross the sunny green meadows, listening for the bells. Usually Matthew did not let the sheep wander far, but sometimes he led them to drink at a stream miles from home. On these jaunts they would often pause to rest, under the lacy shade of a terebinth tree or beside a ferny, flower-filled gully where the water spilled chill and foaming over great boulders into the stream.

And as they walked or lay gazing into the sky, Joachim would tell him the legends and tales of ancient Egypt and Israel. Whimsical, poetic, scholarly, simple, some so beautiful they brought tears to the child's eyes, some so horrible his blood ran cold. Two he would never forget: about the teraphim, those household images considered oracles able to foretell events.

"Egyptian idols in human form. Vile, vile, they would sometimes kill a firstborn child and mount its head upon a plate of gold, with the name of an unclean spirit beneath its tongue."

"No, Grandfather, no!"

"They would put lighted lamps before it and pray to it for answers to their questions. But as Zechariah the prophet warned, 'The teraphim speak vain things.'"

Loveliest was the legend of Yahweh's song: How, when God created the world, he asked the angels, "What do you think of it?" Ah, but it was beautiful, they told him, but one thing was lacking and that was music. "Music?" asked the Lord. "But the birds sing, the brooks babble." "The music of people worshiping you," said the angels. "Wait," said God, "just wait; I will put music in their throats so that they too may sing." But the angels told him, "That is not enough; they must sing with their hearts forever, waking or sleeping, praising you for this wonderful world you have made."

"And that," Joachim assured Jesus gravely, "is why we must never forget to thank and praise our maker from the minute we first draw breath in the morning until we close our eyes in sleep."

Drowsily Jesus lay on his stomach, listening. It seemed all the music of the universe was playing and singing within his own being. The water's soft liquid shouting as it plunged over the rocks . . . the birds trilling, ringing their tiny bells, plucking at unseen harps with little beaks, notes that spilled from their throats in a sweet cascade . . . the gentle rhythmic soughing of the trees. It seemed that his own heart would burst with it, this music of life with which God had drenched the world; he could not contain it. He sat upright and began to sing, a sudden outbreak of song that startled his grandfather, for it had no words that he recognized, only a magical tune that set his own heart dancing.

"Come, Grandfather, sing with me!" the boy said, springing up. "It's right that we can use our throats to praise him."

"Yes, if he has put an angel like yours in your throat," grunted Joachim, "instead of a frog like mine."

"You have no frog, Grandfather, only a good strong bass that makes the melody richer. Anyway, frogs are part of the choir that sings in God's garden."

"Boom, boom, boom!" Joachim laughed. "All right, we will sing together." And clapping their hands and making up words of praise as they went, they began to climb the rocky gorge.

One day they found that a lamb had somehow crept down the cliff and was perched on a rock, afraid to leave. "That boy!" Joachim was frowning as he squatted to peer over. "He's been told not to run off. He will feel my stick." An idle threat, for Joachim never beat his children.

"Don't worry, Grandfather, I will rescue the sheep." Before Jesus could be stopped he was scrambling down the embankment and had reached the rock where the lamb was cringing.

Joachim watched in fear, wishing for a rope. The descent was too precarious for his own weight; if he slipped, all three would be hurled to the rocks.

Jesus looked up, laughing, the lamb in his arms. Nimbly he climbed back, eyes shining. "I'm big and strong, Grandfather," he boasted. "Never be afraid for me."

Beyond lay the high green pastures where Matthew let

the sheep graze, often with some half-wild goats brought there by Rosh, one of his friends. Sometimes the older boys suffered Jesus to join them, even to spend the night with them beside their fire under the stars, singing, playing their instruments, or just lying with the cloaks over their faces, talking. As time went by it was more and more their company he sought instead of his grandfather's.

Joachim would stand shielding his eyes for sight of the boy in vain; or Jesus would appear at the foot of the hill, wave and call out a bright greeting, and then be off, with Jubal, the wild dog he had rescued from a pack of jackals, bounding at his heels. At first Joachim felt resentful, stricken, a trifle shocked. Somehow he had thought Mary's son would be different: not like the others, so cruelly quick to abandon their elders when the blood of youth called.

Even Mary. But no, he must not dwell on that. . . . Stolidly, wincing but trying not to be hurt, Joachim would go back to his plowing. He couldn't blame the boy. It had been getting harder to keep up with him. Joachim's bones ached, his breath gave out, he often had to stop to rest on a pile of stones. I'm getting old, he realized, with a pain in his breast that was appalling. Anxiety clutched him and a shaken tenderness as he thought of Hannah—their dear years of bickering closeness. He thought of Mary, precious Mary, and his other children. But most of all he thought of this grandson.

Joachim lifted his eyes to the clouds coasting overhead. *Lord, just let me live long enough to witness his wonders. Perhaps even to see him free our people, be crowned the true king of Israel!*

Matthew's friend Rosh was about sixteen, a handsome dark-skinned boy who seemed only half tamed, like his goats. He was like the Greek god Pan, playing his flute as he pranced around the fire, a spray of fragrant jasmine in his hair, golden earrings flashing. His teeth were very white, his breath was sweet with cloves. He was something of a desert rat, having followed the caravans with his father, a camel driver. He carried seeds and little sweet dom tree berries, which they would munch while he sprawled on his

side, telling them tales of his travels—often by starlight, the
bells of the tawny beasts clanging—the colorful saddles and
trappings . . . the loads of goods—gems, silks, spices . . .
escapes from lions and robbers . . . teeming marketplaces,
palaces and harems . . . bazaars where, to wild music, slave
girls with ankle bracelets were dancing.

Matthew's eyes glistened to hear him. Matthew was a
plump, amiable boy with a mane of red hair like Joachim's.
Patient and cheerful, he had enjoyed playing big brother to
Jesus. Now he was changing, beginning to chafe at a life of
simply tending sheep for his father. His smile, usually
thoughtful, was quick with Rosh. "See, see!" he would tell
Jesus proudly. "There is a world beyond these hills. These
hills won't hold him long."

There was a pagan excitement about them, fascinating
to the younger boy, yet disturbing. They seemed to have a
secret between them.

One night when he was ten, just as they were lying
down to rest, Rosh came to crouch beside him. "Here, I
have a present for you, Jesus." From beneath his cloak he
drew a slim luminous object and pressed it into his hand.

The boy at up, astonished at its chill weight in his fingers, its pale alluring glimmer in the firelight. An ecstatic
horror smote him, a sweet and nameless stabbing. He was
holding the naked figure of a woman; a serpent entwined
her legs and suckled at her pointed breast. His heart beat
wildly, he shuddered. "What is this thing?"

"You don't *know*?" Both doubled with laughter. "Astarte, you baby," Rosh informed him. "The Canaanite goddess of passion!"

"*No!*" For the sweetness in his bowels had turned to
hell. He found himself running, blindly running, toward
the chasm.

Shocked and scared, Matthew dashed after him,
caught and restrained him at its edge. "Stop, you little fool,
you'll fall!"

Jesus struggled free and hurled the obscene thing from
him. It twisted for an instant, a pearly flash, mocking in the
moonlight as it plunged into the water. Breathless, all three
bent to discern its fate upon the rocks below. It had van-

ished. There was only the roar of the falls, the white leaping spray.

"We're sorry," Matthew said anxiously, an arm around his nephew's shoulder, leading him back. "We meant no harm."

Even Rosh was contrite. "We shouldn't have done that," he said, trotting along beside them. "He's too young. He's different."

Jesus lay awake most of the night, or so it seemed. From beyond the hill came the mournful laughter of the jackals. Ominous, threatening, like the goddess, whose silvery smile drifted all around him, now near, now far, weaving through the sounds, making a hideous sweet music. The music writhed up from somewhere in her breast, coiled glistening into the yelping throats of the jackals, laughing with them, drawing closer. The music was cold and silvery, like chilled water, spewing from the breast where the serpent suckled. . . .

Jesus threshed about, lifted a hand to fend off the smile, now one with the jackals, the serpent. His hand struck the hard ground, prickly with grass. He half roused, innocent yet guilt-stricken, shaking with alarm. Were the sheep safe? Yes, they huddled nearby; he could smell their flat oily odor, was conscious of their occasional restless stirrings in his sleep. And the goats too, those slim-necked creatures with ears like drooping leaves and wonderful amber eyes. Silken in the moonlight, they too knelt peacefully sleeping.

A great love for all God's animals flooded him; he wanted to shelter and envelop them in his own being. He wanted to go to his friends and shelter them as well. No matter that they were older, he wanted to protect them, reassure them. So go now, rise up and go to them! Yet a great weariness overwhelmed him. Shivering, he gathered his cloak closer around him, and huddling deeper into it, he slept. . . .

The sky was rosy with sunrise when Rosh woke him; the fire was crackling afresh with dry grass and thorns; there was the toasty smell of the wheat kernels Matthew was parching in a pan. They greeted him brightly. Rosh was slicing a melon, pink as the sky. "For you, my friend," he said, giving Jesus the largest piece.

Their eagerness to make amends consoled him. But even as he squatted there munching, the howling of jackals again split the chill mountain air. Closer now. Dangerous. Either the beasts were hungry, or already drunk with blood and ravenous for more. Matthew and Rosh sprang for their rods. Alert, experienced, they ran to check their herds: no strays. They stood watching as the pack flowed over the ridge, yelping, leaping, tossing something in the air, then streaking after it. For it was running, desperately running, a small creature already mutilated but fighting for life.

Jesus' heart froze. "We must save it!" He started forward, but Rosh put out a calm brown hand to restrain him.

"Never mind, it's just a dog."

Just a dog. A breed almost as despised as the jackals, for dogs also roamed the hills for carrion or slunk about the streets thieving food. Yet it lived, it lived, and he must save it. He could feel the meadow grass beneath his bare feet as he ran, wildly, instinctively, as he'd run toward the cliff's edge last night. And the other two were following, yelling and howling, brandishing their heavy clubs, beating almost joyfully at the beasts, kicking them, cursing them, driving them off.

It was over in a few minutes. The pack vanished almost as swiftly as the graven image in the waters. Only a cloud of dust and a trail of blood marked their passage. And there at its end lay their prey: a half-grown pup. Small, brown, quivering, barely breathing, but looking up at them with pleading eyes. Its back was broken, its tail chewed nearly off. Blood trickled from its nostrils. Starved, scabby, and almost hairless even before the attack, yet it begged piteously for life.

"Don't!" Jesus cried, as Rosh picked up a rock.

"It's already half dead. Put it out of its misery."

"No, no, *don't*." Jesus dropped to its side. Talking softly to it, he gathered up the dirty battered body. It lay against him, helpless, trusting, gazing at him with its stricken black eyes. Then, as he stroked it to quiet its trembling, he gasped in amazement, for the dog's small pink tongue began to lick his hand.

Matthew laughed, half disgusted. "Filthy thing, what're you going to do with it?"

"Carry it home and bind up its wounds."

"*Home?*" Both boys hooted. "What will my sister say about that?" Matthew asked.

Jesus held the dog closer. "I know my mother would never refuse to help a hurting thing."

Mary cried out at sight of them. Her son's tunic was bloodstained; he was even smeared with excrement, for the poor little thing in its terror could not control its bowels. "A dog?" she gasped. "Oh, Jesus, no!" Yet she held out her arms, as she had for the pigeons and other wild things her children brought her, and warmed it at her breast. Then she bade young Joseph to light a fire to heat water to bathe it. The other children raced about, excited, eager to help, bringing towels and the herbs and salves kept in a cupboard. Their father, hearing the commotion, joined them and sent back to the shop for wood to fashion splints. Still shuddering, the dog lay, heart pounding yet submissive, head on its paws, black liquid eyes beseeching them.

"We'll do what we can to ease its suffering," Joseph said, as he knelt to bind up the fractured limbs. "But we must realize its back is broken; it probably won't live."

"It will live," Jesus insisted. "I know it will live. I have asked God to heal it."

"We hope it will live," said Joseph. "We will all pray for its healing. But if it does we will have to release it. Dogs belong in the fields."

The dog was finally wrapped in a blanket and put in a basket beside Jesus' bed. Later in the night Mary awoke to hear her son sobbing. Carrying a lamp, she tiptoed around the pallets of the other children. The basket, she saw, was empty. The small battered bundle was cradled in his arms. "He came to me!" Jesus said. His face was radiant even as the tears rolled down his cheeks. "He crawled out of his box and dragged himself to me. He is healed, Mother, I felt it, God is healing him! But he mustn't go back to the fields," the boy pleaded, "or the jackals will attack him again. He must live with us."

Troubled, Mary sat down beside them. Her own fingers crept to the warm little head. "That would be very unusual, my darling. You know Jews don't keep dogs; only Egyptians keep dogs."

"Uncle Cleo does."

"Well, yes, Cleo. A few rich people like Cleophas." Mary laughed. Joseph's oldest friend Cleophas rode a horse as high-spirited as he was, and beside it paced a hound he had brought from Cairo. But then Cleo had always been a law unto himself: merry, arrogant, thinking his father's money could buy him anything. At one time, even Mary's hand. Mary smiled to remember. Poor Cleo—his astonishment had been almost comical when her father gave her to Joseph instead. And Hannah was so distraught she took to her bed; she had been so anxious for Mary to have the merchant's son. . . . How strange life was, these battles caused by love. Yet now Cleo was like a favorite uncle to her young.

Mary was stroking the puppy cuddled close to Jesus. "But it isn't the custom for people like us to have a dog."

Jesus sat upright. "Bad customs should be changed, Mother! Dogs are God's creatures. Dogs need people and people need dogs. It's a bad custom not to love and care for dogs."

Joseph relented, of course; he could deny his family nothing. And with a speed that astonished everyone, the dog healed. They named him Jubal for the joy he brought them. Also for the way he tried to join in when they were all singing and tootling away on the instruments Joseph had fashioned for them: timbrels, a flute, some horns, even a lyre. Esau, Mary's blind brother, helped him; Esau had an uncanny feeling for musical things. The candles in the shop burned late as the two labored to make the wood like satin, the metal bright, eagerly testing the tender strings. Joseph had never been happier. Almost every night, after prayers and the evening meal, he would gather his family on the rooftop, and there, head cocked, beating time and smiling proudly even as he piped, Joseph would lead them.

Mary, putting the last dish in the cupboard or laying

the fire for morning, sometimes felt like dancing to hear them, her darlings, like so many birds on a bough. Wiping her hands, she would scurry up the steps to sit beside Joseph on a cushion, listening with her shining eyes and her heart.

It was cool there under the stars; jasmine spilled its white fragrance over the wall, sweet . . . sweet as the sounds they were making, so young and bold and yet plaintive in the night. Her whole being seemed in tune with this music of her life. The very stars seemed to tilt toward her, sparkling, blazing, as if they too were striving to speak or sing. How close God seemed! Mary had not heard the voice of her Lord since childhood; not once since that incredible experience in the shed. Not even the voice of an angel, although, strangely, angels had spoken repeatedly to Joseph in dreams. Yet on such nights she felt as if the whole company of heaven were swirling close, blessing her, blessing her. Compressing as much happiness as possible into these few years.

For deep within her, on quite another level, Mary walked a secret and lonely road: aware, ever aware, of the changes sure to come. . . .

Cleophas often dropped in on these evenings, still darkly handsome in his fine striped silks and jewels, bringing presents for the children. His own marriage had been a sad one. His wife was sickly; she had lost three babies before fleeing in disgrace to her parents in Acre. Cleophas had gone after her repeatedly, to no avail. Mary and Joseph welcomed him. They knew he envied their happiness, yet it comforted him to be near them.

"Cleo! Uncle Cleo!" The children pressed their instruments upon him. "Come join our music!" With a vigorous hug for everyone, he would perch on the parapet, and pretending at first to be confused, pluck clumsily at the lyre. "No, no, Uncle Cleo, you are holding it upside down!" the younger ones would shriek. "Ah, like this?" His eyes, under their sleepy lids, twinkled. Suddenly long sleek fingers flew, rings sparkling, his voice rang out, and oh, such merry melodies as now raced toward the stars. The little dog, lying at Jesus' feet, would lift his head and howl.

"Listen, he's singing too!" the children claimed.

"That pariah?" Cleophas teased. "That bobtailed wretch? He's trying to tell us to take him back to the jackals."

"No, no, we love him, he's beautiful!" They beat at Cleo with frantic fondness. "God sent him to us and healed him! His sores are all gone, see his shiny coat? Even his stumpy teeth grew in straight and strong!"

"He's still limpy," Cleo persisted, laughing as he fought them off. "He will always have a stubby tail."

"At least he has a heart." Joseph grinned. "Not like that cold-blooded hound of yours. Where did you get him, out of a tomb?"

They were always trading insults—Cleophas vehement, often outrageous, Joseph cool, composed, amused. It had been so since boyhood, this mocking affection between them. Joseph had worried about Cleo—his wild ways. Once he had even fought him to the ground over Mary, bloodying his best Sabbath robes. Yet they remained close. Their eyes met now over her head. How small and dainty she still was, after her day's work. She wore a soft little blue garment, tied at her tiny waist; she had wound a ribbon through her dark hair. A few curly tendrils escaped as she moved about, gently but firmly quieting the children. So young, so small and virginal . . . for a moment it seemed incredible that she should be their mother.

Jubal was devoted to them all, especially Mary, but Jesus was his idol. The dog slept beside him at night, and followed him to school, where he would flop down on the synagogue steps and wait patiently until the boys came shouting from their studies. Then, with a yip of delight, he would leap to greet his master.

Toward midafternoon, in the courtyard of her house, Mary could hear him barking, a signal that her sons were coming. In a minute Jubal would hurtle through the heavy drapery at the doorway, eyes bright, tail frantically wagging. Mary hugged him and gave him his bite of the goat's cheese or sweetmeats she had waiting. Meanwhile, her oldest daughter, Ann, helped her pour mugs of milk and portion out the treats.

The children swarmed in, Jesus tallest—nearly as tall as she was now—followed by young Joseph, whom they had taken to calling Josey, and James. Josey was a ruddy, noisy boy, very active and aggressive. He liked to climb, wrestle, throw things, grab things. He was inclined to be belligerent. He was always teasing James, who was more gentle, a shy child who had his aunt Salome's way of looking up at you with a sudden charm from beneath lowered lids. James was often bewildered and frightened at Josey's antics, running to Jesus for comfort or protection. How fast they were growing, Mary's heart protested. Next year Simon would join them; Jude would be at her skirts a few more years. She was grateful for toddlers and daughters.

Jesus hugged his mother, tried to pick her up in the manner of his father and swing her around. "No, no, stop, you'll hurt yourself!" she cried, laughing. The others hurled themselves at her too, vying for her attention. The younger ones sometimes quarreled about it.

Today Josey folded his arms and scowled darkly at his cake. "You gave Jesus the biggest piece!"

"Oh, dear, I didn't mean to," Mary worried. "Let me give you some more."

"Then there won't be enough for Leah," said Jesus. Wiping his mouth, he shoved his slice across the table. "Here, take mine."

"That isn't necessary," Mary said sharply. Sometimes she felt impatient and confused. Why must he always be so sacrificing just because he was the oldest? She loved them all so much, and she tried so hard to be fair. "Stop fretting, Josey, and go help your father in the shop."

"What about him?" Josey pointed to Jesus, who had taken up his flute and gone out to perch on the doorstep in the sun, testing it dreamily, playing a little refrain that came to him, over and over. It sang of the world's loveliness in the green and golden spring.

"Your brother has already spent years working with his father," Mary told them. "Now it's your turn, you too must learn his trade."

Jesus gave a guilty start. He put down his flute. "Come on, we'll all go. Won't we, Jubal?" He snapped his fingers to the dog. In a minute the three boys were traipsing amiably down the hill together, the little dog trotting merrily in the lead.

Mary, still holding her towel, stood in the doorway watching. How beautiful her sons, all of them. Comely, with a casual grace that came from Joseph. Except for Simon and Jude, who were still chubby with baby fat, they were like young gazelles. . . . Jesus, though: How could she define his special beauty? His mop of black curls—more abundant and shining, like a nimbus around his head, it seemed to her sometimes. And his eyes—the mysterious sweetness and radiance of those eyes. At first blue-black, they had lightened to a clear golden brown, rimmed by lashes longer than her own. They were like pools, reflecting all they saw. "Jesus talks with his eyes," Timna remarked one time. "He seems to drink in the world and love it with his eyes."

Jesus was different from the others. Not that they were less dear, Mary hastened to assure herself; not that she loved them less. But there was no denying he was different, no possible way for her to forget. Although in raising her family, she must try.

What did he think about, wandering the hills with his dog, alone or in the company of other boys? What did they talk about? Mary wondered uneasily sometimes. They were old enough now to notice girls; and the girls were very much aware of Jesus, that was plain. Yet in some ways he was still a child. He never returned from one of his jaunts without bringing her wildflowers or some treasure—a shard of pottery, a bright stone, a stork's white silken feather. And only last week a lizard with unusual colors.

She remembered the pleasure with which he had laid it on her palm to admire, its coat glistening now purple, now emerald, now rose, its eyes like tiny jewels. But as they both stood marveling, he had asked suddenly, in a voice of indignation, "How can people do it?"

"Do what?"

"Cruel things. When we have so little time and the

Father has given us such a beautiful world. Yesterday, coming home from school, some boys tried to stone Jubal."

"Oh, *no!*"

"I had to save him again—from *children*. But men, too, beating their donkeys. You've seen them, Mother, we all have. And women, even women at the market, carrying live chickens upside down, their poor heads dragging, eyes so frightened." His own eyes were stricken. "And men hurting each other. The Romans, the terrible things they are doing to the Jews. Even Jews fighting, enslaving each other. God's world is so beautiful, Mother, how can people *do* such things?"

Mary's heart beat faster. "It is not God's will that they should," she said, speaking carefully. "Perhaps, when the Deliverer comes, all this will change. The Messiah—when he comes, surely even cruelty to animals will cease." She was gazing at her son. How much did he already realize? How much should she tell him?

Jesus seemed deep in thought. "Yes," he said at last. "Yes, surely. . . ."

Ann had finished drying the cups. She climbed on a stool to put them away on the shelf, then ran to fling herself against her mother. Ann was much like her grandmother Hannah, quick, fervent, sensitive, curious, with the same lively, deep-set eyes. Arms clinging, she pressed her head with its dark circlet of braids against her mother's breast.

"Why are you crying, Mother?"

Startled, Mary wiped her eyes. "Oh, my goodness, am I?" She returned her daughter's impassioned hug. "I'm crying with love for all my children. I worry sometimes about what life may hold for you. I wish I could keep you like this always."

"Especially our eldest brother?"

"Yes," Mary acknowledged. "For this is his last year in school. That is always a time of change for a family."

"Will he go away from us?"

"Oh, no. Not for a long time yet."

"Then what troubles you, Mother?"

"I don't know," Mary said helplessly. "Except that he will soon be a man. Soon Jesus will complete his first fast and go to Jerusalem with his father and me for the Passover."

"But this time we will all go too!" Ann exclaimed. "Father promised, he promised!" She began to dance around in her delight. "He said that when Jesus is twelve and is presented at the Temple we can go too."

"So he did," Mary remembered. And the festival was barely a month away. None too soon to start preparing for the journey. She must speak to her parents. Joachim always took her brothers. Perhaps this year Hannah could be persuaded to come along. They would stay with Elizabeth, all of them; not just Mary and Joseph, as usual, but the whole crowd. The house was so big and her aunt had often begged them to come.

Ann's excitement was contagious; Mary felt it too, more than ever, as she planned. The mere thought of seeing Elizabeth again always made her spirits soar. They had so much to talk about, they poured out their hearts to each other as they could to no one else in the world. For both of them their annual reunion was the highlight of the year. And this time it would mean more than ever, because Jesus would be along! For years his aunt had been eager to see him, and to have him meet his cousin John; but Joseph, for reasons of his own, had been reluctant to bring him until he was older. Though Joseph hadn't told her, Mary knew it was partly for the child's own safety; her husband was still haunted by the memory of that Passover massacre some years ago.

Well, Jesus was twelve years old now, Mary thought in great anticipation. It was time they took him to the Temple. And, to make the occasion even more joyful, at last the two boys so near in age could get to know each other.

Chapter 4

————◆————

*I*t seemed to Hannah that Joseph had been a fool to promise his family this journey.

Struggling up from a restless sleep, she lay worrying. Joseph had been to Jerusalem often enough himself to know how hard it was. Bad enough for grown people, let alone children, along those rough country roads. Still muddy, some of them, especially through the boggy Plain of Esdraelon and along the Jordan; others dusty, rocky, weed-grown. She thought of the mountains, the treacherous climb through the bleak wilderness of Judea before they could get to Jerusalem.

Carefully, fearfully, Hannah lifted a hand to test her head: no longer throbbing as it had been these past three days. That bitter quarrel between Joachim and Matthew over the sheep! But no, she dared not . . . she had other things to ponder.

Well, she just hoped Joseph took a couple of extra donkeys along so some of the children could ride. One thing certain, Hannah would go this time if it killed her. As she felt, groping for her garments, that it might. Yet she could not allow Mary to cope with the trip without her. I must go along to help her, Hannah told herself, dressing hastily lest she miss the departure. Long before daybreak she'd been aware of Amos and his father tramping around by lamplight, leading up the donkey and trying to keep him quiet as they loaded him with supplies: bread, cheese, blankets, water. Hannah ran a comb raggedly through her hair, slapped her own cheeks smartly to get the blood flowing—and recognized now the real reason she must not be left behind.

59

Didn't she always keep the children while Mary and Joseph made their annual pilgrimage? Except for the years when Mary was expecting, and that time when little Ann had been down with a fever, they had been in Hannah's charge: hers to pet and spoil and make behave while their parents set off like sweethearts to join the caravan. It was good for the two to get away, of course, but how about her? She felt very close to those children; hadn't she earned the right to be along when they first set eyes on the Holy City? Especially Jesus. Hannah caught her breath. Twelve years old now, and being presented at the Temple. That child, that beautiful child whose coming had been such a source of anguish—and blessing. How could she bear to miss it? Her own grandson!

It was going to be a fine day to start a journey. Hannah had sensed it, despite her misery. A thick mist had risen in the night, white as the garments of God, muffling the mountains, blotting out the sheds and fields, but through it birds were already cheeping and chirring. A pink light was seeping across the sky. There was a hiss of wet grass, a smoky smell of tar as Amos stamped out the torches at the door.

He cried out in protest to see her, wrapped in her heavy hooded cloak against the chill. She looked wan but determined. "No, Mother, please, you mustn't try to come! Much as we long to have you." Amos was her third and youngest son, a tall, fair, narrow-featured boy with a pleasant smile but rather anxious eyes. He still clung to his mother, eager for more attention than Hannah could bring herself to give. Even now, when he was sixteen and betrothed, he managed to annoy her. "Remember your head."

"The Lord has taken away my headache," Hannah insisted, trying not to sound impatient with his concern. Her small deep-set eyes peered out almost impishly from the hood. "Perhaps the Lord deems it is high time I too pray at the Temple for my sins." Deliberately, she held out her arms to Amos rather than Joachim to help her mount the donkey. "Especially since your brother will not be with us," she said sharply.

Silently, Joachim tightened the final strap. He wasn't

surprised. He had felt sure Hannah would come, had even made a little seat for her. Pray heaven her anger at him would soon pass. Though it was a serious thing Matthew had done: running off to Magdala with his friend, leaving the sheep with a hireling! And the hireling had fled, evidently before a lion. Three sheep had been lost, one of them torn to bits—a newborn lamb! Joachim was appalled; he wished he hadn't shouted at Matthew when he came home, but it was high time he learned responsibility. Matthew at least must stay behind and try to find the other sheep.

Still, the ache of Matthew's absence was heavy upon Joachim as they set off. He tried so hard to be a good husband, a good father. Not once since his sons were old enough—at least the two who were able—not once even since the massacre, he grieved, had he turned his steps toward Jerusalem at Passover without both of them by his side.

The donkey lurched, picking its way down the steep cobbled hill in the fog. Hannah hung on grimly, every jolt a threat to her still sensitive head. Yet excitement was rising within her. She herself had not been to Jerusalem in years. To get away from Nazareth after so long, to visit her sister Elizabeth once more, enjoy the city, the crowds! . . . This year, she had heard, more families than ever were heading for Jerusalem. For at last things were a little more peaceful for the people of God; a feast was again a time of holy celebration: especially for Nazareth this Passover, when so many boys were going up to be presented. Half the village, it seemed, was pouring down narrow streets and alleys toward the fork where the caravan was to form.

A small crowd had already gathered when they arrived. Through the shifting veils of mist Hannah could see Joseph and his family. Two donkeys, thank goodness. And Salome and Ephraim, who'd had enough sense not to bring their daughter. All laughing and talking, in a holiday mood. Jesus raced up to greet them, eyes bright, curls bouncing under his velvet cap. Mary had cut down an old, rather faded robe of Joseph's for him, but it suited him, it became him. How beautiful he was—surely fairer than any of his classmates gathered around the rabbi—how young and firm and warm to her embrace. Hannah clutched him to her.

"Oh, Grandmother, I'm so happy you're better. My heart would have been sore without you." Jesus was looking eagerly about. "But where is Matthew?"

"Matthew is being punished," Amos announced.

"Matthew is needed at home!" Joachim snorted. He reached over to grip his grandson's shoulder, taking comfort from it. Jesus was compensation; it would be a fine journey, after all.

Hannah slid down from the donkey and hastened to Mary. The children were racing about, bouncing with excitement, and Mary only stood there smiling. Didn't she realize they could get lost in the gathering crowd? Even get stepped on by a mule? Hannah was startled to see several mules—and with a pang she realized, too late, that even Esau might have been able to endure this journey had Joachim hired a mule for him. Poor blind Esau. Oh, she shouldn't have come, shouldn't have left him! For a second Hannah couldn't bear it: the memory of how bravely he had stood waving to them from the door. Hush, now, he'd be fine with Judith looking after him. Judith was a good girl, betrothed too, to a fine young farmer named Saul; there would be two marriages in the family within the year. Oh, the Lord had truly blessed her. If only Matthew . . .

But no, she would not let pity or regret ruin this day. Hannah spread her arms to receive the other grandchildren, who came swarming to her. Playfully she defended herself against the assault of hugs and kisses. "Mercy, have mercy, you will tear me apart!" But she was smiling. Striving to be like Mary, who always seemed so happy.

That smile, those shining eyes: Mary had carried herself about so since childhood, as if she held in her heart some treasure. But now, with a houseful of children to cook and wash for, just carrying all that water . . . ! And the weaving and sewing, mending too—the earnings of a carpenter had to be stretched—it hurt Hannah that Jesus must set off in a faded robe. Why didn't Mary fret and storm like other women? Her cousin Deborah, for instance, though her husband gave her everything. Or even Salome, who was often troubled—Ephraim, she confided to Hannah, was not always so merry at home.

It was a love secret, of course: the thing between Mary and Joseph, the way they still looked at each other. After all these years! They even held hands in front of the children. Hannah envied this bitterly, even as her heart cried out in gratitude that this was so for her daughter. As Mary ran up to embrace her, Hannah held her fiercely.

"Never mind how I feel." She dismissed the questions. "You need me. I'm going with you!"

A small group of men and animals had gathered around the caravan leader, a tough little brown man with a face so deeply etched it was like a map of his travels. He had to shout to be heard. As usual, they would take the long arduous route necessary to avoid corrupting themselves by any contact with the Samaritans, those hated half-blood Israelites from the northern kingdom. Today across the Plain of Esdraelon, then down the Jordan valley, to spend the night in Beth-shan. Beth-shan was a pagan city, also called Scythopolis, or City of the Scyvians, by the Greeks. But there was a fertile, well-watered site where they could camp, as well as a Jewish quarter where some of them could find lodging. The second night they would be far from any towns, but the Paschal moon would be full and their camp-fires merry, somewhere along the Jordan. The third night they must rest well in Jericho, for the following day would be hard, through the steep stony wilderness of Judea. But at its end—Jacob, their leader, paused, grinning—they would see Jerusalem.

"Jerusalem, Jerusalem!" The magical name was suddenly on everyone's lips. Shouting it, singing it, the parade began to move, led by the youths, who were soon far ahead, Amos and Jesus among them.

Their fathers had insisted. "Go now, join them, we can manage the creatures," Joseph said.

"Yes, go on." Joachim had to pull the reins from Amos, who was dutifully holding back, though his whole being yearned. "Enjoy yourself." With a kind of grudging affection

Joachim gazed after his now eagerly running son. "A good boy," he said. "Amos can be trusted. Not like Matthew!"

He told Joseph about it as they tramped on, leading the asses along roads that were not yet dusty, for the dew was still wet, the trees sparkling. People were laughing and talking, harnesses jingled, there was the thunder of many hooves—a few horses and mules among them—and the steady shuffling of sandals.

"I wish I hadn't been so hard on him," Joachim said gruffly, "but he's old enough to know better. I felt he should stay behind to look for them." He blinked hard, eyes remote but grieving. "Tell me," he said abruptly, "did I do right? Maybe now more than ever Matthew needs to pray and ask forgiveness at the Temple."

For a moment Joseph couldn't answer. His own young sons had come racing up from the ranks of women, begging to join the older boys. Their father refused; he didn't think it safe, for one thing, but mainly he wanted Jesus to be free of them. To appease the children he lifted them onto the donkeys and let them ride.

"You know that better than I do, Joachim, you're a more experienced father than I am. I can only hope that someday I'll be as wise as you are in dealing with my children."

"Well, Esau, of course—" Again that fleeting grimace of pain. "What can a man do, with his firstborn son so afflicted? Matthew—I had counted on Matthew to take his place, but now I'm not so sure. I still have Amos, of course. Amos is dependable; I know Amos would never desert me."

They were interrupted by another burst of young voices. The girls, released by their mothers, flew by like a flock of birds. Nervous, giggling, excited, they scurried in pursuit of the youths. For a festival march was the one time they could mingle, laughing and singing and chasing each other, sharing a drink of water at the well or a cold meal beside the road. And at night, when the family tents were pitched, they would build their own fires a little apart, to play their instruments and dance under the Paschal moon.

Watching them, Joachim's grizzled face brightened.

He grinned wryly. "Ah, sons! Let them enjoy themselves while they can. After marriage it's too late."

Joseph too was smiling. "My marriage to your daughter, Joachim, is far from a joyless thing. As for Jesus—yes, a boy grows up too fast." He spoke thoughtfully as they trudged on. "The day will come when he too will have some important decisions to make. Until then, we just want him to be happy. Mary and I have prayed that nothing, absolutely nothing, will spoil this trip for him."

The roads were better than people had feared. Roman crews had been out for weeks repairing them, and erecting new mileage markers. And at every turn, it seemed, new pilgrims waved the caravan down. For this was the season when the men of Israel dropped everything to pay tribute to their Lord. Never mind that the barley harvest was barely over, the wheat crop beginning to gild in the fields; that despite all precautions, thieves might come in the night to steal what they had just labored so hard to garner; that a man with enemies might find them even mean enough to sow tares in the ripening grain. They must go, they must go up to the Holy City, where at last the Messiah might—yes, must sometime—appear.

Perhaps at this very Passover!

For it would surely be at Passover, many priests and doctors of the law believed, when they celebrated their miraculous Pesach, or passage out of the bondage of Egypt. What more appropriate hour for their own Deliverer to be sent, one even greater than Moses? And once he set foot in the Temple . . . ! Just how this would happen, neither the priests nor the people quite knew. Only that Israel's agonies would somehow soon be over, her enemies overthrown; he would establish a kingdom to rival David's, and all the earth would recognize them at last as the one true People of God.

The Galileans realized, humbly, that they were considered notoriously lax in obeying the Law, especially about fasting and washing—actually regarded as little better than heathens by most of Judea. Yet in this one matter they could not bear to be found wanting. When he came, surely they, even they would be worthy. They wanted to be there to greet him.

Toward evening of the fourth day, the caravan approached its destination. The final march had been long and hard, climbing up, forever up through the bleak Judean wilderness. The air, so high above sea level after that of Jericho, was hard to breathe. The women often had to pause to rest, while the men and boys, walking together now and already far ahead, pressed on in their eagerness. They had almost reached The Red Ascent, where each year at Yom Kippur the scapegoat Azazel was led into the wilderness and pushed off a cliff. Through the haze, thrillingly in the distance, the first glimpse of the city could be seen. And as they began to climb the last steep winding limestone ridge that overlooked Jerusalem, their excitement could no longer be contained. At sight of it a mighty shout went up.

"Let us go, let us go too!" Mary's younger sons begged.

"All right, go then." Gladly Mary released them, though Hannah clutched her arm and predicted they would surely be trampled.

They scurried through the crowd to find Joseph, who smiled and reached out to draw them in. He lifted them up onto the donkeys, where they could see. Jesus stood holding the reins, his dark curls blowing, his face set in the direction they all were gazing. The whole procession had halted, breathless and awed. For a little below and beyond them, above the broad green gorge of the Kidon, rose the magnificent City of David. Above its surrounding brown walls it soared, a tawny confusion of rooftops, citadels, palaces and towers, glittering in the rosy fires of the falling sun. While high on the hill Moriah, at its very center, lifted like a blazing golden heart, was the dazzling beauty of the Temple.

"Well, son?" Smiling faintly, Joseph put an arm around the shoulders of his eldest.

"Yes!" Jesus exclaimed softly, heart pounding. He stood for a moment, marveling. Then, wordlessly, Jesus handed over the reins and ran back to share this moment with Mary.

Elizabeth stood on the rooftop of her house overlooking the village of Ein Karem, shielding her eyes from the slanting sun: a tall, older, but still beautiful woman, very intense but warm, joyous, loving. Everything about her had a rich creamy quality—her skin, her voice, her rounded body. There were dimples at the corners of her full sweet lips, which curved upward, giving the impression that something within her was constantly smiling. Her dark eyes had a gentle radiance. Her black hair, once winged with silver, was now striped with creamy white.

All day long—like some anxious child, she scolded herself—she had interrupted her own eager preparations to come out here and lean on the parapet, searching for the distant roads that led into Jerusalem. The roads were always choked with pilgrims at Passover, but she couldn't remember ever seeing such approaching hordes as now. She fancied she could hear them even from here, singing their songs of ascents, and she found herself singing with them: "We will go into the Lord's house! Within thy gates, Jerusalem, our feet stand at last!"

The servants smiled to hear her; they had missed that lovely voice ever since her husband's death. But today as she worked beside them, seeing that all was in readiness—the lamps, the wine, the food, the flowers—their mistress kept bursting into song. Then she would rush to the rooftop and stand gazing toward the surrounding hills.

More and more, Elizabeth had come to live for the Passover, when she would see Mary and Joseph again. They always stayed with her, although Joachim, for some proud stubborn reason, refused. Their annual reunion had become for Elizabeth the dearest, most significant event of the year. But a great hunger for all her family had been growing in Elizabeth, especially since the loss of Zechariah. She hadn't realized how much she would miss him. John had proved little company; their son was a very independent boy. But now her people were coming, just how many she didn't know, though word had been sent by a runner that Hannah might be among them. Her sister who hadn't even seen John!

And Mary and Joseph were bringing Jesus. *Jesus*, that child of destiny who had brought Mary, his girl mother, so deeply into her life. Elizabeth felt almost faint with anticipation as her eyes combed the hills.

But now that the sun was sinking, the streams of pilgrims had thinned. It would soon be dark. She must hasten inside to see that all the lamps were lighted. Thus, despite her long vigil, Elizabeth missed the sight of them toiling at last up the cobbled hillside to her home. A maid came running. "There is a body of people approaching! Even now they are climbing the steps."

Elizabeth herself flung wide the heavy, brass-trimmed oak door. And there they were, dirty, disheveled, footsore, weary but elated, still in the thrall of having at last reached the Holy City. A crowd she did not altogether recognize— all these children, and to her joy, even more guests than Elizabeth expected. Salome and Ephraim insisted they would lodge elsewhere, but no, no, Elizabeth cried, "There is room, there is room and the food and basins are waiting. Come, come, fill this big empty house for me!"

Laughing and crying, embracing, they swarmed in. Happy, excited, yet most of them suddenly shocked and humbled before the luxury of a high priest's house.

Hannah looked pertly, painfully about. She had quite forgotten how her sister lived. These tapestries and alabaster urns. The ornate lamps like jewels on their tall stands or hanging from the ceiling. The soft rugs, the mosaic and marble floors. . . . And Elizabeth! No, no, this couldn't be her sister, she protested, even as, weeping, they fervently hugged. Not this gracious, still stunning woman with only a few flattering stripes in her hair. Why, she is older than I am! She was at least forty when her only son was born. How is it that, though she is fuller to my arms than when last we held each other (when was that? Hannah groped—too many Passovers ago to remember, although Elizabeth had implored her to come), how could Elizabeth's face remain so rich and smooth? Hannah drew back, stricken, feeling by comparison wizened and old. It's being poor country people, she decided bleakly, having so many children, blessing though they are.

Well, at least Mary and Joseph seemed at home here. And she realized, bewildered, that this was, for them—certainly for Mary—a homecoming her mother could never share. *Never has Mary looked so radiant on any return to the home we made for her. Nor held me the way she and my sister are holding each other now. . . .* No matter, it was too late to suffer again the old pain, the dark fret, some blindness within herself, some barrier that kept them apart. For now she was too tired, miserable, excited—let it go.

"John, John, where are you?" Elizabeth was calling out. "Come, make our kinsmen welcome!"

To his mother's proud relief, he came striding across the polished floors, arms outstretched. John was tall for his age and ruggedly built. Not comely. John's features were big and rather rough, his mouth full-lipped; he had a shock of wild wheat-colored hair and strange light eyes. Yet there was a charming vigor about him, a sense of vitality and warmth that attracted people intensely.

All the family felt it, were almost overpowered by it. A stab of actual pain smote Hannah, along with a blind confusion of loving pride. Her nephew's bright poise. The bracelets on his wrists, the gold ring on his finger. And his *robe:* not only of purest white wool but embroidered. Oh, why, why hadn't she herself made a more suitable garment for Jesus?

Then, seeing how the cousins were joyfully embracing, chattering like old friends, Hannah was ashamed. Almost fiercely she ran to hug Elizabeth once more. "What a handsome boy! What a handsome nephew! Isn't he, Joachim?" she cried. "See how tall John is—almost as tall as Amos."

To her distress, Amos was taking no part in the conversations. Amos, who had seemed so merry on the trip, now held back, shy and self-conscious. "The donkeys must be unloaded," he reminded his father in a low voice. "I will go attend to them."

Elizabeth protested that she would send the servants, but there was a general exodus of men and boys. John had thrown an arm around Jesus' shoulders; he must come onto

the roof to see the Temple with the evening star first shining
and the lights of the city beginning to sparkle. The others
brought up the baggage—there was a nervous if happy commotion as their goatskin bags and bundles were dumped on
the marble floors or carried by the servants to their rooms.
How poor and shabby it all suddenly looked. Hannah
winced to think of her modest gifts to Elizabeth: hon-
eycakes like those their mother used to make when they
were little girls in Bethlehem, some special cheeses.

Maids and menservants escorted the rest to their
rooms; one long chamber had been prepared for the children. But Elizabeth herself preceded Hannah and Joachim
down a long white corridor. She was smiling as she drew
back the velvet drapery. "The room I shared so long with
Zechariah. . . . You must sleep here," she insisted as they
hesitated. She now occupied a simple room. "I have kept it
so against the day when at last you would come to see me."

Meekly, feeling awkward yet pleased, they entered. A
glowing brass brazier made shadows on the white walls,
where leafy designs of grapes, pomegranates and other
fruits were painted in vivid colors. Scented lamps
blossomed from chains like dangling flowers.

"Nazareth is so far," Hannah retorted, groaning.
"Nobody knows *how* far until they walk the distance we
have come these past few days."

"Oh, my goodness, I wasn't scolding," Elizabeth
laughed. "Forgive me. I know *I* couldn't do it. Each year I
marvel that so many people come so far to worship. Even
the men, let alone women and children."

"It's the Law," Joachim reminded gruffly.

"For men, yes, but not for us, and you men are strong.
I don't see how women do it, especially at our age." She
hugged her sister. "Oh, your poor *feet*!" she cried to both of
them.

A maid was already at the door with basin and towels.
To their astonishment, Elizabeth took the things from her
and knelt beside them. "Take off your sandals," she ordered.

"No, no, we can't let you!" Hannah protested frantically. Though deeply touched, she was embarrassed. That

Elizabeth should even see their dirty country feet—so thick and calloused and homely with broken nails. She looked helplessly at Joachim, chagrined to see that he was smiling. In his remote dignified way, Joachim bowed slightly and sat down on the couch. With a sigh he shook out a pebble.

"I will be honored," he told her.

Outside, leaning on the parapet, John was pointing north and east to the Temple. "See, its white marble walls seem to have a special glow at this hour. And when the breeze is right—" the boy cocked his big sandy head and sniffed wryly—"there is a special aroma."

Jesus agreed. Ever since their awed approach to the fabulous city he'd been aware of this strange smell. "Incense?" he asked.

John laughed shortly and folded his arms. "No, it's the fires being stoked for tomorrow's burnings," John informed him. "And the smell of the victims' stables: oxen, bullocks, goats, sheep. The smell of their offal, and the smell of their fear."

Jesus was puzzled. "But I thought only lambs were used for the Paschal sacrifice."

"Yes, lambs for the .Passover feast. But sin offerings, too, later in the week." John was grinning faintly. "And bribes to heaven in the hope of favors. And the greater the sin or the greater the favor, sometimes the bigger the beast."

As Jesus winced, John grabbed his shoulders, face joyfully intense. "I'm so glad you've finally come, my cousin. I have dreamed of you for years—and now here you are and we must talk. We need to talk to each other: of things, many things, that would only upset my mother, and perhaps yours too, to hear."

They were interrupted by a summons to supper.

"Only enough to ease your hunger after such a long journey," Elizabeth told them, "for tomorrow night we will eat richly. Dear Joachim, you must lead the prayers. Come, we will all sit down together." Tall and gracious, flushed with pleasure, she indicated the silken cushions arranged before the linen cloth. "It was never the custom of this family to separate men from women at meals." Then, lest Hannah think she was belittling the custom still common in the country, she added quickly, laughing. "There were never enough men!"

Rejoicing, Joachim lifted his arms. And as they began to break the bread, to dip it in the savory stew, to share and praise Hannah's gifts of cakes and cheeses, their nervousness vanished, love bound them. It was so good to partake of such food at last after makeshift meals on the road. The wine was sweet and hot, warmed at a rosy brazier whose lights danced on the high ceilings; a servant kept pouring it into silver mugs. Their tongues loosened, they regaled Elizabeth and John with stories of their trip.

Even Amos joined in. He was a good storyteller when the mood was upon him. His shy face shone. "You would have been proud of my father, leading the singing as we marched through Beth-Shan."

"Singing?" Elizabeth exclaimed.

"Yes, singing, though some wouldn't call it that." He grinned at Joachim, who was chuckling. "'Damn the idols!' my father said. Their temples were lining both sides of the highway as we approached. Women were warning their children not to look. That's when he shouted, 'Damn the idols! Jews shouldn't go slinking through this heathen city. We will lift up our heads and sing.' And so we marched to the Jewish quarter, beating our staves on the pavement and singing as loud as we could: 'The Lord makes us strong, sing praises! Sing to Israel's God!'"

"Sing praises, sing praises!" the children began to chant, delighted, and suddenly Salome, her husband, and the others joined in.

"How I wish I could have been with you!" John was leaning forward, excited. "What did the authorities do?"

Joachim snatched the story from his son. "They came running out of their houses and shops to watch. Most of them smiled, some of them laughed. They considered us just a ragtailed band of Galileans, I suppose, willing to risk arrest for the One we worship. No threat to them. . . . Not yet, not yet," he added, with a small tight smile. "Let them wait. They don't realize—when the Messiah comes—"

A hush fell over the table. "When the Messiah comes," Elizabeth said quietly. Her long fingers were twisting the stem of her goblet. As yet she had not allowed herself to look, really look, at Mary's son. Now she lifted her eyes and caught her breath at his beauty as he sat there, smiling so innocently and proudly, first at his grandfather, then at John, who shot suddenly to his feet. Eyes shining, John began to recite the ancient prayer, asking—yes, demanding— that the Christ, so long promised, appear: "Let your name, O God, be praised and glorified in this world which You have created according to your good pleasure; vouchsafe to establish your reign; let redemption flourish, *and the Messiah quickly come.*"

"Let the Messiah quickly come!" Echoes went up from the table, although Mary and Joseph sat silent. And the children clapped their hands and shouted, "Amen, amen!"

The meal was over; the dishes were being cleared away. John and Jesus again started for the roof; then, seeing Amos' hurt look, they urged him to join them. He sauntered after them, feeling too old for their idle chatter but hating to be left. Mary began quietly gathering up her children to be put to bed. Elizabeth walked with her to their chamber. Holding a lamp, she stood looking in. It felt strange, seeing Mary with her own family. How small she seemed, to be in such control. The boys were sulking: Why couldn't they too go out on the roof? Tomorrow night, she assured them, after the feast. But Jesus—! "Jesus is older." Yes, Leah could sleep with her favorite blanket, it was somewhere among the bags. Mary would find it.

At last they were quiet. Mary blew out the lamps, except for a small saucer burning in a niche, and crept out. She was suddenly so weary she could hardly stand. Elizabeth reached out one arm to hold her. "Oh, my dear, my poor little girl!"

"Elizabeth, *Elizabeth.*"

They clung to each other fiercely for a second, the way they often did. But this time Mary's shoulders were shaking. The face she lifted in the lamplight was pale and, for an instant, young no longer. "Forgive me, it's just that now that we have actually brought him here—!"

"Hush, hush," Elizabeth whispered. "We will talk soon. Not tonight, you are so tired, but soon, when we can find a time of privacy."

Hannah couldn't sleep. The bed was too soft, it would smother her; the coverlet was too slick. And she would surely fall—whoever heard of a bed with legs, gilt ones at that? How could Joachim sprawl there, so promptly snoring? Fearfully, Hannah tested the distance to the floor, and carefully backed down onto it, pulling a woolen spread after her.

Joachim roused up, blinking, not sure where they were. Then he saw his wife, trying to settle herself. "Hannah, what are you *doing?*"

"There is a rug here; it will make a fine mat for sleeping."

Dismayed, but too exhausted to discuss it, Joachim burrowed deeper into the clouds that seemed such heaven to his aching bones. But his wife's voice came plaintively through the darkness. "Joachim?"

"Yes, Hannah, what is it?"

"That gold ring John was wearing—surely you noticed? And his robe, that beautiful robe! Oh, why didn't Mary—or I, for that matter—see that Jesus arrived in a better robe?"

Joachim groaned. "Hannah, please. Life should not be a contest: who is fairer, who is better dressed. We are here for a sacred reason, to thank our God for our deliverance!"

Yet her distress was real, Joachim realized. He reached over, groped for her bony hand, and pressed it.

"You must not grieve over such trifles, Hannah. Try to remember, God has a tremendous mission for our Mary's son. What does it matter now about a ring?" He laughed impatiently. "A mere garment, a robe? When one day he will be a *king!*"

They lay for a moment in silence.

"Pray that we live to see it," Joachim said finally, sighing. "But even if we don't, rejoice, since that is your nature, that then he will have a dozen rings and bracelets, and robes that will put his cousin's, or even Solomon's, to shame."

* * *

John dashed off before daybreak, for he assisted the priests on festival days. Last night he had urged the men too to leave early, if they hoped to avoid the long lines before the booths of the money changers. They laid their coins on the table as he spoke, anxious lest they had not brought enough. The rate of exchange had gone up, he warned; the thieves were charging worshipers more than ever to trade their Roman coins for the clean Hebrew shekels needed to purchase animals for the sacrifice. "Even the price of beasts is higher. I'm afraid there'll be stiff bidding for the best." It was all fearful, deplorable, yet somehow exciting.

Mary awoke that morning, startled to see that Joseph's place beside her was empty. She realized the household was already stirring—she must run to see about her children's clothes. To her surprise, her younger sons were already dressed in the brightly colored garments she had woven and mended with such care; they stood awaiting her inspection. Hannah, scolding and fussing about keeping close to their father and staying clean, was triumphantly tying a final sash. "They've all washed and said their prayers," she announced briskly. "We decided to let you rest."

Mary turned to Joseph in astonishment. "But I thought they were coming later with me."

"They've already waited long enough to see the Temple," Joseph said. He felt guilty at having held them back from their brother so often on the trip. He must compensate; the last thing he wanted was enmity among his sons. "Passover," he claimed heartily, "is the time for men of all ages to do these things together."

Mary straightened her sons' little velvet prayer caps: ruby, turquoise, green. They were like small bouncing flowers. And now Jesus, all in white like Joseph, was putting on his own scarlet cap. He looked eager if a little nervous. He kissed his mother and held tight to her for a moment. Then they were gone: Joachim, Ephraim, the lot of them, marching down the hill through the sunrise, while their women watched from the roof.

Of a sudden a sense of freedom swept the house, the

release of women alone together. Elizabeth told the servants they would not be needed; she herself brought bread and figs and thick mugs of warmed goat's milk to the small table around which they huddled, in a sunny chamber she used for sorting flowers. It smelled of pots and stone vessels, and the spicy fragrance of the multicolored lilies which everywhere bedecked the house.

Now, at last, delicious woman talk: News of the family, for which Elizabeth hungered. The aunts and uncles and cousins—why didn't more of them look her up when they came to Jerusalem? Elizabeth asked. Had they thought her too fine, as the wife of a priest? It would mean even more to her now that she was a widow. . . . Illnesses, marriages, babies. Cousin Deborah had the biggest house in Nazareth, they told her, and four children, but unfortunately all girls.

"As you know, I have only one child," Salome acknowledged forlornly, "and that too a daughter."

"In time, in time," Hannah said. "If you can ever get away from your in-laws. Smithies," she informed Elizabeth, on a note of contempt. "What can you expect of smithies?"

"Nice pots to cook with," piped up Ann, who was enjoying this as much as the women.

But no, now, the morning was going too fast. Time they too dressed and started for the Temple; the feast officially began right after noon. Where was Mary? She must have slipped back to her couch. Together, Hannah and Elizabeth went to call her. But for a moment they could only stand gazing at the slight figure lying with one arm shielding her face. Suddenly their eyes met, and wordlessly they gripped each other's hand. Then gently, very gently, Hannah shook her daughter.

Chapter 5

———————————————

The walk to the city had never seemed so far to Mary. Only four miles—nothing compared with the long marches of the past few days, or that last hard hot climb through the barren wilderness—but today it seemed endless. Her feet, she found, had swollen; it was all she could do to squeeze them into her sandals. Her head felt light. She kept trying not to limp, not to let the others know.

Jerusalem too: the mad confusion of walls, rooftops, courtyards, markets; the incredible stench; the racket—donkeys, camels, carts, vendors. "Water, fresh water!" the sellers screamed as the merciless sun beat down. Buffeted and jostled, the women paused to drink. All about them were mobs of shoving, shouting people pressing toward the Temple, but laughing and calling out to each other too, for however sacred the festival, it was also a time of high spirits. They could hear trumpets, wild and golden in the distance. There was a frantic bleating as flocks were driven by. So many pilgrims had come this year the Temple stables could not contain all the sheep; boys with sticks were darting about, herding them from nearby pens.

"Are we late?" Hannah asked anxiously, as the trumpets drilled the air again. "Will they let us in?"

"The ceremonies go on all day," Elizabeth said, "but it would be well to hurry." She strode a little ahead, beckoning, smiling, knowing her way—through the immense stone wall, along deep covered passages, to the massive, richly ornamented Beautiful Gate.

After the heat and din of the streets the Temple seemed a refuge, despite its own seas of people and noise.

Hannah gasped at its splendor; she had almost forgotten—it
had been so long ago—this assault of cedar, marble, and
gold. The soaring blue and white columns garlanded with
vines and grapes. The porticoes and pillars and arcades.
And the white marble steps and tiers that led up and up to
the very house of God, all gold, purest gold, almost blinding in the sun, its glittering topmost spikes piercing the
deep blue heart of heaven.

In the Women's Court now: shrill babble of voices and
the press and smell of women's bodies, mingling with the
heavy odor of incense and smoke drifting down from the
highest tier where white-clad priests were swarming. At
the front, two boys stood guarding a marble bench: friends
of John's, wearing the short white tunics of Temple aides.
Waving, one of them ran to escort them through. Feeling
privileged and relieved, the women sat down.

Here they could look up fifteen curved steps into the
Court of Men. Impossible to pick out their own among that
crowd of males whose backs were turned, anxiously though
they tried. Never mind, for up more steps, on the final
court, the solemn procession of priests was forming, the
high priest at its head. An awed hush fell as he moved forward in his magnificent blue robes: a towering man made
even taller by his turban, which was encircled with a golden
crown. The lesser priests, in spotless white linen and tur-
bans followed, then the Levites, playing lyres: *O, give
thanks to the Lord; for he is good, for his mercy endures
forever!*

Hannah was so excited she wanted to weep; it had
been years since she'd witnessed such a spectacle. Even as
she prostrated herself and joined the prayers, she was trying to remember how it was, so she could describe all this
for poor blind Esau. Yes, and Judith and Matthew—how she
missed them, especially Matthew! Oh, how thankful she
was that Salome had come along. And Joseph had been
right in bringing all his children.

The high priest was approaching the balustrade, the
twelve gems on his breastplate flashing. They represented
the twelve tribes of Israel—so precious they were kept in
the custody of the Romans, Elizabeth said, released only for

this occasion. (Such arrogance, how dared they?) It was also said the jewels would never burn their brightest until the Ark was returned. Yet it was hard to see how they could blaze more brilliantly than now.

The priest's robe was decorated with scarlet and blue pomegranates, his thick waist girded with a sash of blue silk and spun gold. They could hear the tinkling of little bells as he spread his arms for the blessing; the sleeves of his garments looked like wings. He had been very close to Zechariah. Seeing Elizabeth, the elegant figure bowed in recognition; his holy eyes smiled a gentle welcome to her guests.

Hannah's heart nearly burst with pride. Then it occurred to her to search the hosts of other priests for a possible glimpse of Abner, a Nazareth youth of priestly descent who had once been in love with Mary; after her betrothal he'd come to the Temple to study. But no, never mind, for there was a stirring, a sense of anticipation in the Men's Court just above. Aides were lining up the fathers and their sons to ascend. How young and fair the boys were, nervously inching forward, but none so fair as Jesus. Hannah strained for a sight of her darling far down the line. Would he spare a glance for them as they walked past? No, for when at last he and Joseph appeared, to climb the steps where the high priest waited, there was no time.

Impossible to hear what Joseph was saying, but they knew: "I am Joseph of Nazareth, and this is Jesus, my first-born son." The priest leaned forward, murmuring something and smiling before he placed his hands on the boy's curly head. It seemed to Hannah his prayer for Jesus was longer than for the others.

Her daughter's son! Did the priest realize? she wondered wildly. Priests, high priests, had special powers; they were closer to God. Perhaps even now he sensed who this was. An awful impulse came over Hannah; she wanted to leap to her feet and shout. Shaken, she glanced at Mary, who was staring straight ahead, hands locked in her lap. It was Elizabeth who turned proud wet eyes to meet Hannah's hungry gaze. . . .

Overhead, a hundred silver trumpets flashed as they

were tilted toward the sun; their golden throats wrenched the skies again.

Dry-lipped, heart pounding, Jesus stood waiting. The sheep tied to cedar posts were being released. There was a renewed bleating and blatting. Their little hooves rumbled as one by one they were led or shoved up the ramp, to be given over to each boy who had just been blessed. It had been deemed that on this day he would walk beside his father to deliver up the sacrifice.

The unblemished yearling lamb Joseph had purchased this morning was put into his arms. The boy could feel its warm body lunging and kicking against him, its heart beating wildly for life. It knew—it knew!—and was bawling piteously. "Hold him tighter, son," Joseph said as they strode forward, "lest he escape." Jesus struggled with his burden, terrified. Its wool was soft, its black nose brushed damp and chill against his face.

"Forgive me, Father, don't think me unmanly, but I cannot, I cannot—!"

Wordlessly, Joseph grabbed the frantic lamb and handed it to a short bald priest in a bloodstained smock, who carried it up to the marble table. The small head was tipped back, a knife flashed, the first blood spurted and was caught in a copper chalice, to be dashed upon the altar. Fresh-faced young Levites leaped to drain the remaining blood into a gutter beside the platform, where it would run, scarlet and foaming, on into the Kidron River. All was accomplished swiftly, the skinning and the gutting and the slashing of the little still-jerking limbs. The Levites snatched the entrails and ran to wash them in the hall of the spring. Running back, they were presented to the barefoot priest, who added them to the flesh and fat he was arranging on a golden platter. Dashed with the salt of the covenant, sprinkled with incense, the offering was then lifted to heaven and carried to the horned altar where the sacred fires burned.

It was soon over. In a few minutes another young priest made his way through the hubbub and down the steps to them, carrying a large package wrapped in palm leaves. He was tall and gaunt in a gown that was likewise bloodstained.

He had deep, kind, friendly, yet somehow lonely eyes. Joseph cried out softly at sight of him. "Abner!"

"Joseph!" The priest was grinning faintly. "And this is your son." He turned to the boy. "Jesus, son of Mary, I watched for your coming. Like your father, you look strong. Here, you can carry the Paschal lamb for your family's feast."

Jesus took the package. The lamb, so recently warm and fighting for life, had not seemed heavy; but now that it was only raw dead flesh, he could scarcely hold it; descending the steps he stumbled with its weight.

At Elizabeth's, the ovens were already hot for the roasting of the lambs, one to each family. Carefully, so as not to break their bones, the small pink bodies were inserted, and soon the delicate savor of their cooking flesh filled the house.

John had not yet returned from his duties at the Temple. Jesus sat alone in the high-ceilinged room they shared, his head in his hands. His face felt damp, his brow was flushed. He started guiltily as Joseph came seeking him. "Forgive me, Father, but the smell of the meat sickens me. I'm afraid I cannot eat this Passover lamb."

"Come now, you must try. You know it is a sacred commandment."

The boy looked up, stricken. "But I *held* him, Father. I felt his heart beating against my heart, yet I let them take him from me!"

Lightly Joseph shook his shoulder. "You must put aside such thoughts. It will spoil the festivities for the rest of us. Come, don't worry your mother or distress your aunt." His own voice was more jovial than he felt. He had been afraid of this; in fact, had dreaded it ever since Jesus first started to school. Now, too late, Joseph realized how grievously he had failed in not bringing the boy to the Temple long before, and accustomed him gradually to the rite. At first it was partly for the child's own safety, Joseph reasoned. He had not dared dismiss the possibility, however remote, that there might still be danger from Herod's henchmen; or, more likely, the threat of another uprising, with the horrible consequences he himself remembered so well. So be it, he had done the best he could. . . .

Jesus was struggling with himself. What was the matter with him? He had witnessed the necessary killing of animals on the farm. And each year at Passover, while his parents were away, he shared the Paschal lamb without hesitation. One of his uncles who couldn't go would have killed it, and one of his grandmothers roasted it on a pomegranate branch, over an open fire. He remembered the fat hissing onto the smoking coals. A pitcher of the lamb's blood stood nearby. Then, when the meat was crisp and brown, someone—Uncle Cleo or Esau—once Joachim, when he was too ill to make the long march—would dip a hyssop branch into the pitcher and bring it forth dripping with bright red blood, which he solemnly dabbed on the doorposts as the people of Moses had done.

But this mass butchery! He was unprepared for the terrified bleating of innocent creatures being shoved, dragged, even kicked to their doom. What had they done, what was their crime? Did the sins of man really ride in their blood? Were they carrying man's guilt and error and vileness to be burned in the fires? Then why did people continue to sin? Why did they leave these very altars to cheat and fight and fornicate? He had seen them in Nazareth; even here in this beautiful city he had already been sickened to see them, cursing, drunken, mounting women in the gutters like dogs.

What did the Father want with their cruel sacrifice? There was a mystery here that he must solve. . . .

To Joseph's relief, John burst in upon them. Rough, boisterous, looking tired, but to their surprise he was beaming. "I'm hungry!" he cried. He lunged playfully at his cousin and pulled him to his feet. "Come on, we will worship God with wine and song and outeat all the others."

The unleavened bread had cooled, the sauce and the wine were ready, yes, and the crisp brown lamb. And Jesus rallied, joining hands with the rest of them gathered around the table. He swallowed the salted water in remembrance of the tears their forefathers had shed; he ate the bitter herbs and devoured the lamb that was slain for them. But the wine was sweet on his tongue, as glass after glass of it was passed from hand to hand. By the third, the goblet of benediction, as they were singing the hallel, such a thrill of wonder and promise rose in him he could scarcely contain it. "Not to us, Lord, not to us the glory; let your name alone be honored!"

A shock of love and joy possessed him, an agony of loving. He saw Joachim's grizzled, life-toughened, kind old face, and the tart-sweet burning eyes of his grandmother. His sister Ann, so innocent and small . . . his restless, wriggling brothers . . . And Amos and Salome and Ephraim . . . Elizabeth and John. . . . Marvelous, unreal, their faces loomed and receded; he longed to reach out and touch them, confirm them with his fingers. And his parents—he caught his breath at their beauty, as if seeing them for the first time. They were bathed in radiance: Joseph, like some graceful young god of the pagans; and Mary—her dark hair in its coronet of braids became a nimbus, and small golden butterflies sprang out of the fluttering candlelight to dance across her cheeks.

But it wasn't only these, his people, but the servants and the priests and all the people in the Temple as well. And the beggars and the Romans on the streets. They were being born to him, somewhere in his being, yet he had known them all since the beginning of time. Every breath and bone of them, every experience of birth and death, every sin and hope and dream and fear. All this ran singing and sobbing through his own blood in this instant of awareness. And as the fourth and final glass was raised in joy, his young eyes filled with tears.

"Blessed is he who comes in the name of the Lord!"

Exhausted by all the excitement and emotion, Hannah slept. The men were again at the Temple. And Salome had taken Mary's children into Jerusalem; they'd been teasing for days to see the shops. Ephraim and their grandfather had given them each a handful of jingling coins to spend. "Sister, you rest too," Salome urged as Ann and the boys rushed down the steps. "You look pale. Remember, we still have a long journey back."

Now, except for the muted voices and footsteps of servants, the cooing of pigeons on a ledge, an occasional rattle of vessels, all was quiet. Eyes shining with anticipation, Elizabeth turned to Mary. "Come, at last we can talk!"

"Yes, oh, yes!" It was the hour they both lived for all year—their talks, their precious talks. Mary felt almost faint with her sense of release.

And following her aunt onto the balcony, she remembered their first reunion five or six years before, her first trip to the Passover with Joseph, when the children were small. How, while others were at the festival, they had escaped even as now, desperate to share what was on their hearts. "Oh, Elizabeth, I have wanted to tell you this so long," she cried then. "That time we first brought Jesus to the Temple—the time of my purification, when he must be dedicated—"

"I will never forget the time. I was aware of it even then, almost to the very hour."

"There was no way to see you," Mary rushed on. "That was my dearest wish, to see you again. To see your precious baby, and to have you see mine. But we dared not; we had to hurry, we were in great danger."

"Of course I know that, darling." Elizabeth leaned closer to clasp her hand. "Zechariah and I heard about the slaughter in Bethlehem. All Judea knew of it. That beast, that monster!" Her eyes blazed; her full sweet face, usually wearing its little half smile, was grim: "We were nearly crazed with fear for you. We hired people to search for you. To think that here we were, our own child safe, while you, who had become like a daughter to us—" She brushed away tears. "Oh, thank God, thank God you were spared!"

"And there is something else," Mary said, her own eyes wet. "I have never spoken of it to anyone save Joseph—not even my mother. There was a man in the Temple that day, a very old man named Simeon. He was waiting for death, he told us, but he knew he could not die until he had beheld the Messiah." Mary was trembling; it was a minute before she could go on. "The Holy Spirit had revealed this to him, he said, and led him into the Temple to find us. Then he took our baby in his arms and blessed him. And he

predicted—he predicted—I shall never forget his words—
'*Behold, this child is set for the rising again of many in
Israel.*' But then he turned to me and told me, '*Yet there
will be pain for you, his mother, and a sword shall pierce
your heart!*'"

Elizabeth had held her that day and rocked her. Spoken words of comfort. "Old men say strange things, Mary.
Zechariah prophesied too. When at last his tongue was
loosed, he too spoke in the Holy Spirit. How I wish you
could have heard him," she said, "for it was a beautiful
hymn of thanksgiving. It was quite long; I remember only
parts of it. But I know it promised that we would be saved
from our enemies, that we might serve God without fear!"
Elizabeth was smiling, her voice cheerful, in part to comfort
and convince herself.

"And our sons?" Mary asked. Sitting upright, she
wiped her tear-streaked face. "Did he speak of them too?"

"Yes, of course. In fact, the last of his beautiful litany
was addressed directly to John. It was the day of John's cir-
cumcision. I'll never forget how his father took the baby
from me and gazed into his little face. '*And you, child, will
be called the prophet of the Highest,*' he said, '*and go before
the Lord to prepare his ways.*' He said that John would
teach the people they must repent if they expected salvation, and that a tender and merciful God was sending a
great light for those who walk in darkness."

Elizabeth paused, regarding Mary. "You alone know
who that is, Mary. You and Joseph."

They had spoken of this endlessly, each time they saw
each other, wondering, marveling. Yet those were the years
when their sons were still precious and small, playing with
other children, going to school. The future seemed mysterious and far away, surely as filled with promise as with
threat. Just being together made it so, here where they had
often sat working on mosaics, while their babes were safe in
their wombs. The same little table was still there, the same
little reed basket with its bright familiar tiles.

But now, suddenly, inexplicably—overnight, it
seemed—their sons were twelve and thirteen years old! On
the brink of manhood, Mary realized. The trip to Jerusalem

this time—her mother, even Joseph, thought Mary's exhaustion was due to having the children along. How could she explain to them the inner thing that had fastened itself upon her about midway, heavy, dark, anxious, so that every step was leaden? And the nearer they drew to their destination, the greater her dread. A kind of panic beset her, shameful, absurd. She had wanted to snatch Jesus and flee with him into the hills. And when at last the caravan ascended the final ridge and paused in awed excitement to gaze across the broad gorge of the Kidron to where the fabled city rose, Mary covered her eyes. She turned and sat beside the road, busying herself with a sandal. A strap was broken; she must fix it somehow before she could go on.

She blurted this out to Elizabeth now. "Am I strong enough to face . . . whatever it is God wills for him? To stand by Jesus and help him? I am so torn sometimes; God has also sent me other children. I mustn't fail them either." She was struggling to make it clear. "You have told me often what Zechariah prophesied about our sons. But what of us, their mothers? Did your husband and my uncle prophesy of us as well?"

Elizabeth sat considering, her fingers playing with the tiles. "No," she said, regretful and yet resigned. "Nothing." She rose then, arms folded, and walked to the parapet. She was wearing a dress of some soft light stuff, silver-threaded like her hair. The sky was hot and very blue. Plumes of smoke still rose from the Temple—a glimpse of gold in the distance—and drifted lazily toward Herod's palace, ironically darkening as they approached it, sometimes obscuring the palace face.

Pigeons still crooned and strutted on the ledge below. Absently, Elizabeth reached for a crust someone had left and began tossing crumbs to them. They swarmed up around her, luminous, begging. A small breeze had risen, stirring her hair, sharpening the faint ever-present odor. Suddenly, dusting her hands and fending off the pigeons, Elizabeth came swiftly, gracefully, back to the table. "Mary, listen to me," she said, sitting down. "Every word that your uncle uttered is true; the Holy Spirit does not lie. John *is* destined to be the forerunner of Jesus. The messenger warning people to listen. But what the Spirit did not tell us is that our sons will be rebels! Breakers of images. I can see it already in John. John is—difficult. Even you may have noticed. I am frightened by him sometimes—his ideas. I don't know how to handle him."

Elizabeth paused. Her rich throaty voice was troubled.

"Mary, I'm not surprised at your apprehension. To be chosen of God as you and I were chosen, and as our sons are chosen, does not mean life will be easy for us. Any of us. Quite the contrary. Anyone who goes against tradition is persecuted, suffers terribly. There is jealousy, terrible jealousy between the Sadducees and Pharisees, even among the priests. The fight for honor and position is appalling. And the women don't escape. How well I know that, as the wife of a high priest! For you there will be jealousy even in Nazareth, I'm afriad. Even among his brothers and sisters, his own family."

"Oh, no!" Mary cried. "Not my children."

"You must be prepared for it, Mary. And you must be prepared for danger. Actual danger. Anyone who threatens authority—" Elizabeth's voice was not quite steady. She rose again and began searching about for something else to feed the birds. "I thought surely there was more bread lying about. No matter." She drew a deep breath, stood bracing herself against the stones. With an effort she went on. "We both have seen the crosses, Mary. And I—pray God you never will—but *I* have seen beheadings." She shuddered. "That old man who spoke to you in the Temple—Simeon— was right. A sword will indeed pierce your heart." Unconsciously she touched her own breast. "Already I feel the sword in mine."

Elizabeth turned then, and seeing Mary's white, strained face, rushed to kneel beside her. "Forgive me, I'm just a foolish old woman saying wild and foolish things!"

"No, what you say is true. I'm a grown woman, I must know."

"Yes. You're no longer the little girl who first came to me—or so you seemed then." Wistful but smiling, she lifted Mary's chin—her niece, her dearest friend, the daughter she had never had. "We're both grown women now, Mary, and we are strong. God would not choose weak women to bear and stand behind strong sons."

She gave Mary a fond little shake. Suddenly laughing as well as crying, they sprang up. For the pigeons had come pecking about their feet. And Hannah stood in the doorway, yawning and grimacing as she shielded her eyes to look for them. "Come, sister, join us," Elizabeth called out in her usual rich sweet voice. "But first ask a maid to bring us some bread for our friends."

Jesus lay on his couch, appalled at what John was saying. Yet why am I so shocked? he wondered. It was as if he had heard these same words long ago, experienced the self-same scene. This moon shining beyond tall arched windows where long white draperies were stirring . . . the damp nighttime fragrance of the garden, subtly flavored even now with the acrid scent of burning. Even the thump of his cousin's dropped belt and sandals, the sight of John's already hairy young body as he pulled his shirt over his shaggy head. Every brisk, merry, half-mocking gesture, every toss of that wild yellow mane. . . . Where have I known and loved and been rudely shaken by this boy before? But no, reasonably, had they not been together hours on end this week? And in this very room?

"I reject the Temple," John said, blowing out the lamp. "I reject the priests, the entire priesthood."

"But your father, Zechariah, was a priest!"

"Yes, a high priest. Obviously much favored by the Lord." John laughed shortly, flinging himself down. "You know, of course, the circumstances of my birth? My mother shared them with me shortly before my father died."

"I know only you were considered a great blessing, since your parents were along in years."

"I was considered a miracle!" John laughed. "Quite literally, my father was speechless. He was a good man, my father, a true servant of God, incorruptible. Yet even my father was blind to the injustices, the corruption. He accepted without question the moneymaking in the Temple, the tithes and taxes and offerings. To glorify God? Ha! Tell me, does the One who owns the universe need money? No,

only the scribes and Pharisees who run the Temple. And
the priests. Ah, the priests! Luxury for the priests. Luxury"—he snorted—"while other people starve."

John sat upright, made a sweeping gesture of contempt
for the room: its golden candlesticks, gleaming in the moonlight, its graceful Greek chests and chairs and tables.

"I reject this luxury for myself. True, my mother is accustomed to it, and she has earned it. She has given her
whole life to the Temple, training the virgins, most of them
from very poor homes. She has taught them, helped them
to make good marriages. She has worked hard; she deserves
it." John lay back down. "It would be unthinkable to disturb
her. Mind you don't ever tell her what I've said."

There was silence for a long moment, though John
threshed about. Finally he spoke again. "Jesus?"

"Yes, cousin John."

"I mentioned my own birth—there were all sorts of
prophecies and predictions, though I wonder sometimes if I
can ever live up to them. But you—do you know the circumstances of yours?"

"My mother has told me very little. Except that I was
born in Bethlehem. My parents had to flee into Egypt; it
seems there was a slaughter of newborn babies."

"But why did Herod command that slaughter?"

"The man was mad."

Both boys were sitting up now, staring at each other
from their separate beds. John gasped. "You mean to say—
good heavens, you are telling me you don't know?"

"Know what?" Jesus demanded. His head was reeling.
It was as it had been during those first days at school; he felt
lost and drowning in something too vivid to articulate. . . .
A stable, he could see and smell it—the hay and the beasts
and a small red fire. And a great light, a star blazing . . . and
music, thrilling music from somewhere, beyond and yet
blending with the song of suffering which came from a girl
who struggled moaning on the hay. . . . And yes, he knew,
had known forever and yet did not know, quite know, who or
what had brought this travail upon her. Only that he loved
her, he loved her, and so did the man who knelt beside her,

though both of them wept and yet rejoiced at what she must achieve.

Blood then, hot blood spurting. And a baby crying. His own voice crying. . . . The boy threw a hand across his cold wet brow.

"But you must know!" John said. He came, almost angrily, to perch beside his cousin on the couch. He sat there, staring into the tormented face. "You were born with the knowledge. You are the one who must save us."

"I am but twelve years old!"

"We will soon be men. We are men already in the sight of God. And we both have a thing to do. But I am nothing compared to you," John said bluntly. "I will simply go ahead to prepare the way. When the time comes I will tell the people who you are."

John sprang up abruptly and plunged to the window. All his bright bravado had vanished. His shoulders were hunched together, bowed, as if under some intolerable burden; he seemed very young and defenseless as he stood there, gazing out into the night.

Jesus waited, shaken. It was hard to breathe, such fear, such sudden terrible fear for his cousin clutched his heart.

John finally turned to face him, but it was a moment before he could bring himself to say the words: *"You are the Messiah."*

Chapter 6

*B*erating his own curiosity, Nicodemus, the Pharisee banker, found himself pushing through the Temple gates—a tall, bald, patrician-looking man with a kindly erudite face. He would not tarry long, he told himself, for the caravan from Egypt, due days ago, had been delayed by the pilgrim-choked roads; it had arrived only last night, and the traders would be storming his place of business. He would merely stay long enough to see if the boy his friend had described was still there. Not only listening, Joseph of Arimathea had said, but astounding the older men with his questions. He called himself Jesus—from Nazareth, of all places—and was barely twelve, yet challenging some of the best minds in Jerusalem.

Nicodemus grinned . . . or so they thought.

The mobs that had jammed the courts during the festival had thinned; only a few faithful were here bowing and murmuring, or prostrating themselves on the marble floors. Only a few sheep still kicked and mourned in their stalls; the sellers sat listless, yawning. The wonderful place stank of offal and burnt flesh, but high on the horned altar a single fire smoldered, while a brisk young priest, looking bored and almost impatient, offered up a dove for some poor couple holding a babe below. Yet Nicodemus could hear voices and sense unusual activity in the Men's Court beyond.

With a ridiculous sense of anticipation, Nicodemus hurried up the steps and through the final gate. Evidently word had spread. He had seldom seen so many rabbis and scribes and doctors of the Law—many of them members of the Sanhedrin like himself—or such a crowd of Pharisees and their rival Sadducees, standing amused or amazed or looking indignant, some of them, as they listened to the bright voice that was ringing out even now.

Nicodemus pressed to the front where he could see and hear this strange boy, who was perched a few steps above the men. Joseph of Arimathea was right; there was something unusual about him, beyond the fact that he was tall for his age and beautiful, very beautiful, with his mop of shining black curls and those eyes—never had he seen such huge, sweet, beseeching, yet fervent eyes. There was a boldness about him, along with a trembling near humility. Evidently his period of submissive listening and questioning was over. He was speaking with a kind of shy passion, an outrage softened by courtesy.

He also seemed very young and vulnerable in his poor robe—and this touched Nicodemus. The robe was clean but faded and a trifle too big for him.

With a nod, a pudgy warning finger, Joseph made room for Nicodemus on a bench directly in front. Joseph was a tough, keen, heavyset old scribe, wise, alert, much respected. Today he was hunched slightly forward, eyes narrow in their fleshy pouches, listening intently. He seemed to be both confronting yet subtly encouraging the speaker.

"Why do men slay and sacrifice the ox?" the boy was asking. "The faithful, gentle ox! I have driven, yes, and ridden my grandfather's ox. Would it please God that I bring it here to be burned?"

He wiped away angry tears. "Farmers need their oxen! Israel needs its asses and its oxen to cultivate the land that God has given us. Why—tell me *why* each year thousands of beasts are brought here to be butchered and burned? Yes, and sold here for handsome profits? To line the coffers of the Temple, while the land lies fallow and people starve?"

There was a noisy reaction; Joseph of Arimathea lifted a hand to still the crowd. "Now, now, hear him out."

"Forgive me," Jesus pleaded. "I mean no disrespect. I am eager to learn—as you know, I have sat listening and asking other questions for hours. But now I must speak out. How is it that the priests, with their generous portions, can eat meat daily, while the farmers who raise the animals are lucky to have meat on their tables once a week? And the tithes and offerings," he rushed on, over angry protests—especially from the Sadducees, for many of them were priests themselves, or descendants of priests. "My grandfather is a farmer, my father a carpenter—they can barely pay the taxes demanded by Rome. Yet our own religion gives us no relief; instead, it only compounds the misery with even worse taxes. Plus the tithes, the merciless tithes."

The scribe spoke up then, his phlegmy voice patient but stern. "You challenge sacred scriptures, son. The tithe goes back to Moses. Our God himself commanded that the firstfruits be offered up, rejoicing."

"Yes, but the Father said also, '*You are to feast on all the good things I have given you, you and your household, and with you the Levite and the stranger*.' Those firstfruits were not simply to be devoured by the priests! They were returned to the people who produced them. But now—how can there be rejoicing when the authorities have so cruelly twisted and multiplied those tithes? Turned them into forced tributes?" he demanded. "Fees to be collected on every little thing—from the eggs in the nest to the smallest plant, even a piece of dill! Surely this was never our Father's intention."

The scribe's big hands were poised lightly on his parted knees. Now the hands flew upward. Shaking his head, yet repressing a smile, Joseph of Arimathea turned to gauge his friend's reaction. He could see that Nicodemus was shocked but intrigued. Although speaking Hebrew, the boy was obviously Galilean. His accent, the sprinkling of Aramaic phrases. Just a poor lad from the north country, home of the hated *am-ha-aretz*, low-class people who did not observe the Law. A place where the Syrians and other pagans mingled with the Jews, corrupting their thinking, mangling their speech. Yet how charmingly intense he was to be so young; and how courageous, considering—

A voice from the back echoed some of what Nicodemus was thinking—abrupt but good-natured, only mildly mocking. "But aren't you a Galilean? Don't the people up where you come from sacrifice pigs to idols?"

"They are not my people," the boy declared, eyes flashing. "My people have nothing to do with them. But if we did, I would condemn them for such practices. The One who made us gave life to *all* his creatures; he would not have us destroy that life without good reason, even the lowly pig."

Without good reason. Nicodemus felt a start of excitement. There was something hauntingly familiar now about the boy. He had a sense of urgency, of something important impending.

Joseph was pressing his fingertips together, beating them thoughtfully against his own porcine lips. Blinking, he leaned forward to resume the argument. "Like the tithes, our Hebrew rites of sacrifice are also very old. They too have come down to us from Moses. Even David sacrificed ten thousand oxen at a time. And Solomon far more."

"Yes. *Solomon offered a sacrifice of peace offerings, which he offered unto the Lord*," the boy quoted quickly. "According to the book of Kings: *two and twenty thousand oxen and an hundred and twenty thousand sheep.* But that does not make it right!" he cried. "David himself deplored the custom, and the prophet Isaiah detested it, telling us that the man who really pleases God is the humble man with the contrite heart. Was Jacob saved by his sacrifices, or by his prayers and penitence? The prophet Hosea too, did he not proclaim in the spirit, 'For I desired mercy, and not sacrifice, and the knowledge of God more than burnt offerings'?" Jesus caught his breath. "Wise as our ancestors were, they had little choice, for the time was not yet come when there would be no further need for animal sacrifice."

"What then?" demanded the scribe. "Will we no longer worship God?"

The boy was silent for a moment, his eyes pondering. "The Father will have shown us another way," he said then. "When the Messiah comes he will take the sins of men upon his own shoulders; he will bear our iniquities, *he* will suffer for our transgressions." Sweat had broken out on the young face; he wiped it away on his sleeve, obviously shaken by his own words.

"Tell me—" Nicodemus could no longer refrain from asking—"how do you know these things?"

The boy turned his gaze upon him, full and sweet. "I have a good rabbi," he said modestly. "I have studied the Scriptures, and my father and my grandfather have taught me." He paused, still regarding Nicodemus, whose heart was pounding absurdly. "Yet there is more. The Lord himself reveals the truth to those who ask for it."

"Where were you born, son?"

"In Bethlehem. The birthplace of my father. It was the year of the census, when Cyrenius was governor of Syria. My father had to return to Judea to register; my mother went with him."

There was a mass gasp of surprise and disbelief.

"But that was the year when all the babes born in Bethlehem were slain!" Joseph scolded slyly. "Didn't your parents hear the edict from Herod? They were supposed to give you up to be butchered—like the animals whose slaying you so eloquently protest. You *did* escape the slaughter?"

"I'm here!" Jesus laughed with such innocent wonder the crowd joined him. "I'm told they fled into Egypt. I'm afraid I can't swear to any of this, gentlemen, because I honestly don't remember. I was still in swaddling clothes."

Again they laughed. But Nicodemus had a sudden belated flash of recognition. "Haven't I seen you in the Temple before?" he asked. "With a husky light-haired boy who comes here often? A boy named John?"

"He is my cousin, the only son of the priest Zechariah."

"Zechariah, the high priest who died last year?" Nicodemus exclaimed. It was hard to believe. "Then you too are of priestly descent?"

"I am related to the priestly line only by marriage. Zechariah was the husband of my mother's aunt, Elizabeth."

Even *so*. Anyone even remotely associated with a high priest—especially Zechariah! Nicodemus himself had been in the Temple on the day the revered old man had emerged from the inner sanctum white and shaken, unable to con-

tinue the services. He had thought nothing of it until the
stories began to circulate. Something about an angel's ap-
pearance, shocking the aged priest dumb. Something about
his at last begetting a child. Legends, probably; people
were so eager to believe such things.

But the favorite story had come from guests at the
christening, where Zechariah was said to have prophesied
about his son—John, his father called him, breaking with
tradition—that John was destined to be a great spiritual
leader, he proclaimed. . . . Nicodemus shook his head.
How wrong fathers could be, even a high priest; for the boy
was rumored to be something of a trial to his mother, in
some ways already a renegade.

John, that must be it! Nicodemus snapped his fingers.
That explained a lot. For an instant he was both amused and
disappointed. "And this cousin," he prodded, "you get
some of your—forgive me—wild ideas from him?"

"I admire my cousin," Jesus said steadily. "He has
opened my eyes to a number of things. But I speak out of
my own convictions. And the questions I ask of you, gentlemen, are surely put upon my heart by the One who sent
me."

There was a moment of puzzled silence. Nicodemus
and his friend exchanged glances. "Your father?" Joseph of
Arimathea asked.

"Our Father, yours and mine. The Father of us all."

"Be careful not to blaspheme, son!" the scribe warned.
He turned, in some concern, to assure the others. "He
means no harm. He's young, he will learn." Cupping his
hand, he spoke privately with Nicodemus. "He has a fine
head. A pity he can't just stay on here and study with a
rabbi like Hillel or Shammai, have access to our libraries—"

"Perhaps if we spoke to his parents," Nicodemus said
on impulse. Again that sense of urgency, that he must never
lose touch with this boy. His own son, the only son God had
allowed him, had died of a fever before he was two years
old. Since then—nothing, not even a daughter. Other blessings, yes; prosperity, position, but to have no *son!* There
was an actual aching in the banker's loins. Had the child
lived he would be about this boy's age. The man's lean face

tightened. He bit his lip, for it was trembling; he had never wanted anything so much. "I will find them!" he declared fervently. "I will adopt him if they'll let me. I will give him every advantage—"

It was then they heard the commotion in the Women's Court below. Someone was calling out. "Jesus!" A cry both desperate and thankful, echoing from the marble walls. "*Jesus!*" Startled, everyone turned and looked down to discover its source: a tiny woman in a blue wrap. She was beautiful, they saw, even disheveled, her dark hair tumbled down, her eyes distraught. Unable to approach them further, she stood there with her arms outstretched. She was sobbing in relief.

Jesus had leaped to his feet. He looked dazed for a moment. Then a smile of great joy lighted his face. Eagerly he waved to her. "It's my mother!" he told the men, eyes shining. "I must go now." He gave them a courteous little bow. "Thank you for being so patient with me." He darted through the crowd and down the curved white steps.

Nicodemus made an anxious move to follow, but was restrained by the quick grip of his friend. "No," Joseph of Arimathea ordered brusquely. "Never!"

The two stood watching as the boy held his mother against him, gently, with great concern, patting and consoling her as if he were the parent and she the child. Then they went off together through the Beautiful Gate.

"I found him, I found him!"

Joseph heard Mary even above the commotion and din on the street. Giving a choked little cry, he came running, dodging camels and donkeys, beggars, peddlers, rattling carts. He too looked stricken and unkempt, his gray eyes circled from loss of sleep.

Wordlessly, fighting back tears, Joseph embraced them both. Then anxiously he drew back to examine the boy. "Are you all right? Where have you *been?*"

"In the Temple," Jesus said innocently, but he was pale and stricken, astonished at their alarm. Never had he felt such confusion or such pain. "Please forgive me," he pleaded. "Something drew me into the Temple. And I became so absorbed in the discussions, I didn't know at first the caravan had left."

His father drew a long shuddering breath. "We had traveled a day's journey before we missed you. We thought you were up front again with your friends. But when Amos came back that first night to say you weren't there—!"

"We've searched for you for days," Mary broke in. "We've been nearly crazy with fear." She felt suddenly limp, as if she would collapse from the strain. Then she turned on him; she couldn't help it. "Why have you *done* this to us? Why have you treated us like this?"

Jesus was gazing at them bewildered. "I didn't mean to hurt you. I thought surely you'd know where to look for me. So I didn't leave the Temple, not even to go back to Aunt Elizabeth's." He stood for a moment, bewildered. They must understand. He loved them both so much. He felt, quite literally, that he would cut out his heart for either of them. Yet there was a thing he must do, a thing that had held him, blind to all else these past three days.

"Forgive me," he begged again. "But why did you look for me anywhere but in my Father's house? Didn't you realize I must be about my Father's business?"

BOOK TWO

Young Manhood

Chapter 7

---

*J*esus strode ahead of the sheep, leading them through meadows still wet and sparkling with morning, uttering the familiar gurgling cries of the shepherd: "*Hoo-hoo . . . hoo-hoo!*" It was good to have them following him again, knowing him, his favorites responding to their names—Lisby, Coco, Imar. With his crook he pulled Imar over to walk beside him. Even Bezer, the king ram of the flock, a quarrelsome beast with immense curling horns, marched docilely at his heels, as if glad to have him back. Although Amos had warned that the old devil had been attacking the young rams.

"He even went after me last week," Amos fretted anxiously. "I had to beat him off. Be sure you have a stout staff."

Birdsong and tinkling bells, the bleating, the pattering of little hooves, and Jubal bounding joyfully at the edges of the flock, nipping and yipping to establish his authority over any would-be strays. Jesus, nearly eighteen now, was glad when he got these calls from Amos for help with the sheep. A welcome change from the racket of saws and hammers and the ever-present haze of dust in the carpenter shop. Only the other day this urgent summons from Amos had come.

Joachim was ailing again, Amos said—grieving more than ever over Matthew, it seemed, and he, Amos, just could not manage everything. The crops had to be harvested, and Judith and Esau could not handle the sheep, however they tried. That wretched ram—it wasn't safe for them. And most of the ewes were in lamb; they would have to be watched, some of them might drop. And they really

should be led to farther pastures, kept out—if Joseph could
spare Jesus—until the new moon.

And they must be well fed, Jesus was thinking, plan-
ning his route as Amos talked. He had inspected them all
yesterday and found some of them too thin. He would lead
them to distant pastures by way of a grove of pomegranates
where they could feast their fill. There were wild grapes
there too, although now toward summer's end the pigeons
would probably have robbed the rich purple clusters. Such
gluttons! But weren't all wild creatures mainly walking or
flying stomachs to be filled? He grinned in affectionate
amusement. The birds and animals were so totally brazen
and unembarrassed by their incessant need, feeling no guilt
whatever when they fought each other for a morsel or
devoured each other to survive. Strange that the Father
had made them so—innocent, incapable of blame. While
man . . .

There were lush and verdant growths too in the hills
beyond. Enough to last for weeks. He patted Imar, who
seemed a bit too scrawny, trotting by his side. He would
tend his sheep like a mother. Like David, son of Jesse, as
the ancient writings said, he would "set tender grass before
the lambs for food, to the old sheep give soft herbs and
tender grass easy for them to chew; while to the middle
sheep whose teeth were strong he could give the tougher,
older grass, feeding each according to its wants and
strengths."

He had thought of David often, striding over the hills
these past few years, calling or piping to his sheep. And on
those nights when Jesus kept the flocks, he felt a special
kinship with David lying under the stars on the hills of Judea—near Bethlehem, he marveled, where both of them
were born. David, composing his psalms even as a youth.
Jesus' heart stirred. He felt a sense of familiarity and communion, as if he himself had known or even been that boy.
With a thrill he remembered what had also been written:
"*And the Lord said, 'David, who is able to care for the
wants of the flocks entrusted to him, will be able to rule
properly over my flock, the people of Israel.'*"

These thoughts he had had for years, but only when

with the sheep, never with his brothers in the commotion of the carpenter shop. So he welcomed these urgent calls for help from Amos whenever his father could spare him.

Joseph was usually glad to release him. Jesus was no longer needed so much. The younger boys were being apprenticed, and there really wasn't enough work for them all. Jesus had been a big help in teaching them, but this was not always appreciated, especially by Josey. His own eldest son had resisted almost from the day Jesus had tried to show him how to hold a hammer. "I know, I know, I can *do* it!" Angrily Josey had run to his father. He wanted instruction only from Joseph, to be close to him the way Jesus had been those first few years, before Josey was old enough. . . . Or so Joseph surmised. Impossible, of course. That relationship was different. It had a special quality of its own. Like Mary, Joseph kept reassuring himself, he did not love his other children less; they were his own flesh and blood, how could he? Yet he could only share himself as best he could, divide himself up among them. This was not easy, here in such small crowded quarters.

James gave him no trouble. James was a more placid, generous, happy child, and he adored Jesus, tagged him about, was eager to learn from him, beamed in his praise. Simon and Jude, though more congenial than Josey, also kept striving for their parents' attention, and joined Josey in targeting Jesus for their frays in the shop. Taunts, complaints, sawdust fights—sometimes merry but often furious. Jesus held his own as they grew up, ducking, laughing, throwing back, chasing them and stuffing their shirts with shavings as they had stuffed his, or sometimes merely submitting to their attacks. It hurt Joseph, this seeming hostility, but Jesus had begged him not to intervene.

"Please don't punish them, Father. I can take care of myself. They mean no harm, and it would only make things worse."

They did not understand their brother's strange ways. For one, his passion for scrolls. He had acquired quite a number from his grandfather, the rabbi, and others, which he studied during free moments at the shop, or sometimes carried with him into the hills. He devoured them voraciously, not only the Psalms and the Law and the prophets, but other writings too, ancient learned commentaries like the Midrash, which searched the Scriptures to reveal their true meaning. Yet he read with the thrill of recognition, as if all these truths and tales he knew already; they sang in his blood, were one with his breath, a part of him before time's beginning. Yet he wrested new meanings from them, exciting discoveries of his own. There was good news here that he must share: that we do not please the Father by slavishly obeying the letter of the Law but rather by obeying the spirit behind it. And in obeying God's second greatest commandment, that we truly love each other—as much as or even more than ourselves!

At night the lamps often burned late while he pored over his books, which he discussed endlessly with Joseph. Mary would often listen, sometimes vouchsafing a comment as she folded garments or prepared dough for the morning bread. Her sons knew Jesus had taught her to read—very strange in a mother. They weren't sure whether to be proud of this or embarrassed. But they sensed that it had given her a deeper bond with Jesus, which puzzled and troubled them.

And the way he always lingered in the Temple on their trips, sitting at the feet of the learned men there. That first experience seemed to have unleashed some new fever within him. Each year as the family set out for the Passover, to sit with them seemed to be his main objective, more than the ceremonies and prayers, or certainly the still painful sacrifices. He didn't debate with his elders as before, he confided to Joseph, for now he recognized the virtues of silence. To listen, to learn, to absorb knowledge, that was imperative for him.

This too dismayed his brothers, when there was the whole exciting, colorful city to be explored: bazaars and carnivals and markets, the processions and games and dancing in the streets. Fortunately, Jesus never again lingered long enough to miss the caravan. That experience had been a shock for them all, although briefly it had brought the family closer. In their own way the other children loved Jesus fiercely too. They had gone white with fear when he couldn't be found; they could not imagine life without him.

Or again, Jesus would put away his books and be off with the young people of the village, leaving his brothers behind. Places they could not follow. He was very popular, handsome and lithe and merry, and how he could sing! His beautiful voice brightened many a sheep shearing, grape treading, or wedding feast. Not a hint of the sober scholar. Few people even knew of his studies—only that was different. Eccentric. For, incredibly, he also spent as much time with people who were old or ill or very poor. The hurting, the downtrodden, even the despised. His pockets were always empty; every cent he had, which was little enough, he shared with them. Their worries became his worries, their wounds were in his eyes.

Joseph was uneasy about him. Most of Jesus' friends were getting married, while Jesus was not even betrothed. It was plain the girls were mad about this immensely likable but strange young man. Yet, musing, Joseph smiled at his own discomfort, remembering how he himself had worried his parents in the same way years before. The girls, the eager girls and their fathers hinting, sometimes pocketing pride and custom to come directly to his father, Jacob, who was flattered no end at their offers. Yet he, Joseph, had moved coolly among them, stubbornly waiting for Mary. Who or what, he wondered, was Jesus waiting for?

Joseph did not bother Mary with his concern. It was not his nature to share any problem he was not yet ready to resolve.

For Joseph it was almost a relief when Amos would call on Jesus for help in the fields or with the sheep. Joachim, however, fumed. It was another blow to his already injured pride. Oh, shameful, shameful that he could no longer rise with the dawn and till the land, but only hobble about, beset by such excruciating pains in limb and back. But even worse was this humiliation—that Amos, who had been so eager, yes, determined to take over, was now browbeating him. Trying to keep him inside with Hannah on the days when he *did* feel up to at least helping to winnow the grain. "Stop babying me, dammit!"

"Very well, Father," Amos would say, wounded. "Since you insist."

Yet when Joachim was there among the men, it was too hot, he soon discovered; the sweat ran down his face, the dust began to clog his lungs, he choked, felt faint, and they must set him on one of the beasts like a woman and support him as it was led back to the house.

There were other things: Amos' going into the village and hiring workers without Joachim's approval; or setting fire to the stubble before his father thought it dry enough. One day, hearing a sudden explosion as it caught, Joachim stalked to the door to see the bright flames already dancing across the field. "He hasn't left enough to dry out for the ovens!" he stormed. "And I've told him and *told* him to dig around the roots of those trees before laying dung for the soil."

There was bickering, lashing out. Amos was often sullen, sulking for days because he wasn't appreciated. His wife, a sly little thing who seemed to thrive on trouble, delighted in relaying his complaints to Hannah. As if I can't see for myself, Hannah thought testily. This feud between father and son—she was weary of the whole business. It only fueled her smoldering resentment toward her husband. She had begun to blame him for Matthew's running away; Joachim had been too hard on him. And now this!

In her anguish over Matthew, Hannah had fastened on her youngest son to fervently defend. Though she herself was exasperated with his moods of martyrdom, the things Amos did to antagonize his father, she felt compelled to boast about him lavishly. "See how much hay he has put up today," she would point out to Joachim. "And the sheep have never been so fat. We will make enough to pay our taxes from the tails alone."

"The sheep have never looked worse and you know it," Joachim snapped. "If Amos is doing so well, why does he go running to Joseph? It's an imposition on Joseph and an insult to me. Matthew would never have done it," he said grimly. "Matthew would have been too proud."

"Matthew isn't here!" Hannah reminded him bitterly.

And they stared at each other at such times, sick with the memory: Their return from Jerusalem when Jesus was twelve. To everyone's dismay, Jesus could not be found. While his frantic parents went back to look for him, they had come on with the caravan, to comfort and care for the other children. They had arrived home, already worried and exhausted, only to be met by a trembling, white-faced Esau and his sobbing sister, Judith. And they knew at once that something had happened to Matthew.

His sheep had been discovered wandering. A neighbor had rounded them up and brought them home. Other neighbors had been searching for their brother in vain. His friend Rosh also had disappeared. . . .

Nearly seven years ago. All those days and nights of waiting, wondering, Where, oh, where? . . . The sleepless hours of staring at the ceiling or leaping up at a crackling branch or possible footstep and racing prayerfully to the door. The nightmares: of seeing their son lying bloody beside a road, beaten, in prison, starving, suffering. Or dead—long dead—and nowhere to mark his grave. . . .

At such moments the pain that contorted her husband's face was too much for Hannah. Inconsistently, she couldn't stand it. "Don't look like that!" she pleaded, and dug her nails into his hand. Then, fiercely, "It's not your fault. Matthew deserted us as he deserted his sheep!"

On and on Jesus led the sheep. Beside the still waters, where the gentle natures would not fear to drink. Through the green pastures, scarcer now that summer was waning. Then up and up, where they would be free of the tormenting gnats and flies that swarmed up from the grasses. Here in the lowlands he had to stop almost every day to anoint their heads with the oil he had brought in his leather knapsack. It also held a knife to free them from thickets or to ward off attacks from wild beasts.

Jesus crouched this day beside a sparkling stream. Cupping his hands, he drank to test the waters. Good, it was cool and sweet. The flock were thirsty, but he could not allow them to drink at the stagnant pool a few miles back. In their own wisdom they had shied away from it anyway, for it had a smell of phosphorus. Blatting plaintively, yet docile, they had followed him here and now were nosing around, hunting for water nooks where the stream was still. "Sheep will not drink from swift-running water," his grandfather had taught him years ago.

Hastily, he began gathering stones to construct little nooks to hold the water. Joachim and Matthew had taught him that as well. "Hoo-hooooo!" he called, and soon there was the pleasant almost dainty sound of the sheep's lapping.

There was shade here too, where the sheep could lie down and rest. But the nose flies that had driven some of them nearly mad with their biting and stinging were already attacking. Jesus sat down and took out his horn of oil, a pungent-smelling concoction of olive oil, sulphur and spices. It was almost gone. He must use it sparingly, for it must last the rest of the week. In the morning he would lead the flock up into the mountains. It was harder to graze them among the rocks: a few would always stray, and there was greater danger from lions. But the air would be cool, and they would be delivered from these pests. They crowded up, sensing relief, and he must shove some of them away and order Jubal to separate them, that he might take the warm woolly heads one by one onto his lap and firmly massage in the oil.

He enjoyed the feel of their bones under his fingers, their black silky faces, the warm black leaf-shaped ears against his palms. They gentled under his touch, and he knew it was not the oil so much as the massaging and stroking. They were comforted, they nuzzled him, making soft little love sounds in their throats. Presently most of them were drowsing.

Jesus wiped his sticky hands on his tunic, filthy now, after weeks with the sheep, and torn from brambles. Though he washed himself as best he could, according to the laws of Moses, he knew that he stank, for he was sweaty, and his nose was no stranger to the smell of the other shepherds he sometimes encountered. There was a rude sheepfold along the path he intended to follow tomorrow, a place where nomads often gathered to share a common fire and a jug of wine and to spin tales half the night. It offered protection from marauding beasts—they kept watch for each other—but best of all was their company after so many nights alone under the stars.

Nights when Jesus would lie thinking about the patriarchs: Abraham, Isaac, Jacob. All the famous men of the Bible with their sheep and cattle and goats and wives, moving, ever moving. A time when to be a shepherd was a proud and noble profession. Less so now, for the size of the herds had dwindled. But to be responsible for sheep was still a thing to respect, even for women. Though of all the shepherdesses, the Torah named only Rachel: "And while he was still speaking to them, Rachel came with her father's sheep." Beautiful Rachel, for whom Jacob gallantly lifted the heavy stone from the well, that her sheep might drink: showing off his brawn, for he had fallen in love with her at sight. In fact, Jacob kissed Rachel and wept. And he worked for her father, Laban, seven years that he might have her, but he was cheated into marrying the older sister, Leah, first.

Jesus bridled at this outrage. . . . But Jacob also finally wed Rachel, his own true love, and it was with both wives and two maidservants that he fled Laban's household. And by these wives and their maids, Zilpah and Bilhah, he became the father of one daughter and twelve sons: thus the twelve tribes of Israel. It was sacred history, it was true; yet the thought repelled him.

How could a man who truly loved a woman lie with another at the same time? In the same tent! Horror, half enticing, possessed him, almost as on the night Matthew's friend had pressed into his hand the naked figure of Astarte. . . . No, *no*. Jesus' fists beat the earth. For the scene had become a nightmare, a vision of his father Joseph actually leading a second wife or concubine into their house.

Restless, Jesus threw off his cloak, got up, and stirred the fire. Then, leaning on his crook, he stood gazing at the sky. Above Mount Hermon's white crest, the stars were brilliant, a tangle of diamonds that trailed off like jeweled ribbons among the blue foothills. The stars seemed close enough to touch. He reached out a hand as if to try, to feel their chill beauty, bring a few down to carry in his belt as he used to carry his childish treasures back to Mary.

Thinking of the patriarchs this night disturbed him. "It is not good for man to be alone," God had said when he created the first woman for Adam. How warm and sweet she must have felt to his arms. Longing quickened, rose up within him, as it did so often now at marriage celebrations. And at christenings—he sometimes held the baby, tiny and kicking, like the newborn sheep. . . . Two of the ewes had dropped and lay even now beside their lambs. How does a ewe know her own lamb among the sameness of the flock? Yet she does; should one of them stray she finds it and noses it back to nurse. And should one fall ill, she seeks out the shepherd, bunting his knees.

Yesterday, before its mother could stop it, a lamb had swallowed some of the stagnant water. He had had to purge it, and when it was finished heaving it was so weak it staggered; he had lifted it up and carried it on his shoulders while the grateful mother followed.

Love flooded him. A vast tenderness that made him want to save them all, carry them safely across the meadows and over the rocks and through the streams, every baby, every calf and kid and lamb. He was different. He had always known that he was different. . . . But there comes a time when it is not another man's lamb or another man's child you hunger to hold.

Desperately Jesus searched the stars. "Father, Father, what is it you want of me?" he cried out in a loud voice, for there was no human being to hear.

There was no answer. No sound but the fire, which suddenly began to crackle, and the distant melancholy baying of a jackal—though Jubal, startled, raised his head and came bounding to his side. Jesus threw more branches on the coals; the yellow flames leaped high. He stood warming himself to still his trembling. Then, wrapping his cloak more closely about him, he flung himself again onto the hard ground.

As he lay there he could hear the earth's heart beating, feel every point of light that glittered overhead, feel the secret life force pulsing in the meadows, the wind, the

stream, the precious sheep he was tending. . . . Why was
he here? Why was any man or woman or child or creature
here at all, to live and suffer and die? . . . A number of the
sheep had risen, as they often did on a clear bright night,
and were cropping the cool dew-wet grasses. Poor things,
seizing this opportunity to stuff themselves after some of
the miseries of the day. So beautiful and somehow pathetic,
bending their heads so trustingly in the starlight, knowing
he would look out for them. They were his children. The
world and its people, were they not his sheep and his children? He was responsible for them, he was one with the
Father who had created them. He must somehow help
them, he must comfort and carry them all.

And he heard again the words that John had said that
night, turning from the window in Ein Karem—words that
had haunted him for years: *You are the Messiah*.

Jesus shuddered. It is not good for man to be alone,
he thought. I have been out here too long alone. Early in
the morning he would set off for the sheepfold on the side of
the mountain; with luck he would find someone else there.

It took more time than he had hoped to reach the fold.
Cooler, and free of the punishing flies, the sheep were playful and inclined to wander after the sparser grass. Several
times he had to scale ledges to rescue a stray and bring it
back to the path. All day his eagerness mounted, and his
anxiety, lest the place be deserted. The sheepcote was very
old and had long been abandoned except for temporary
shelter; its walls were crumbling. But there was a well there
and a solitary tree. Jesus' heart sank as he approached, for
he spied no herds. Then to his great relief he smelled
smoke, heard voices, and as he drew nearer he saw two
mules and a donkey tied to the tree.

Their owners were squatting before it, playing dice.
Another man riding a donkey appeared over the ridge from
an opposite path. "Abdul!" Jesus yelled, recognizing him at
once as a small farmer who lived near. Joyfully the two
waved and shouted to each other, while the other men
leaped to their feet, bowing and uttering cries of welcome,
offering him the hospitality of sharing the meal they were

cooking. The fire was already smoldering in a pit. With a great clanking and splashing, they began drawing up buckets of water for his flock.

"And you had best drive them into the shelter for the night," advised Abdul, a slight gap-toothed man who kept hugging him with lively affection and concern. "There is a killer lion stalking these parts—in the company of a bear, unlikely as that seems." One or both of the beasts had snatched lambs or young kids from their flocks, the other men put in. They had formed a posse and come here this night to track the devils down. They were excited; they could hardly wait for darkness. But come, the meat was almost ready; they would help him bed the animals, then they would eat. He must be as hungry as they were.

Jesus washed his hands and drew a little apart, gazing toward the east to pray. Then he squatted with the others beside the fire. The small brown things they were roasting smelled delicious, crisp and succulent, their fat sizzling as it dripped onto the coals. His mouth watered, he was very hungry, and it would be rude to refuse. But for a moment he was torn. These were coneys, rock rabbits, furry little creatures he had sometimes caught and petted and played with as a boy. Though it was not that; didn't he eat equally gentle creatures: fish, pigeons, lamb? Coneys, however, were forbidden; ruminant, yes, but without cloven hooves, and so considered unclean.

Unclean? Ridiculous. Jesus laughed. The greater sin, if sin it was, would be to offend his hosts. Surely it was not what went into the belly, or even the dirt from unwashed hands, that made a man clean or unclean, but how he treated his fellows. These men whose food he now was so gratefully devouring—their hair was shaggy, their teeth were stained, like him they stank. Yet they were kind and generous. They had drawn water for his flock, helped round them up, and seen that there was plenty of hay on which the sheep could lie down. And now they were eagerly sharing their meat and drink. Thanking God for their company, Jesus ate their coneys, drank their wine, and joined in their songs until darkness, which fell quickly.

The first stars appeared, and a tiny new moon, arched

like a smile. The men got up and began gathering their weapons from a pile they had heaped: stout rods and clubs, stones for their slings, knives and daggers that flashed like their eyes as they stuffed them in their belts. Jesus felt their mounting excitement, the heady dread and thrill of danger, the lure of the chase, their fierce sense of power and pride. They had families to feed; a man must protect his family. His own heart was pounding. Though he had often driven off wolves and jackals, he had not yet been challenged to savage attack. But he did not want to fail them.

"I will go with you."

"No, no," Abdul protested fervently, "you must stay with the sheep." He threw a fresh bundle of thorns and brambles on the fire, which burst into brighter flames. His small dark face was beaming. He hugged Jesus once more. "Sleep well, son. Your sheep will be quite safe. We have tracked the bear's footprints to a nearby cave. Before morning, if all goes well, we will be back with a prize or two to show you."

After some noisy argument and discussion among them, they took two of the donkeys and disappeared into the shadows. Jesus banked the fire. It was unbelievably cold here high in the mountains; frost was already gilding the ground. Yet warmed by the food, the fire, and the wine, he fell asleep almost at once. His dreams were of David: at first of David and Michal, the king's daughter; then they drifted to Saul's skepticism about David's ability to slay the giant Goliath, and David's bold claim: "Your servant used to look after the sheep for his father and whenever a lion or a bear came out and took a sheep from the flock, I used to follow him up and strike him down and rescue it from his mouth; and if he turned on me I seized him by the hair at his jaw and struck him down and killed him. Your servant has slain both the lion and the bear. . . ."

Hours later, he was awakened by Jubal's frantic barking and the smell and glow of approaching torches. He could hear voices and the rattle of hooves on stones. The men were returning, leading the donkeys. A huge tawny body was draped across the back of one. The other supported the half-prone figure of Abdul. His dirty turban was gone, his head drooped, and from it flapped a bloody thing that could only be his scalp. His dusky face was pale in the moonlight, like some dusky lily, as they lifted him down. His striped robe was drenched.

Jesus helped carry Abdul into the fold, which was warm from the huddled bodies of the sheep. They cleared a place for him on the straw and built up the fire beside the door. On it they warmed a bucket of water with which to bathe his wounds. Jesus could not bear to look toward the body of the lion, which they had dragged onto some brush nearby.

But it was not the lion that had hurt Abdul, the men told him. They had already killed the lion—a female—surprising her in the very act of devouring another lamb. The lamb was still in her jaws when she turned, snarling, just as they attacked. No, it was the bear, a huge black bear that had come sniffing up to the mouth of the cave, drawn there no doubt by the smell of food. The beast had reared up and felled Abdul with one blow as they came out, then set about mauling him.

"We stoned that bear and beat him, we slashed him and tried to pull him off with our bare hands but he wouldn't stop. Not until we torched him. He ran away then, yelping, with his tail on fire." The tall burly one named Kulaf gave an angry laugh. "He was smoking, scorching, oh, but we burned him good; he was a torch on legs! He's probably out there dead by now, we didn't even want to bring him back."

The rest of the night they ministered to their brother, suffering Jesus to help a little with his salves and prayers to his God, since he was Abdul's friend. But they were unable to stanch the blood spilling from Abdul's clawed face and belly. Even the sheep were becoming stained with it; Abdul saw this in moments when he was lucid and begged them to move him outside. He died at daybreak, just as they were putting him down beside the fire.

The gray sky was turning pink, the sun was rising in a hollow between the surrounding blue cliffs. Silent, the men drew more water to help Jesus. Then they broke camp.

They must get Abdul's body home as soon as possible. They seemed to have forgotten the lioness, although Kulaf went over and kicked it. He gazed indifferently at the buzzards already circling overhead. "They will make short work of this one," he remarked, with a shrug.

Jesus too was anxious to leave. But first he went into the fold and gathered up the bloody straw to be burned. He then went back and crouched beside the golden length of the lioness. Her amber eyes stared at him, her mouth was open, and for the first time he saw that something was jutting from the clenched teeth. A small foot—two small feet! Prying the jaws apart, he reached in and drew forth the hindquarters of a new lamb. And the words of the prophet Amos, who had also been a shepherd, spoke to him: "Like a shepherd rescuing a couple of legs or a bit of an ear from the lions mouth . . ." Jesus stared at what he held, knowing from its tightly curled fur that the lamb had been barely two days old.

"Why, why, *why*?" Jesus pressed the back of his hand against his lips. But he reached out to touch the beast. She smelled raw and acidic, but her sides were smooth and silken to his gentle stroking. Her ribs jutted. Except for her swollen belly, he saw that she was very thin. His hands went to the bulge she carried; he felt the hard tiny shape of the two cubs there. And he wept again. . . . She was so hungry. She was only trying to feed them!

Then, as he rose to leave, he noticed a faint rippling and jerking of her flesh. Shocked, he dropped to his knees to make sure. It was true; under his fingers the thrusting movement came again. At least one of them still lived! He could save it; if he got out his knife he could take it from her. But his soul was in conflict. Why should he? It would only die anyway if he left it behind. And he could not take it with him. No ewe would ever feed a lion cub; true, he could offer it milk from his fingers, but even if it survived and grew, it would live only to devour his sheep.

And he was so weary, so anxious to start the long trip home. He wanted to get back to Nazareth before the Sabbath.

Biting back tears, Jesus sprang up and called brokenly

to Jubal. The dog stood panting beside the old ram, Bezer, who was tossing his horns, impatient to lead the flock back down the mountainside. They set off, bells clanking in the crisp morning air. The sky was cloudless, very blue, alive now with black circling vultures. Looking back, he saw that they were beginning to drop, uttering their own raucous cries. And suddenly he could not bear it. Sensible or not, he cried out to Jubal and Bezer to halt the flock; they had reached a ledge where they could graze. Then he turned and ran back up to the camp.

The birds were already swarming around the carcass. Jesus had to hurl stones, beat them off with his crook. Then, breathless, he knelt and pulled his knife from his girdle. It was swift and sharp. He had taken dead lambs from moaning ewes. The lion's blood was still warm; so was the amniotic fluid that cradled the babies. Gently he brought them forth, warm and damp, the larger one struggling, and placed them on the grass. The cubs were not yet mature, yet completely formed, even to their tiny tails. It was already too late, he saw, for the smaller one; it lay quite still. The other nosed around blindly, its little paws groping, making faint mewing sounds.

Sobbing, Jesus held it against his cheek. It was very weak. Yet he longed to save it, to give it enough love to make it live and grow and become his child, like one of the sheep. Enough to protect it from its own nature, to change it, so that it would actually lie down with the lambs and usher in that blessed time when all creatures would love each other. And as he wept and crooned to it, the slits of eyes opened. They gazed at him for a long moment, as if in communion with his thoughts. Then, with a slight shudder, they closed for good.

He dug a hole in the rocky soil and placed the two cubs in it. On top he piled enough rocks to keep the vultures away.

That was the day Jesus turned the sheep toward home.

His brothers saw him coming, preceded by Jubal, barking joyfully to herald his return. They were just closing the shop. "Jesus!" the cry went up. "Jesus is back!" They rushed out to embrace him, join in a general playful scuffling. Feuds were forgotten, they really loved him, he was their hero despite the quarrels, he brought a sense of adventure with him. Josey's arm was across his shoulders, walking up the steps to their house. Josey's big face was ebullient. He no longer felt threatened; he had been in charge these past few weeks, and almost inseparable from Joseph, who praised him highly.

The others trailed behind or swarmed about, eager to tell Jesus everything that had happened during his absence: One day when their father had taken them along to fell some trees, the woods caught fire and they had helped him put it out. . . . A man carrying a heavy beam along the streets had struck Uncle Cleo in the eye. . . .

"Hush, he's too tired to listen now," Josey scolded, grinning. It both shocked and amused him to see his handsome brother like this, hair and beard shaggy, his robe in rags. "You look like a beggar."

Jesus grinned back. "And probably smell like one too. I'm filthy, I must bathe."

Merrily, holding their noses, they agreed. "And there's blood on you," Josey pointed out. "What happened, did you tangle with a lion?"

"Yes, but I don't want to talk about it."

Mary gasped at sight of him, but ran into his open arms. "I knew you were coming!" she cried. "I told your sisters to make extra bread, for you would be hungry. And to bring extra water. There is a warm jug waiting for you. I felt sure you would be with us this night."

"And I'd hoped to surprise you! You sound just like Grandmother Hannah."

"I mean to. The heart always knows when a loved one is coming, she believes, and she is right."

Mary too noticed the bloodstains but did not mention them, for she also noticed, as his brothers had not, the spots of pink where Jesus had tried to wash them away in some stream. She touched his hair and beard, stiff in places where blood had dried, sensing that he did not realize it was there. There were fresh towels and garments ready, she told him, and soap—little Leah had made up a batch with the help of her grandmother Timna only yesterday.

Ann, looking radiant, brought him the basin and pitcher of steaming water. She was tall now, slim and dainty like her mother, with a breathless prettiness that was actually enhanced by Hannah's quick, deep-set eyes. She adored Jesus, as she did the man she was betrothed to, another joiner named Naboth, whose father's shop was not far from their own. "Our wedding date has been set for spring!" she couldn't wait to announce. "You will have competition, my brother."

"For business or for your affections?"

"For customers, of course. He's almost as good a carpenter as you or our father." Briskly, Ann poured the water for him, and smiled at him as she shook out the sun-sweet towels.

Shyly their little sister presented the soap. "Smell it," she urged, beaming. "We perfumed it just for you."

Jesus sniffed its spicy fragrance, praised it lavishly, and kissed them both. A few minutes later they thrust modestly from under the drapery a tray containing scissors and blades and a jug of oil. Jesus bathed and dressed, feeling cherished. How good it was to shed the grimy garments— he kicked them aside—to scrub his big tough hairy body with the soap his little sister had made; it was very mild and soft and sweet and somehow innocent, like the child. To wash and comb and attempt to trim his beard and hair, hunching down, for the mirror of polished brass had been hung too low for him. Nobody seemed to realize he had grown taller than his father; if he didn't stop he would soon brush the ceiling. To massage into his big curly head the precious oil. It too was fragrant, smelling of jasmine. Ann had given it to him for his birthday.

A man surrounded by loving women. This house—how hard they surely had worked all day, making it pure and orderly for the Sabbath. Swept and scrubbed and shining, not a cushion out of place. Fresh mats, fresh flowers; he had been intensely aware of it all, walking in. And the warm thrilling smell of food: of bread baked, at least a dozen round flat loaves, the largest glossy and braided, for tonight's supper. Of tomorrow's meals all cooked and set aside, neatly in a cupboard, to be eaten cold. But tonight, ah, tonight's almost ready, the sumptuous meal of the week. . . . Fish prepared as only his mother could, with herbs and onions. His mouth watered. A stew of vegetables from the garden and the flesh of a tough old rooster from his grandfather's farm, though she would have made it tender over the fire. And hard-boiled eggs and shiny olives, and a platter of fruit—perhaps a pear, how he longed for a cool juicy pear—but above all for the cakes of figs and nuts and honey Mary always made for the Sabbath.

He could hear the vessels rattling above the gentle voices of the women—they were laughing about something—then Ann's light dancing footsteps running to the door, her joyful greeting to their father: "Jesus is home!"

Home. To be home with your own. Jesus stood quite still. Surely this was heaven, the kingdom of heaven right here on earth—a man with his kingdom of home. To reign there with the beloved, to eat and sleep and love there surrounded by your children.

The sunset had been brief and bright. Dusk was creeping on, softly, softly, as if holding its breath for the first three stars of Sabbath to come peeping through. Any moment now he would hear the shofar blowing from the roof of the synagogue. Ah, there it was, the mournful yet exciting blatting. Two quick blasts, calling the farmers from their fields. Jesus could see the first star from the window. Two more blasts, warning the merchants to leave their shops—although by now most of the men would be home, making themselves clean, donning their best garments. And the third, and somehow the dearest, those final notes telling the women to light their Sabbath lamps.

Jesus saw Mary walking to the window, carrying her "lamp of joy." Leah, moving cautiously, followed with the burning brand. With a little smile of approval, Mary took the flame from her and touched it to the wick. The lamp sputtered, burst into light; he saw his mother's delicate face in silhouette, and the looming shadows of his brothers on the whitewashed walls. Taking his little sister by the hand,

Jesus led her out onto the steps to see the other lamps of Nazareth suddenly blooming up and down the streets, climbing the hills, scattering on up into the mountains, like a vast garden of fire flowers.

Or they were like children lifting their tiny faces to the stars, and the stars smiled down upon them, very much as Mary had smiled upon Leah with her little torch. God and his children, for whom he created the world anew each week. Children of the heavens and children of the earth, merging, twinkling, calling out to each other—another beautiful symbol of a covenant made even before the beginning.

Their grandmother Timna had set her own light in the window and toiled up the hill to join them, as she always did for Sabbath meals. Her once magnificent body was heavier now, she had to lean on a stick, but her white hair was still a crown and her voice and bearing gracious. Joseph's mother brought a special blessing.

The prayers, the wine, the songs. All of them gathered together, bathed and feeling new in their best clothes. What a joyful thing. Filling themselves with this bountiful feast before the cold, self-denying fare of tomorrow. The talk, the laughter, the lamps with their dancing shadows. . . . Though Jesus had missed it before on his sojourns, never had it seemed so precious as this time. He had observed the Sabbath alone as best he could, drawing water whenever possible ahead of time for the sheep, not moving them on the day of rest, sitting beside them studying the Scriptures. Yet God had made no such covenant with his creatures. They got sick and must be tended, fell into caverns, bore their young. Well, now once again he had brought them safely back to Joachim and Amos, in time for the fall shearing. Let others worry about them. The sheepshearing was always time for dancing and celebration. Perhaps it would cheer his grandfather and his uncle up.

Cleo came in just as the women were clearing away the meal—the only work they might do until after sunset tomorrow. The family had all been hoping Salome and her husband would also drop in, the way they used to. But Aunt Salome and Uncle Ephraim were having some trouble, Ann whispered to Jesus. Nobody knew just what. Salome wouldn't say, she was so proud and loyal—hadn't said a word even to her own sister or her mother—but there was something new and strained, almost frightened about her; her eyes were sometimes red from crying.

Cleo was wearing a patch over one eye. On Cleo it looked jaunty, for he had had it cut from a golden cloth and adorned with a jewel. "If a man must be hit by a beam on the street, he may as well call attention to his wounds!"

"Uncle Cleo, you are terrible!" To everyone's surprise, Ann burst into tears. She ran to him and began to beat at him, the way she and the other children had done when he teased them about Jubal. "You are only doing this to shame me."

"Oh, no, my pet, no, no," Cleophas cried, astonished. "You think this is because it was your betrothed who hit me?" He caressed her and look pleadingly toward her father. "Surely you don't think I would do such a thing? It was a windy day, and the dust was blowing in Naboth's eyes; he didn't see me."

Joseph went to them in his composed, almost casual way and patted both of them. "She's in love," he smiled. "Women in love are sensitive. Hush now," he soothed his daughter. "You should know Uncle Cleophas better than that. He'll do anything to get attention. We all know he's mad—ever since he fell off his first horse and was kicked in the head, long before he was felled by a mere beam!"

Laughter, the healing gift of laughter. The whole family laughed, including Ann. But even as Jesus joined in, a torment of love filled him: love that went beyond the sheep and the lambs and the lion, slain with her still-living cubs in her belly. His own wife to gaze at across the Sabbath table, his own daughter to comfort as Joseph was teasing and yet comforting Ann. To have them about him, wife and children and friends. . . .

To be human, to be as other men.

Chapter 8

———————•◆•———————

Joseph lay awake worrying about his son.

Mary's son. God's son. No matter, were not all men sons of God, including himself? Young or old, male or female, children of the Nameless One. If only there were some word, some dream, some sign. . . . But of one thing Joseph was certain: He was responsible for the earthly welfare of this child, who was no longer child but man.

Joseph pulled back the covers, and careful not to wake Mary, moved from her side. He put on a robe, for the night was cold.

Mary missed him at once, however. They were so close, she felt his absence. Most of the night they lay entwined, or when one would turn away for comfort, the other would reach out and they would clasp hands. She sat up, for a moment bewildered. Something had been troubling him for a long time. She sensed what it was and dreaded asking, but it must be discussed—for the sake of all of them.

Wrapping a shawl about her shoulders, she slipped out of the house and down the moon-washed stones of the path that led to the garden. Summer was almost over, the orchard was heavy with fruit; fat olives ticked softly among the leaves as they fell to the ground. The air bore the tang of distant bonfires and the winy scent of the grapes. Joseph was silhouetted against the crumbling wall, one foot planted on a bench that was there, his chin in his hands. He turned at sound of her footsteps.

"Forgive me," he said. "I couldn't sleep."

"What's bothering you, Joseph?" She gazed at him, distressed. "Don't keep this from me any longer. It's Jesus, isn't it?"

He didn't answer for a minute, only strode up and down the path. Mary watched him anxiously from the bench. Yet she admired him as he paced thus in the chill of the night, graceful and somehow composed even now in his concern. "Yes," he acknowledged at last, coming to stand before her. "What's to become of him? Tending his grandfather's sheep, working for me in the shop—a fine young man, an excellent carpenter, better than I am—but is that *all*? What of his future, his purpose; how is it to be achieved?"

Mary drew a deep breath. "We must be patient. We must have faith."

"If only we had some direction!" Joseph exclaimed. "Why doesn't the Lord speak to us? He spoke to the patriarchs—Abraham, Isaac, Jacob—he guided them. He spoke to the prophets, he spoke to Moses. He told them what to do; they knew what was expected of them." Joseph's arms were folded, his gray eyes searching her face. "And he once spoke to us, Mary. He chose us—you, at least, you are the very mother of his son." Joseph's voice was grave. "And even me, humble as I am—his angels spoke to me in dreams. But what of now?"

"Perhaps the Lord no longer has need of us. Perhaps he is speaking to our son."

"How do we know that? Jesus has given us no indication." Joseph hesitated, then plunged on. "I feel sometimes—don't you ever feel sometimes that what happened, so long ago now, twenty years and more—that it was all only a dream?"

"Never. It is as real to me today as it was then. It will come to pass."

"But when? *When?*" Joseph asked. "Meanwhile, I have a responsibility as his father. He is a man; he should live as a man."

"What do you mean?"

"You know what I mean. It's time Jesus was betrothed."

"No!" she cried. "Not Jesus."

"Yes, Jesus. The eldest. People are wondering. I have

heard your mother and mine discussing it, and other people too. His brothers will soon be ready. Josey is ready now; he spoke to me about it yesterday. There is a girl he fancies, perhaps you already know? Eve, you must have seen her in the synagogue—a very tall girl, daughter of the shoemaker Levi. Josey has asked me to go to her father, as I will, if you agree."

"Josey?" she protested. "Why, he's barely sixteen."

"Your brother Amos was married at seventeen. Most men are."

"You weren't."

He sat down beside her. "I had a very special reason for waiting, Mary." He sat silent a moment, holding her hand. "And my parents were very troubled; they felt disgraced."

"At what happened to us?"

"Oh, no, no, no, not that. Only that I was twenty and still unwed. It was a reflection on my father. You know the duties of a Jewish father to his son: to teach him the Torah, teach him a trade, and find him a wife."

"Jesus doesn't want it," Mary said calmly. "He is different. He fancies no one."

"What he wishes or fancies doesn't matter. The Law is very explicit. This must be done within ten years after his puberty. Jesus is how old now? Twenty, past twenty. That gives me very little time for anything so serious."

"No, no," Mary kept saying, "it is not right for him. He has a destiny that goes beyond the Law." Suddenly she thought of John. "John is older, six months older, and not yet married or even preparing to be."

Joseph looked at her, dismayed. He gave a short laugh. "John? That wild thing? Why, Elizabeth doesn't even know where he is any more. Surely you don't want our son to be like John?"

"It isn't what *I* want," Mary said. "Or what we want. It's what the One who sent him to us wills for him."

"If only we had some guidance," Joseph said again. "Some proof, some sign—even if we were tested in some way. Not you, you have already done your part. But me—I am a man, a stepfather responsible for a very special son. It is my duty to think of his future. Will it be as a common laborer here in Nazareth? A man alone, without a wife? How long, how long?"

"Don't forget he is also a scholar," Mary said.

"Yes, and that scholarship should not be wasted. He could be a teacher, a rabbi, but only if he is married."

"Jesus is destined to be much more than a rabbi."

"It is specifically stated in the Mishnah that any rabbi or teacher must be married," Joseph went on. "It is the Law."

"There are men who choose to be celibate by vocation: the monks, and it is said the Essenes—"

Joseph jerked upright. "Do you want him to be a monk? Surely you don't think God would perform such a miracle as we have both experienced, send his own son to earth to *withdraw* from life?"

He took Mary in his arms, there on the bench beside the wall, and held her close to warm her, for she was trembling. He tipped back her head and stroked her hair and kissed her. In the moonlight she saw the deep love in his eyes as he told her, "Mary, listen, the laws I've been quoting from the Mishnah are based on the most sacred law of all. The first law given to man by our own Creator—to be fruitful and multiply. Would you have any child of yours miss that, my darling? Would you have Jesus miss what we have had?"

"No," she whispered honestly, clinging to him. But she was torn. "That is the most precious thing in life. To love as we have loved, to create children together. But Joseph, we both know Jesus is not the same as our own sons. His life can't be confined; it will go far beyond a wife and family. He was meant for a greater love."

Joseph sat silent for a time. Mary's herb garden was here beside the wall; he could smell the thyme, the mint, the marjoram, a pleasant half-acrid savor along with the fragrance of the ripened grapes. "There *is* no greater love," he said bluntly. He bent and plucked a sprig of mint and crushed it thoughtfully between his fingers. "There is so much I don't understand. After all we went through in the beginning, after all these years, I still don't understand. But this I do know: Love was God's most precious gift to man. A mate to fulfill his most basic needs—a man isn't complete without it."

Their talk drifted off, resolving nothing. Yet they sat a while longer, feeling closer to each other because of it. The wind had shifted, stirring the trees; a few leaves blew across their feet. "Come, my darling," Joseph said at length. "You have lost enough rest because of me. I must put you back to bed."

Smiling at each other, they arose and crept back through the silent house. But when they had kissed and lay drowsing, hand in hand, Mary spoke again. "Joseph, don't ever leave me," she cried softly into the darkness. "I need you, Joseph, I will need you even more as the years go on. Even when I sometimes oppose you about Jesus, please don't ever leave me."

"What are you saying?" Joseph turned to her, aghast. "You know I would never leave you!"

"Yes, yes, surely. Yet sometimes I lie awake worrying about Salome. This thing that is happening to my own sister: It has something to do with Ephraim. I am going to my mother's tomorrow to learn more about it and see what can be done."

"What is it you're afraid of?"

"That he may be putting her away. There are rumors."

"No. Impossible. I can't believe it." He gathered her in his arms. "I will speak to Ephraim; there must be some mistake."

"Oh, Joseph, I *depend* on you so. I keep wondering—what if this were happening to me? How could I face even a day of life without you? And I keep thinking of Jesus, how desperately he's going to need us, both of us, when his time comes. And the other children, all of them. What if they were deprived of you, how would we manage?"

"Pray heaven you never will have to," he said, drawing her to him. "So long as there is breath in my body you never will."

"Tell us," Hannah was pleading with her daughter before Mary arrived the next afternoon. "Mary will be here soon. Please tell us now, before she comes."

"Mother, Father, forgive me, I can't, I can't. It is too painful for me and it will be for you. You have already been hurt so much."

"Hurt?" Hannah groaned. "What do you think we have been feeling for you all these months? Don't we see the change in you? We are your parents. Joachim, speak to her," she ordered. "You are still her father; she can't refuse to tell you."

"My little girl," he said gruffly, and limped over to where Salome sat rocking back and forth on a little stool. He had made it for her himself, he recalled miserably, when she was but a tot. Now, tall and mature as she was, rounded by womanhood and the mothering of her daughter, it tore him to see her crouched there, head low, hugging her knees. "Please don't grieve, let us know," he said helplessly. "Otherwise we suffer more. We want to do what we can for you."

"I don't want Mary to know. Married to Joseph, who loves her so much. Mother to all those children. Five sons!" Salome began to sob. "While I—"

"Your daughter Naomi is beautiful," Hannah claimed fiercely. "And Mary—why, of all people, you know your sister would be the first to defend you."

"I need no defense!"

"I mean to stand by you, help you. Mary is grieving for you too. Her heart breaks for you. Please, please," Hannah begged. "Have I not been through enough? Your brother Matthew gone all these years—though he will return!" she declared, her little eyes snapping, bright as coals. "One day, just you wait, he will come back. I see him often in dreams, making his way home to us."

"Never mind about Matthew." Joachim grunted. "Tell us, Salome," he urged kindly. "What is this trouble between you?"

Before she could answer, Mary appeared, and to her parents' relief, Salome plunged into her arms. Gently now, as quietly as possible, they sat down while she stated it flatly, wiping her eyes. Ephraim had tired of her—that joking, seemingly amiable man. "Oh, it was probably my fault, I couldn't seem to please his mother—any of them." He resented her coming home to be with Hannah so much, berated her, would not speak to her sometimes for days. And now—Salome was hanging her head in the old way, her voice so low they could scarcely hear—that was another. A woman named Abigail.

Joachim paled; his heart nearly pounded out of his chest. For once, years before, shortly before he met Hannah, he had been mad with desire for a woman with such a name. Had even seen her a few times on the streets of Nazareth since: fat and dull, to his surprise, making him grateful for the spare little tiger to whom he was safely wed.

"He wants to bring her home as a second wife."

Joachim was jolted; he gripped the arms of his chair. "Never," he growled. "Never! An outrage. A second wife, no, no, that was never God's will. For the patriarchs, yes, there were reasons, they had to be sure God's people would survive. But not today, not any more. The few that still practice this despicable custom—" He spat. His face was grim. "Let him go, let it be. My daughter must never submit to such an arrangement."

Salome began to weep again, so wildly it surprised them; she had been able to keep her dignity so long. "But I *love* Ephraim! I want him—almost enough to share him. Isn't half a loaf better than none?" she pleaded.

"No," Mary said kindly. "Father is right. Marriage is a sacrament, a covenant between two people and God. It can never be divided."

Salome shuddered, fighting for control. This was costing her dearly. "To be *repudiated* . . . it is so shameful, for you as well as me! It is why I didn't want you to know; I kept hoping you might be spared. Though Ephraim says this is not repudiation, since he wants to keep me as well."

Joachim's eyes narrowed; he was leaning forward, listening carefully, trying to restrain his anger. "Daughter, tell me why. This desire for another woman surely goes beyond the things you've spoken of."

She nodded, though it was a long time before she could bring herself to answer. Finally she lifted her shamed and stricken eyes. "They say the girl is beautiful. Quite young, but already full-breasted. He thinks—" she whispered, "my husband thinks she will bear him children, bear him sons."

"Bitch, bitch!" Hannah's mouth curled with contempt. "Like a bitch dog."

Joachim silenced her with a wave. He sat scowling, considering, struggling to harness his fury. His astute mind saw at once a motive he didn't want to share with Salome, lest she misunderstand his own. No letter of repudiation would mean that Joachim would not have to pay back the money he had received at the time of their betrothal, but that Ephraim would not have to pay the usual *kethubah*, or indemnity for putting away a wife.

"You cannot stay with him," he declared sternly. "You and Naomi must come home. The law at least gives you the right to keep your child."

"But this house is crowded already." Salome looked plaintively at her mother. "And I will have no money."

"We will make room," they both assured her, they would manage.

Suddenly it seemed a blessing. A kind of righteous excitement bound them, love enhanced by indignation. Hannah could hardly wait to tell the others; she scurried into the yard to see if she could find someone—Judith, Esau, Amos, or his wife—a mother hen rounding up her chickens. And to have one of them back for good, safely by her side to console and defend. To have this new responsibility and source of stimulation to keep her from brooding over Matthew.

Yet suddenly now, through the challenge, the drama, the fierce call to action on behalf of Salome, came flashes of dismal reality. To have a daughter of hers rejected! She thought of that terrible time when half the town had whispered about Mary. And now this. People would gossip. It was not easy for a woman put aside by her husband. Though the tractates said she was free to live as she chose, even to remarry, who would have her?

Salome had to return to her husband that night. Joachim was determined to go along to confront him, but Salome wouldn't have it. He was in no condition to make such a long walk. Esau was out of the question, and Amos was still in the fields. "Come home with me," Mary insisted. "We will get Joseph."

It was hours before Joseph returned from taking Salome home. Mary had fed her family without him. Jesus, by the light of a single lamp, was bent over his books. He was reading the psalms, he would never forget, the words were burned into his brain: *Take pity on me, God, take pity on me, in you my soul takes shelter. I take shelter in the shadow of your wings. . . .*

"That scoundrel!" His father was fuming. "Ephraim was in high good spirits, would you believe it? He is like a youth with his first love. He actually spoke to me at length, privately, about how fair she is." Joseph flung himself into a chair, exhausted. "He is determined; I could not talk him out of it. But at least one thing was already settled. He will not humiliate Salome, or cheat your father, by bringing the woman into the same house." Joseph laughed dryly. "Ephraim's mother and sisters won't have it—after all, they consider it their house."

Jesus had been listening, appalled. "And what will happen to Salome?"

"He will give her a bill of divorcement."

"On what charges?"

"He hasn't decided. He will have to consult the doctors of the Law. Perhaps taint of defilement," he said as Mary gasped. "Which could mean anything: not being lovable any more, a shrew, not cooking what he likes, or even the truth—that he thinks he's found a better-looking wife." Joseph kept shaking his head. "At least a few rabbis consider that sufficient reason."

"But that's *unfair*," Jesus said hotly.

"My son, there are many unfair things in life."

"Will there be a trial?" Mary asked. "Will she have no chance to protest?"

"No, and a good thing too," Joseph decided. "It would be unspeakable for a decent, modest woman like Salome to have to face public charges before a body of men."

A week later, Salome received the letter. A young man who seemed embarrassed by his mission handed it to her father, then, kicking his donkey, rode quickly off. Bitterly Joachim broke the seal and unrolled the scroll. He could not bear to look at his daughter, huddled in the doorway. "Shall I read it to you?" he asked. Salome shook her head. But she reached out and snatched it from him. She could not believe this, she refused to. She had some blind conviction that if no one ever told her what the message said, the words would vanish; that if she but kept it close enough, warmed it with her blood, the whole thing would go away. . . .

Salome went into hiding. She would go nowhere. She lay dry-eyed on her couch, or got up sometimes and disappeared, walking alone for hours in the hills. She would speak to no one except to Hannah and sometimes to her daughter, a pale frightened girl still unmarried at eighteen. Even Mary could not reach her sister, although she went to her parents' house almost every day, knowing her presence was a comfort to all of them. Together the women would do the work—Mary, Judith, who lived just down the road, and Amos' wife, Rebecca—laughing and chattering as if nothing were wrong, trying to make things brighter, especially for Hannah. Or they would lower their voices and sit discussing it, this grievous problem.

Something must be done. Salome was wasting away, literally dying of grief, and dragging Hannah and Joachim toward the grave with her. This terrible concern, together with their never-ending worry about Matthew, could soon be more than they could bear. . . .

One fall day when Jesus was mending a fence with Amos, he saw his aunt in the distance, climbing a hill just beyond the olive grove. Alone, so alone—like a homeless animal, leaning into the wind with her shawl blowing. Jesus straightened, put down his heavy stone. "I must go to her," he said.

Amos shrugged and said it would do no good. They all had tried to talk some sense into her; she wouldn't listen.

Yet Jesus ran after her, caught up with her, and took her hand. She returned his pressure slightly. She did not draw away. They walked in silence through the sere dry grasses until they reached the crest of the hill. It overlooked a gulch where a stream was winding. The wind was blowing harder here; overhead dark clouds were sailing. Soon the rains would be falling. His heart was filled with compassion. He felt that if she did not revive before the autumn rains began she would be swept away in the torrent like a tossing stick—he could see her bones—or that she might dissolve, be obliterated in the storms of her anguish.

"Aunt Salome, please don't grieve," he said at last. "Human love isn't everything. Think of the One in heaven who loves you. Human love is nothing compared with the love of God."

She turned on him suddenly. "How do you know?" she demanded scornfully. "Have you ever loved a woman— other than your mother? Look at you: past twenty, way past twenty, and not yet even betrothed. What do *you* know about love that you should try to comfort me?"

He was staggered; he could only gaze at her helplessly. "I'm sorry," he said. "Yes, the love between a man and a woman is important. That much I have learned from my parents. All my life I have been blessed to live in a home where there is so much love. But I am a man now, as you say, I've seen other couples, and I know that the kind of love my mother and father have for each other is very rare in Israel."

"My own parents," she went on. "Your grandparents. They cleave to each other, no matter how they quarrel. Only death could ever separate them. While I—!" she gasped. "My husband has cut me away from him as surely as if he had meant to kill me. He *has* killed a part of me, chopped away this unwanted flesh and thrown it away to die . . . with this, with *this*!" To his amazement, she clawed into her bosom and pulled out a tightly rolled parchment.

Her bill of divorcement, Jesus realized.

"Read it to me," she demanded. "Let me hear the words for myself. Perhaps I was wrong not to hear them. Perhaps this isn't even true; perhaps there has been a mistake."

Jesus unrolled the thing and saw them, the ugly words and accusations. He sickened. "No. No, Aunt Salome, no. This is a vile document. An abomination in the sight of

God. It is a blessing you cannot read it, and you must not keep it further to torment you. Let me destroy it."

"No, no, it's mine," she cried. "I want it, let me have it!"

"Then you can only want your own misery and what you consider your disgrace."

Before she could stop him, he strode to a boulder on the ridge of the hill and began tearing the letter to shreds. Even as he did so, a few drops of rain began to fall, spattering the strips of parchment he was flinging into the wind. They writhed and circled like serpents on their way down into the gully and the little stream.

When he returned, Salome was sobbing violently, face in her hands. He held her against his strong young body, turning to shelter her from the wind. Her shawl had gone awry; he put it straight. "Good, good," he soothed, "it is good for you to weep, good for you to talk." He stroked her gently, and she quieted under his touch. Her convulsions stopped. She caught his hand and pressed it feverishly against her wet cheek. "Thank you, Jesus, you have helped me."

"God has helped you," he said. "Not even a sparrow falls that he doesn't know—and care. He felt your pain; he didn't want you to go on suffering as you have. You will be well now. Sometime, when all this is long past, you will find love again."

"No, never," Salome said vehemently as they began to walk down the hill. "Love hurts too much when it's gone. Even if another man would have me, I could not risk the pain of losing love again."

"There are worse pains," Jesus said. "The whole world is filled with terrible sin and suffering, Aunt Salome."

"What has that to do with me?" she retorted. "All I know is what *I* am feeling. True, there are probably worse things, as I will discover as life goes on, and I will have to face them. But no suffering will ever surpass this one."

"Then you are sorry you married Ephraim?"

They had reached the olive grove and halted there to take shelter; the rain was pattering down on the silvery leaves. "No!" Salome's voice was shocked. "How can you say such a thing? My husband's love was a treasure, it enriched my life for years, it gave me a daughter who will enrich my life for years more. How could I regret having had the treasure? No, no, only its loss."

Salome was gazing at her nephew as if seeing him after a long absence. "You are very wise for your age, Jesus. You study, you are preparing yourself to help people, even more than you are helping now. I have sensed that for a long time. But no matter how much you study, you will never know what human happiness or pain is until you have known that kind of love."

Chapter 9

*A*mos strode through the sunrise, rejoicing. Never had he felt so loved, so secure. A son, another son, he thought—a third and perfect son! Only an hour ago Hannah, determined to act as midwife despite her age, had wrenched it from his wife Rebecca. And his father, usually that dear stubborn adversary, had not only paced the fields with him but had entered the chamber and with trembling arms held the boy close, to be consecrated upon his knee.

Never had Amos seen a more beautiful dawn. What a fine day it would be for the threshing! The pink light claimed the sky even to the west, and the mountains held up their massive shoulders like kings emerging from misty baths to draw on their mauve and purple robes. Softly, softly yet excitingly the sweet light fell, touching and turning to magic the blue fields of flax, and nearer, the golden wheat. A rippling treasury to be harvested and sold for profit. Enough to sustain the whole family for another year. What a wealth of grain—and sons!

Rebecca slept now in the little house he had built with the help of Joseph and his own sons, just down the hill. Overhead the very heavens exulted, as if Yahweh himself were spreading his brilliant banners to proclaim, "Well done!" And now the sun appeared, as rosy and round as the little boy's face. Like himself, his father's third son and heir.

At last they realize, Amos thought, with a twinge of pain. There was no longer any denying all he had accomplished since the disappearance of Matthew. The years of seemingly thankless work, fighting locusts and weeds and dust, and rains that would tear the rich earth away. He paused and gazed with satisfaction at the stone terraces that stripped the green of the hilly land. Joachim had let the terraces fall into disrepair; Amos had not only mended them but added new ones. And the crop that would be reaped today! Joachim had admitted that never had he seen a more promising stand of wheat, and never had the family needed it more.

The more people, the more mouths to feed—and this included Salome and Naomi. That rascal Ephraim wasn't contributing a shekel to their support, and Joachim was too proud and embittered to demand the money—never mind that their presence meant a bigger burden on Amos. Not that he minded, he loved his sister and his niece, bent over backwards to be generous, make them feel wanted, although Rebecca fretted sometimes that it meant taking food out of his family's mouth. Also that Naomi dawdled, didn't carry her share of the water. Women! Being in charge meant he had to be a peacemaker too.

Amos paused at the shed, where a pile of sickles lay bright and gleaming in the rising sun. It had taken courage to carry them to Ephraim's shop to be sharpened; he hadn't told his father, who'd have been furious. But no other smitty could give cutting tools such an edge. A lucky stroke! Because when Amos reached into his girdle to pay, Ephraim, shamefaced for once, but laughing, had waved the money aside. "I guess I owe your family that much."

It pleased Amos to remember with what contempt he had stood regarding the man. "You do indeed," he said coldly. "Although this was not my motive in coming, on behalf of my sister and your daughter, I accept."

Testing a blade against his fingers, Amos thought of Matthew, who never could have achieved what he had. Matthew was a lot like his father, although Joachim could never see it. Careless. Yes, careless, that stern, dignified, hard-working man. People didn't realize, even Amos hadn't realized, not until he was given some authority, how careless Joachim was about some things. Why, this family might have prospered years ago if his father had worked the land as Amos did. Goaded the ox harder to break up the clods, plowed it over and over to prepare the soil. Amos would never forget their arguments about this, Joachim claiming it wasn't necessary, just get on with the sowing.

And the sowing! When Amos and Matthew were children it was fine to trudge along behind the father, a hero to them then, broadcasting seeds willy-nilly, then stooping to cover them with their hands. No wonder so many fell among the rocks and thistles, or were blown away to be eaten by the birds. Not until he was older was he able to prevail upon his father to use beasts to tread the seeds in. "Their hooves will not only press them into the earth, their droppings will provide nourishment for the soil."

Joachim had snorted. "You are informing *me* of a method of farming that has been used since Isaiah!"

"It is still the best method, Father," Amos had said respectfully, controlling himself. Since Joachim refused to use the ox, he had taken his own money to rent a yoke of cattle, and the following year the crops of barley and wheat and flax were so much thicker even Joachim was impressed. Since then he had not resisted. And now look! There would be enough not only to pay the laborers and the taxes but also to lay by for other needs, and of course to share with the poor.

Amos felt the thrill of the harvest season: the joy of the new wheat to be baked into bread, of the storehouse replenished. And this year both a new son and a new threshing floor. To think his father hadn't recognized it himself years ago—the perfect place, a rock shelf at least fifty feet in diameter, halfway up the second hill. Open to the mountain winds that would help blow the chaff away, yet sheltered on one side. No longer would they have to haul the sheaves of grain to town on carts and laden donkeys; what's more, others would soon be paying them fees to use the floor. Another source of profit.

The sun was now warm on his back; it was drinking up the dew, gilding the waiting grain. He could hear dogs barking, and the sound of voices and tools. Good, the reapers were at the gate. Hired hands were seldom as anxious as the owner to get started. Amos wanted the wheat cut and ready for threshing by noon. Joseph had promised to send whatever sons he could spare to help with the winnowing. Beaming, Amos strode across the yard, calling out the traditional greeting "The Lord be with you!"

"And the Lord bless you," the men answered. And this too was part of the happy morning, that these rough men, some of them *am-ha-aretz* who paid little attention to religion, were so respectful, responding to a salutation that was often neglected. Unconsciously Amos glanced toward the house, as if to receive his father's approval.

"Follow me," he ordered. Leading the procession, he began to assign them their tasks. As they worked he moved about the fields, giving directions. He didn't want the stalks too short: "Just a little below the ears." He grabbed a handful with his left hand and demonstrated with a brisk stroke of the sickle. The binders, following behind, were not only to bind the sheaves, they were to pick out the weeds or tares and tie them in separate bundles. He himself squatted here and there to make sure this was done.

Most of the men were older than he was, and a number had worked for Joachim. A few of them exchanged glances, bemused, long-suffering, yet they had a grudging admiration for this energetic, anxious, and yet courteous young man. They wanted to please him. Some had brought their children along to help. It was a good cool bright day, with a pleasant breeze blowing and the wheat smelling toasty in the sun. There was the crisp clean slash of the sickles, the rustling of the stalks, the braying of donkeys, the rattle of carts soon to be hauled up to the new floor. . . .

Joachim had toiled up to inspect the place. He wanted to be there waiting with the ox and the husking sledge when the first sheaves were delivered. Like Amos, he was very tired from the long night's vigil, but proud: his new grandson sleeping, his bins soon filled to overflowing. Below, he could see a little parade of women moving from the house—Judith, Naomi, Salome, Ann. The sickles were silent, the men resting in the shade. The women were carrying jugs of wine and fresh water, baskets of food. Word had just gone around: the reason Amos' wife was not among them was that she was suckling a newborn child. "To your wife and son!" the men called out, lifting their cups to Amos.

Joachim could not hear them but he smiled, waiting there with the ox. He sensed Amos' half humble yet pleased strutting about. Also that he was probably nervous about getting the threshing over before nightfall, which Joachim could understand—all this wheat! There was always the danger of fire or thieves. To his relief, he saw Jesus loping toward the group, followed by Josey and James at a more leisurely pace. Good, with family to help, things moved faster.

Well, Amos deserved credit. If only Matthew . . . ! Joachim's fists clenched; he had to bite his trembling lip. *Good riddance*, he had tried to think when they had discovered another appalling truth: Matthew had not only run away, he had stolen his own inheritance to take with him. But Hannah had been so frantic they had continued to search. Every rumor sparked new efforts. Matthew had been in Sidon, Tiberias, even in Egypt. Nothing definite, although for years they had hired lookouts from caravans passing through Nazareth. Prayed and hoped. Too late now, too late. . . . Joachim blinked hard and wiped his eyes. True, he had been spared far more than most; the Lord did not deem it good for a man not to have his portion of sorrow and pain. But oh, to have his family reunited just once more before he died.

Joachim braced himself, steadied the ox. For now, creaking and swaying, the carts and wagons were coming slowly up the hill to dump their golden cargo. The ox, unmuzzled so that he could share in the feast, began to drag the sledge, ridden nimbly by his grandson James, who enjoyed the job of keeping it firm. Soon the whole floor was covered by a dry dusty confusion of husks and straw and grain, a deep rustling mass of gold to be tossed into the air by the three winnowing forks.

Joachim watched the men with pleasure, their strong dark bodies leaping and hurling, like pagans performing a dance to their gods of plenty. And Jesus the tallest, strongest, most lithe among them. His teeth flashed white in his sun-browned face; he was shouting and singing as he flung the stalks high. His eyes were sparkling as he spied his grandfather, and the smile Jesus sent him seemed bright with some strange secret.

Doubtfully, trying to suppress his own excitement, Jesus had taken Amos aside to speak to him before they left the field.

"I have something important to tell you. Good news— at least I hope it's good news."

Amos frowned; for some reason he felt alarmed. They walked over to a fig tree and sat down in its shade.

"We think Matthew has been found, and is coming home."

"When?" Amos gasped. "How do you know?"

"Soon. He may be on his way even now."

Amos sat stunned, torn between joy and dismay. Something about Egypt, a man of his brother's description there—in Giza, the same small town where Mary and Joseph had once lived. Something about Joseph's friends there sending word.

"Several weeks ago," Jesus was saying. "They were pretty sure they'd seen Matthew, although he'd fallen on hard times. We didn't want to say anything too soon; your parents would only worry or get their hopes up; it might not even be true. But we've been questioning people on every caravan from Egypt since. And yesterday we learned that a man of that age and name had started with them, but dropped off about a day's journey back. He said he was very tired and wanted to rest before setting out again. For Nazareth."

"Matthew!" Amos whispered. "I can't believe it. Not after all these years."

"Don't tell anyone just yet," Jesus warned. "Your mother and father have suffered enough. It would be too cruel for them to be disappointed."

"That's right," Amos said tightly. He was gazing into the distance. "Matthew will never know how much pain he has caused them." Dazed, he got to his feet, trying to sort out his emotions. He wished he could be grateful, enthusiastic, and a part of him was indeed thrilled at the possibility of seeing his long-lost brother again. Yet another part was shocked, even stricken. Matthew, the plump, amiable one, always favored by their mother. Amos felt bewildered, suddenly and foolishly threatened, his own influence crumbling, even now.

"It would seem their prayers have been answered," he muttered. "But if he does come home I hope they remember he's already had his inheritance. And probably squandered it!" Half ashamed yet defensive, Amos turned on Jesus. "I know this doesn't sound very generous of me, Jesus, but you're not married; you don't know how it is. I have a wife and children to support."

He stalked off then to help load the carts. . . .

The breeze was blowing the chaff into Joachim's beard and hair. He sneezed, his eyes watered; the lack of sleep was catching up with him; he was suddenly too tired to stay. But he bent to scoop up some of the clean smooth kernels and sift them through his fingers. With a kind of stodgy playfulness, he threw several handfuls at his grandsons, then took up his stick and started off down the hill. He had promised Hannah he would not stay long.

Joachim had almost reached the house when he had to pause to rest. He stood a moment half dizzied by the sunshine. It made the yard ripple in places, creating illusions the way it did on the desert. Standing thus, getting his breath and his balance, he was sure he saw a figure approaching along the narrow path that led up from the shed. A gaunt, weary-looking man carrying a bag over his shoulder. One of the poor come early, Joachim thought, to glean the corners of the field. "That way, that way!" he hollered, waving his arms and pointing the opposite direction.

But the poor beggar came on, and as Joachim stood watching, shielding his eyes, he gasped; his shoulders began to shake. He saw the face now, and it was like seeing a ghost. His heart nearly stopped. "*Matthew!*" he croaked. Then somehow he was hobbling swiftly toward him. They were clutching each other, laughing and crying and kissing, then drawing apart to embrace again.

"Father, Father, forgive me," Matthew was pleading through his tears. "I want to come back, if you'll have me. I have hurt you, I have shamed you, I am unworthy, but I'm tired and ill. I will sleep in the barn with the beasts if you'll only have me; I will serve you—" He sagged; he could scarcely stand.

"Hannah!" Joachim bellowed. It was all he could think to do. "Hannah, Hannah, our boy is home!"

His wife stood frozen in the door, eyes huge. "I knew it, I knew it!" she claimed, one hand to her throat. Then she too came running.

Together they got him inside and knelt to bathe his feet. They were nearly beside themselves with joy; it was hard to think. Fresh clothes—he must get out of those dirty rags. While Hannah drew more water, Joachim pawed through the chest and brought forth his finest Sabbath robe.

Hannah's heart shriveled to see her son's body—this once pudgy boy like a skeleton now, his poor flesh covered with bruises and ugly sores. What had happened to him? Oh, he was so hurt, feverish, exhausted.

They put him to bed and he slept deeply while they took counsel. A kind of madness possessed them. They must get word to Mary and Joseph, and Joseph's mother. And all the cousins, the neighbors, his friends. They must celebrate! Food? There was already extra food for the reapers; they could borrow or buy more. It was too late to kill the fatted calf—or was it? The butcher didn't live far. They would summon the butcher to slaughter it; if the fire was started at once it would be ready within a few hours.

It was almost dark when Matthew awoke. He could hear voices, many voices, chattering, laughing, singing. And music—the melody of timbrels and lutes. There was the tantalizing aroma of meat roasting. Could he be dreaming? He sat up, stupefied. A shadowy figure turned from the window, a tall young man he didn't recognize. "Who is it?" he cried sharply. "Where am I?"

"It's Jesus, your nephew, remember? I've grown up since you left." Jesus stood over him, smiling, and bent to kiss him. "Hello, Matthew, welcome home!"

"But what's going on? What are they doing?"

"They're having a party for you. They've invited in all

our relatives, and the neighbors, and your old friends. They are having a feast in your honor."

Matthew shrank back, aghast. "No, no, this is impossible. We must stop them. I don't deserve this. I betrayed them." Matthew groaned. "I stole my father's money!" He lifted his tormented face. "Jesus, they don't realize—I have lived with *pigs*! No, please don't let them. I want to run away and hide. I want to die."

"You *were* dead," Jesus said gently, marveling. "But now you are living. That's all they can realize right now. That's all that matters. Let them. Don't spoil this for them, Matthew. Come, put on your garments, go out to join them."

Groggily, still cringing, Matthew reached for the clothes. It was impossible. The sandals, gemmed with small inexpensive jewels, must be Esau's. His father's gold ring. And the robe—dear heaven, after all these years, Joachim's cherished, well-preserved, multicolored Sabbath robe! He could not believe it. He plunged his face into his hands and wept.

"Come on now, come, come," Jesus encouraged him, and the eyes of the two met. Those incredibly beautiful eyes, Matthew remembered; even when Jesus was a little boy, tagging him about with the sheep, he had been haunted by the special shining beauty of those eyes.

"It's going to be a great feast," Jesus was saying. "Grandfather went to great effort to have a calf he was saving killed in your honor this afternoon. And no small job it was right now, during the harvest season."

"That's right, the harvest—"

"They're all waiting for you," Jesus said. "Mary and my father and brothers, my sisters, Grandmother Timna, Uncle Cleo, even some of the reapers. Esau, Judith and her husband."

"And Amos? I want to see Amos."

"Amos hasn't come in yet. He's probably still up on the hill, cleaning the new threshing floor. Or maybe storing grain. I'd better go look for him."

But when Jesus ran hopefully up the road, he found the harvest floor deserted, its rock foundations swept clean.

The place, humming with activity only a few hours ago, was silent except for the rustle of a few stray husks. Surrounding it, like pyramids glistening under the first stars, were the neat stacks of fragrant hay. Praising God, he stood drinking in the scene for a moment as he caught his breath. A day's work well done, a precious life returned! Yet what had happened to Amos?

In the distance he could see the lights of his uncle's cottage. Feeling apprehensive, Jesus raced back down the hill in their direction. To his distress, he saw that Amos was pacing the yard. "Amos, hurry," he called out. "Please come on, we don't want to eat without you."

Amos halted, his face cold. "Never mind, go back to the celebration," he said bitterly. "It doesn't matter, they've all forgotten me."

"No, no, they are *calling* for you. Your brother is very anxious to see you. Your mother and father want you."

"Nobody even bothered to *tell* me!" Amos accused. "I heard the commotion while I was picking up tools in the field. I heard the voices and music. I had to ask one of the workers what was going on." Amos brushed away angry tears. "No, no, it doesn't matter—never mind that my wife has just given them another grandson. Never mind that we have just harvested the biggest crop this farm has ever had. On a new threshing floor!" he blazed, and shook aside the sympathetic hand Jesus put on his shoulder. "No, no, go on back and join the party."

"Amos, don't," Jesus pleaded. "Your parents have already suffered so much because of your brother. If you love them, surely you won't want to hurt them more by refusing to welcome him home."

"If my father wants me, let him come for me himself!"

Joachim had opened the gate and was limping toward them, looking concerned. He had heard. "Son, I have come indeed," he said humbly. "Please don't stay apart from us on such a joyous occasion. I entreat you, please come with us."

Amos turned on him, eyes glaring. Poison, bottled for years, spewed from him. "Listen, Father, I've broken my back for you. Never once have I disobeyed you, though I've often had to go against your stubborn will in order to improve this place. And I *have* improved it, you've had to admit it yourself. But praise me?" he demanded. "Not that I remember. Reward me, given me a party? Killed so much as a goose for me so that I could make merry with my friends?"

Joachim stood stiff and dignified before the tirade, but his face was ashen, his thick lips trembling like a child's—a berated and stricken old man.

"But when this son of yours who has treated you abominably shows up, this son who's spent your money on harlots and God knows what—not even been in touch with you for years—what do you do? You treat him like a king, you summon the whole town to celebrate, you kill the fatted calf!" It was too much; Amos covered his face with his hands and wept.

Joachim watched helpless for a minute, too shocked to speak. Finally he reached out his hand. "Forgive me, Amos," he said. "If I have failed to show appreciation, I am truly sorry. It is not my nature to praise. But you are always with me, and that is a comforting thing. And you know, surely you know, that all that I have is yours." He waited for some response. "But your brother is *home*—your own brother whom we thought dead. He was lost and now he's found! It is fitting that we rejoice and make merry. For Matthew was dead and now he lives!"

Amos fought to get hold of himself. He nodded, wiping his tears on his sleeve. "I'm sorry," he said thickly. "Of course I'll come to welcome my brother. But don't wait for me, go back to your guests and begin. I must wash and put on proper clothes." He plunged off into the house, ashamed. He loathed himself, yet the sense of injustice would not go away.

Joy now, relief from worry, thanksgiving. The whole family together again. For the first time in years, Hannah and Joachim held hands, laughed together, were kinder, more patient with each other, at peace.

Matthew mended rapidly, and put on weight. They refused to listen to his protestations of remorse or his tales. If he must get them out of his heart, let him talk to Amos. And he did, pouring out his shame and sometimes his adventures as they worked together, desperate to make amends. This pleased Amos, whose heart was aglow with forgiveness and the thrill of teaching his own elder brother the new ways of farming the land. They had never been so close.

The parents rejoiced to see them setting off on their tasks together, or to hear them laughing and talking on the roof, sometimes far into the night.

Yet one thing troubled Joachim. He spoke of it to Hannah one day, to her surprise. "I want to give Amos a party. I've been thinking of it a long time. A big dance, a feast with music and dancing. He deserves it. I must make it up to him." And he thought he knew the perfect place for it: the threshing floor.

Joachim toiled up one hot muggy day to inspect it, though Hannah had warned him about the heat. Missing him, in late afternoon, she sent Amos and Matthew out to look for him. They found him, broom in hand, sprawled on the hard rock floor where the chaff had begun drifting again. They knew, even before they ran to him, that their father was dead.

Chapter 10

———————•◆•———————

*T*he return of Matthew and the death of Joachim brought a new atmosphere into the family, a new awareness of their own mortality and need for each other. At first Hannah wandered around bereft; then she set about weaving herself more deeply into the lives of her children. Leaving the care of her own house to Salome or a daughter-in-law, Hannah spent weeks at a time with Mary and Joseph. She identified them most closely with Joachim; being near them brought back a period she loved to dwell on. Ironically, the very pain and problems of their courtship had become dear to her, with its drama, its need for her and her husband to protect their own. And how magnificent Joachim had been! Hannah did not spare herself in the recollection, but took comfort in exalting her husband. No, no, she had been the foolish one.

Sometimes, when there was no one else to listen, she would put on her shawl and go down to share as much of this as she dared with Joseph's mother, who kept to her bed a good deal these days in the room behind the shop. "I was so wrong about Joseph," Hannah never tired of confessing. "The Lord himself couldn't have chosen a better father for Mary's son. *All* their children," she hastened to add. "Always so kind and patient, but firm too, just like Joachim was, teaching them their little prayers—'Cause us to turn, O our Father, to your law. . . . Forgive us, our Father, for we have sinned'—I can hear him yet and their little voices; I hear them through Joseph's children." Hannah often moved herself to tears. "And how good Joseph is to Mary. Oh, Timna, they are so happy, it is the joy of my life to see them, so affectionate, just the way Joachim and I were!"

147

Timna, waiting courteously but a bit wearily for her turn, would try. "Joseph is very much like his father. Jacob and I were very much in love; not a day passed that we didn't—"

But she seldom got to finish a sentence. Hannah was only catching her breath. Although Timna was actually a year younger, Hannah considered her an old woman to be dominated, a perpetual audience for her own now seemingly eventful life story.

Mary and Joseph also had the largest family, whose betrothals, marriages, and birthings kept Hannah busy. Ann, Josey, and Simon were all married now, and had added two great-grandchildren to her score. It might have been three, but Ann's first baby had been stillborn. Hannah would always blame herself; Ann had gone into labor one day while Mary was away and Hannah still visiting with Timna. Hannah should have known better than to leave the poor girl, who must have been crying out for an hour. Hannah was getting a little deaf, and what with all the noise of hammers and saws in the shop she hadn't heard her.

Mary's other children were still at home; James and Jude, like their eldest brother, Jesus, seemed in no hurry to marry, a fact that Hannah knew troubled Joseph, much as he valued their help. They were becoming fine artisans, especially James. His fingers were like Joseph's, skilled at fashioning cabinets and tables. The others were better at building the hard, firm scaffoldings and outside staircases for houses. They were all jaunty but much respected youths, proudly wearing behind their ears the wooden chip that marked their trade.

Jesus remained the only misfit: now working cheerfully beside them, now out in the hills with the sheep, sometimes simply vanishing for days—off to the sea of Galilee, or climbing some mountain, or just walking to distant villages, they scarcely knew where.

"Where have you been, what are you doing?" Hannah probed, knowing it was none of her business, but concerned. "We miss you. We—you'll never know how dreadful it was for us, worrying about Matthew when he was gone."

"You mustn't worry, Grandmother, I'm sure my parents understand. Mostly I'm just studying. And thinking, and praying. Or making friends with the fishermen along the lakeshore. They're wonderful men; they've taught me to swim. What a great thing, swimming—no boat, no oars, no sails, just the sheer force of your own arms propelling you through the cold water! It's like flying; I sometimes feel I could rise right up and fly."

"Don't you ever try it!"

"And I love being out with the sheep. I feel very close to God and to Grandfather, when I'm out there under the stars with his sheep." As Hannah's face broke he leaned down to kiss her cheek, wrinkled and soft as butter to his lips. "To me they will always be Grandfather's sheep."

"You are a fine shepherd," she told him. "You will be a fine shepherd of men."

"If that is God's will for me," Jesus said. Their eyes met, and for a moment they gazed at each other in silence, expressing things that could not be said. He smiled then and pressed her hand. "I must know soon. Pray for me, Grandmother."

His brothers were less easily put off. They often discussed it scornfully among themselves. What was the matter with Jesus? Still wasting his time, a man his age. No steady job or prospects of any, it seemed. Wandering around like some beggar or tramp. Consorting with fishermen, a rough lot—and probably worse. A wonder their father didn't kick him out; instead, both parents seemed to prize him, put some special stock in him. Look how they acted when he did come home—almost as crazy as their grandparents had when Matthew finally showed up. Bathe, rest, eat the best food! Sing, dance, rejoice, come with us to the synagogue. For he always managed to arrive in time for Sabbath supper, and to charm everybody at the services. His eyes shone, his beautiful voice rang out in the songs, and when he was called upon to read, people leaned forward in expectation, for he seemed to bring a special power and magic to the words.

Jesus was different, he had always been different. He was a contradiction. People knew that and still loved him.

Strange. It was no use even trying to understand him. His brothers were torn between envy, resentment, embarrassment, and a curious pride.

The night before it happened, Jesus could hear his mother and father laughing and talking softly together on the roof. They seemed very merry and free on this lovely spring night. They had just taken Hannah home, walked with her to the farm and persuaded her to rest there with the others for a while. Hannah had gone willingly, at first a little hurt, yet scolding herself that she hadn't realized sooner that they needed to be alone. Life was short, she thought bleakly, chattering all the way to keep them from suspecting the pain heavy on her heart. If only she had taken more time to be alone with Joachim. . . .

Mary and Joseph had hurried to the roof at once. Jesus smiled to hear them as he prepared to leave. Simon and Jude had already run off to mingle with the excitement of the camel caravan that had arrived this afternoon. The first since the long winter rains. It was on its way to Egypt from east of the River Jordan. A long procession of the tall tawny beasts, bells jangling, their burdens swaying, riders waving from their brightly colored saddles, and among them an unusual number of jovial people swarming the village with fish or trinkets to sell and items to be mended. Jesus could see their campfires on the newly green hills and hear their music as he pulled on a clean tunic and tied his sash to join them.

"Come with us," he called up to his parents.

"No, thanks." Joseph came to the roof's edge to peer down. "The boys and I are leaving early in the morning to cut some timber. If you see them, remind them not to be late."

"I won't be late either. I'm taking the sheep out to pasture."

He stood a moment, reluctant to leave. The night was cool and sweet, with a smell of rock roses and wild geraniums mingling with a whiff of the fires. Sounds of singing came from the village. There was a clatter of hooves on the street below as Cleophas rode toward them, a somehow lonely figure on his horse. Like a youth, he too was out seeking some excitement from the caravan. Pulling up, he waved. "Come along," he invited hopefully.

Mary and Joseph stood beside each other now, waving cordially but shaking their heads. "Wait, Uncle Cleo," Jesus shouted, "I'll go with you!" He ran down the steps and sprang on the horse behind him.

As they rode off, Jesus turned to look up just as his parents were embracing. A star went streaking across the sky; it seemed to land between them, on his mother's breast.

The whole family was up early the next morning. Joseph had hired a mule and wagon for this excursion into the forests along the slopes of Mount Tabor, some miles away. Jude and Simon were going with him; his older sons, who lived nearer the site, would meet them there. In a couple of days they could cut enough trees to supply the shop with all the lumber they would need until winter: oaks and sycamores mostly; the wagon would bring back the trunks. Now, at daybreak, Jesus was helping load it with their tools—axes, hatchets, saws—and with the food and blankets Mary had prepared, for they would spend the night.

Jesus wished suddenly he hadn't promised Amos to take the sheep. He wanted to troop off with his father and brothers on this mission, with the wagon rattling merrily along the waking streets and Jude proudly driving the mule. To go with them up into the dark scented forest where it was always cool and the trees murmured together, a thrilling and faintly ominous sound. To feel the ax biting into a trunk when his strong arms swung it, and to hear the squealing protests a great tree made before it crashed.

He also felt uneasily that he was needed. "Father, listen," he offered impulsively. "I'm bringing the sheep back Friday night. If you could wait until next week—"

"No, this is the best time for cutting, before the trees are too heavy with leaves."

Mary came running down the steps, a slight figure in the soft gray light, bringing them a jug of warmed milk which she urged them to drink before setting off. "Be careful, all of you," she told them. "You too, Jesus."

He drank it miserably, his regret and disappointment growing. Even now, if there was time, he would race up to the farm and ask Amos to get someone else to graze the sheep. But he knew his father was anxious to get started. Scolding himself, filled with a curious anxiety, he could only stand with Mary waving goodbye. Then, incredibly, when they were out of sight, he had a childish longing simply to stay with her. Again he considered getting someone else to tend the flock, or leaving them where they were for a few days. Amos' sons were old enough now, at least to graze them near the farm. Still, most of the boys were in school. . . .

Jesus felt better once the flock was at his heels. Penned up for months during the rains, the sheep were like children on a holiday, blatting and bunting, bells tinkling, a few wanting to scamper and scatter. It was all his latest dog, Benjamin, could do to keep them together. Jubal had died quietly in his arms several years before. Jesus had wakened to feel the beloved body stiff and cold against him. "No, oh, no, don't leave me!" Jesus had implored. "Wake up, I command you, come back to me—live!" For one long desperate moment he had believed: the eyes would surely open, the warm tongue lick his hand again. Then, berating himself for his delusion, Jesus wept.

Benjy appeared at the door a few days later, as if sensing that he too would find haven here: a yellow cur, starved and cruelly beaten. One eye was swollen nearly shut, he still bore whip marks on his nearly bald hide, and, like Jubal, one leg dragged. At first he snatched his food and ran, whimpering and cringing when they tried to approach, but soon he too lay docile before the family's ministrations and leaped for joy at their love. Ben too was jubilant at once more bounding over the hills.

Spring had come early this year. Even in January, when the high mountain ranges were still white with snow, spring began to creep over the valleys and up the slopes on little green feet, as if eager to mate with winter. And the heart of winter was melted; dry creek beds became foaming torrents—Jesus had to take the sheep farther than ever to find still water—but their banks exploded with grass and flowers. Lilies of the field in colors of pink and white and gold; anemones and cyclamen, rock roses, asphodel, blue lupis, wild gladiolus, scarlet and yellow tulips, daisies and chrysanthemums, snapdragons of a dozen hues. The fingers of God had embroidered the earth like a tapestry and scented it with his headiest perfumes.

Jesus took out his pipe and played as he walked through these fields of beauty. His heart ached with a kind of tender wonder as he remembered his parents, so close last night, now parted for even a day. . . .

Jesus was not sure how much he slept that night. He could hear the sheep stirring, and the sounds of the fire, and the nighthawks making their curious cry. And it seemed to him he heard the voice of his father speaking to him gently and firmly about taking a wife. The love of his parents for each other was a part of his semiconscious state. He saw the star that seemed to fall on his mother's breast, and it became a baby, for he could see his father bending over her tenderly, the way he always did whenever a child was born. To love like that, to find a woman whom he could love like that, his own wife who would bear him children to nurse at her breast! . . . Restless and stirred, yet lying remotely apart, Jesus dreamed.

He was no longer himself but Jacob rising up from his pillow of stones to climb a ladder of stars. And the top of it reached to heaven, and behold angels were ascending and descending. And the Lord stood above it, speaking the words he had spoken to Jacob: "I am the God of Abraham your father, and the God of Isaac; and I will give you the land on which you lie, I will give it to you and your seed."

"But Father, I have no seed!" Jesus cried out, in a voice so loud he half awoke and lay, heart pounding. Then he found himself somewhere else, wrestling with an angel; like Jacob it seemed to him they wrestled all night long, trying desperately for some foolish reason to learn each other's names. The angel kept laughing at him, but just before he awoke, the angel promised to tell him.

What was it, what was it? Jesus sat up in a cold sweat.

Then to his relief it came to him: Temptation. He had been wrestling with temptation. . . . He lay a few moments longer, thinking. What was temptation? Had he not been tempted many times? The girls at the grape treadings, young and lovely, sometimes unsteady from the very smell of the wine. The girls who came into the shop on pretext of some tool to be mended for their fathers—their flirting eyes and sometimes casually touching hands. The matrons who walked the streets of Nazareth, hips swinging seductively, no matter how many little ones might be clinging to their skirts. . . . Was the yearning in his loins evil, or merely nature's response to the vital instinct God himself had planted in males that the race might survive?

Jesus threshed about, both yearning and rejecting. He would not, he could not. He was different; he had always been different. Something restrained him.

Squatting before the fire the next morning, he had a strong impulse to turn back. Perhaps if he hurried he could even yet dispose of the sheep and spend at least one day in the forest with his father—or with Mary, if she preferred. They had had so little time together these past years with Hannah so much about. Even the long evenings they had once shared, discussing the things he was reading, had somehow been lost in the commotion of the family. But no, he had promised. Jesus stamped out the fire, loaded his knapsack, and took up his rod. Ben had already rounded up the flock, but he continued to run about barking, his signal that something was wrong.

Groaning, Jesus began to count. Sure enough, one of them was missing, probably the restless ewe Amos was keeping for a neighbor. Always running off and giving him trouble, yet it must be found. The search took an hour; the ewe had wandered down a steep ravine and was perched on a rocky ledge high above a rushing torrent. It was afraid to go farther or try to come back. Grabbing at roots, rocks, and branches, Jesus scrambled after it, risking his own life, for the ledge was narrow, the sheep heavy, and a misstep would have plunged them both into the raging stream. Ben's incessant barking only aggravated the rescue; Jesus kept ordering the dog to stop as he struggled with the frightened sheep. It was heavy; he must maneuver it around and push and shove it up the steep bank that was also slippery in places. At last he boosted it over the rim, and grabbing a branch, hauled himself up.

"Hush!" he scolded the dog. "You know better than to bark when I'm going after a sheep." Then he saw the horse pounding toward them. "Cleophas!" he cried out in amazement, "Uncle Cleo, what's wrong?"

"Thank heaven we found you! We've ridden half the night." Cleo's handsome, dark, heavy-lidded face was serious. "It's your father, Jesus. He's had an accident. Never mind the sheep. One of Amos' boys came with me; he's waiting with them now; he'll drive them home."

Dazed, Jesus climbed onto the horse behind his father's friend. It seemed to him strange that only two nights before, they had ridden thus toward the music and merriment of the caravan.

It had been past dark when the wagon returned, carrying Joseph home. The streets of Nazareth were almost deserted, silent except for the creaking of wheels and the clopping of hooves on stones. Mary, trying nervously to embroider by lamplight, heard the sounds approaching and put down her needle. She knew it had not been their intention to return with a load of logs so soon. Of course it might be some other wagon passing late. Denying it, desperately denying the apprehension that had haunted her all day, she ran to the door and looked down.

It was a clear night, with a new moon sharp as a sickle in the sky. It shone down on the steps leading from her house to the shop. The steps were strewn with petals, blown today from the trees. A lamp burned in Timna's quarters. She saw her mother-in-law emerge, white-haired in the moonlight, and stand for an instant frozen, like herself, staring down.

The mule-drawn wagon had stopped. Her sons, who had been walking beside it, looked up to where the women stood. Mary tried to go to them but her feet were wooden, as in a dream. She had to clutch the rough stone wall for support. In its crannies she saw cyclamens and anemones still blooming, where they had found shelter from the icy rains. James came running up the steps to meet her halfway. "Father's been hurt," he said. "A falling oak. He'll need a doctor. We're sending Jude."

"And Jesus!" Mary cried. "Oh, dear heaven, please send someone to find Jesus!"

Somehow she was beside the wagon as they lifted Joseph from the straw. There were bits of twigs and leaves in his hair. The street was coming alive with lamps and running feet. Carefully, very carefully, grunting with his weight, they carried Joseph to his bed. His face was covered with blood, but his eyes opened slightly as they put him down; he mumbled something and strove to touch Mary. "Don't move, Father," Simon choked. "The doctor is coming."

A frantic Ann and her husband arrived; they lived above their own shop just a few doors away. Ann set about helping her sister heat water to wash their father, while their grandmother mixed oil and wine for his wounds. There was only one doctor in the village, and he was often not to be found; it might be hours. They must make Joseph as comfortable as they could. But when Mary pulled aside Joseph's garments, she waved the women aside. She could not bear for even his own mother to see how brutally his body was crushed and torn.

The doctor came within the hour: a big, earnest, very devout man wearing a tasseled prayer shawl; phylacteries were bound to his forehead and one arm with wide leather straps. He never visited a patient without them, nor would he even examine the patient until he first gathered the family together for prayer. Then, carefully removing and folding the shawl, he knelt by the pallet where Joseph sprawled.

Even the doctor was shocked. He rummaged among his bag of potions and salves, wondering what to do and how to tell her. Finally he beckoned Mary aside and said kindly, "He will be in great pain when he wakens, for his ribs are broken. Give him this, along with more wine to quiet him. But it isn't the chest that concerns me, it is his legs." One was badly broken, he told her, but he thought it could be fixed. The other one was crushed beyond repair. The doctor stood rubbing his big troubled life-scarred face. Finally, drawing a deep breath, he told her: The leg would have to come off.

Mary was staring at him blankly. "What?"

"Mary, you're a brave woman," the doctor said. "Your husband's leg is too badly injured even to try to mend. Barring a miracle, it will have to be removed." She still stood white and silent, as if she hadn't heard. "Barring a miracle," he repeated. "Unless it is better by morning, I must cut off your husband's left leg."

She still didn't seem to understand. "That won't be necessary," she said simply. "We are sending for Jesus." The doctor looked mystified. "My eldest son. You must have heard him read sometimes at the synagogue."

"Oh, yes, a fine young man, very handsome, though not yet married."

"He has more important things to do," Mary defended quickly. She put out a hand to reassure him. "Don't worry, Doctor, Jesus wll be here soon. He will surely be here by morning. He will be able to heal my husband."

The man looked puzzled. "Is he studying medicine? If so, perhaps I can help him."

"No, he is studying the word of God."

It was a chilly morning. Though a fire burned in the brazier, Mary was huddled in a blanket as she sat beside Joseph. She could not get warm, and she had not slept all night. But she would allow no one else to come near him. At last her head dropped; she dozed, still holding tight to her husband's hand.

Jesus found her thus when he tiptoed in. He stood a moment staring at the torn, bruised face on the pillow. Suddenly, sensing his presence, Mary started. "Praise God you are here at last!" she cried softly. She hugged his waist fiercely, then very cautiously got up, wiping away tears of relief. "I sent the doctor away," she whispered, sounding confident. "I knew he would not be needed."

"Not *needed*?" Jesus gasped.

Mary's head was thrown back. She was almost smiling. "I knew you would come in time to save him."

Jesus stared at her, incredulous. "Mother, Mother, what are you saying?"

"Why, that you will heal your father," Mary stated simply. "We can't let him be butchered as the doctor wanted; we can't let him die. You must heal him."

"Mother, only the Father in heaven can heal him."

"But you—!"

"I can only pray for his healing. And that I have done; from the moment Cleo first brought me the news, every breath has been a prayer for his healing."

"But you are God's special child," she cried. "He sent you to earth to save his people. Surely he will grant you the power to save your own father!"

As he only stood there appalled and stricken, she clutched his arms so hard he winced.

"Heal him," she ordered. "I command you, heal your father, Jesus. I know you can—you must!"

"You don't understand. . . . I am not yet ready!"

She wouldn't listen. She began to shake him angrily, like a child. "Ready? What has being ready to do with it? He's *ill*!" Mary bent to fling back the sheet. "See how his limb has swollen—it's black, and his brow is like fire. His eyes are glazed; he doesn't even know us. He will die if you don't put out your hand and heal him!" Desperately, she began to sob; never had she prayed for anything so hard or believed in anything so much. "You have the power—God must have given you this power. *Heal* him," she demanded again. "Heal Joseph your father."

"Mother . . . Mother, don't." He couldn't bear it. He turned away, covering his face.

Mary was rocking back and forth, pleading now through the sounds of her grief. "Jesus, Jesus, please. If you really love your father—"

"Love has nothing to do with it," Jesus said. It was a moment before he could go on. . . . Or everything to do with it? If he loved enough, if he loved with the power of the One in heaven. . . . "You *know* how much I love him!" Jesus knelt by the pallet and took Joseph's hot puffed hand. "And he knows how much I love him, don't you, Father? I told you last night in a dream; you came to me and I told you. And I have told you with every breath since the news was brought to me this morning. Our Father in heaven knows too, for with every breath I was also praying. But I can't—" he said brokenly. "Not until God wills it. Not yet. Not yet. Not until my time has come."

Mary had walked to the window. She stood there a moment staring blindly out. "He may be dead."

"Yes."

They were both calm now, gazing at each other through tear-wet eyes. "Mother, you're very tired," Jesus said helplessly. "Go to sleep now, let me tend to him."

"*No!*" she cried sharply.

"Let me help you. Give me at least the comfort of staying with him, caring for him while you rest."

"*No!*" There was no sound but Joseph's labored breathing. "If he sleeps I will be beside him, if he stirs I will know and care for him, and if he dies it will be in my arms." Then she took pity on her son and made a little movement with her hand. "Forgive me, but I want to be alone with him."

Joseph died that night.

In the shop where he had taught them, Jesus and his brothers hammered and sawed until dawn, building him a bier of finest cedarwood. Toward noon they hoisted their precious burden to their shoulders, and taking turns with Cleophas and other men who loved him, carried him, praying aloud, up to the cave in the rocky cleft where the body of Joachim lay. His mother Timna was too crippled to lead the procession with the other women—Mary and Hannah and their daughters, for as everyone knew, it was the woman Eve who had brought death into the world, and thus women should lead death's victims to the grave.

Jesus, wearing Joseph's prayer shawl, lifted his arms and uttered a prayer of his own composing before the stone was rolled to seal the tomb: "O Lord of all mercy and help and healing, you who created our mother Mary to be the wife of this good man, send your army of angels to comfort her now and to comfort us, their children; above all, comfort the soul of our father Joseph as he leaves us to be with you, let your angels march with him as they lead him to a life of everlasting joy until we join him."

Mary and Hannah supported each other, creeping back down the long hill to the farm. The men would follow when they were finished. Mary was shivering; the tomb had been damp and chill. Her face, like her mother's, was set. She could cry no more. Let people think what they would. Let other women wail and moan and beat their breasts. They had not slept in his arms or kissed his mouth or borne his children. The grief that consumed her was too deep for sound; one who will mourn forever cannot expend her strength in screaming.

The hired mourners were waiting; at sight of the widows they set up their howling afresh. "I wish they would stop," Mary said. "I wish they needn't follow us home."

Hannah nodded. She seemed dazed. "It will be over in a week. Everything ends. Except memories," she added.

On the final day of mourning they took off their rough black sackcloth and scrubbed the ashes from their faces. Hannah's cheeks were streaked with blood. She had been caught up in the organized frenzy of grief, after all. She had rent her flesh and her garments and screamed. Now, exhausted, faint with fasting, she was a little ashamed as she remembered Mary's composure all week—bravely trying to comfort her weeping children, and just seeing to all those guests! Such a turnout for Joseph. Never before seen in Nazareth, it pleased her to think. Except, of course, for Joachim . . . *Joachim.* Fresh pain struck her, pain so genuine she doubled over with it, there on the bench where she was putting on her clothes. Fiercely, Hannah sat hugging herself, as if to crush it from her breast.

"Mother, don't. Please don't." Mary came to stand beside her, to stroke the pitifully balding head.

"But where *are* they?" Hannah moaned, lifting her tiny tormented face. "Joseph and your father?"

"I don't know," Mary said. "But Jesus does."

"Will we ever see them again?"

"Yes. It's what Jesus promised when we stood at the cave. That is part of the good news he was sent to bring us."

Mary drew her mother to her feet. "Come, we must eat something. We are both weak."

"How does he know?" Hannah pleaded. She was clutching Mary's hand. "How does he *know*?"

"We must not forget who he is," said Mary. "He is God's son."

"Then why—?" Hannah hesitated, filled with dread. Yet she must speak of it, express it somehow, the question that had taunted her all week. And it came to Hannah that perhaps her screaming, all her screaming, had been only for its answer. "Mary, I can't help wondering," she groped. "I have heard of—healings. The holy men, the prophets, sometimes even the rabbis—it may not be true, of course, but I . . . it has been said such men sometimes do miraculous things." Miserably then she blurted it out: "Surely Jesus is greater than any of them. *Why didn't he heal them?*"

Mary closed her eyes, fearing that for the first time she might break. "Nobody loved his father more," she said quietly after a moment. "Or his grandfather either. Oh, Mother, don't you think he would have saved them if he could? But he couldn't, he couldn't, not yet," she moaned softly. "We must be patient, Mother, we must wait. His miracles will come when the One who sent him is ready."

"I may not live to see them," Hannah whispered.

"Yes, you will! And they will be miracles such as the world has never seen."

Chapter 11

Mary never slept that she did not reach for him, never woke that she did not feel the emptiness beside her, never prepared a meal that she did not listen for his step. These feelings she kept to herself. She did not want to burden her children. She was grateful for their ability to go on with their lives. Jesus, more than the others, was suffering. And so she was glad when he prepared to leave once again with the sheep. She knew that this was vital to him, now as never before, and so she did not restrain him, although she could scarcely bear to see him go. He was so much like Joseph— far more, it seemed to her, than any of her sons.

The day of his departure she arose while it was yet dark and kindled the fire that he might have hot bread. She set out a bowl of fresh figs and a mug of hot milk. She filled his knapsack with extra loaves and ran her fingers along the seams of his cloak; she had mended them only yesterday, but was it warm enough for cold nights in the hills?

"I wish you were going with me," Jesus said from the table.

"So do I." She was hugging the cloak against her. "I used to enjoy the times when my father let me tend the sheep. Never overnight, of course, or far from home. There was little danger, although I did have to throw my rod once at a snake."

"You, throwing a rod?" Jesus smiled. "It's hard to believe."

"I was quite strong. He had made me a little rod to carry—much like that first one your father made for you— and taught me to throw."

162

"Did you hit the snake?"

"No, but I scared it away!" They both laughed, but their eyes were suddenly wet. Mary pressed a fist against her trembling lips. "Oh, Jesus, I miss them both so much!"

Jesus came to her and held her. "I can't leave you, Mother, not yet. I will get someone else."

"No, you need to go. I can see it in your eyes. You eat almost nothing. I hear you pacing sometimes, late at night. Jesus, *you must not blame yourself.*" She drew back to search his face. "It is not your fault that you were not with your father that day. Or that you were not—" Mary hesitated, groping for words—"prepared to do—what I was foolish enough to beg you to."

"You mustn't blame yourself either, Mother. That wasn't foolish, it was your love pleading for him."

"Yes," she agreed, blinking fiercely. "I could do nothing else." She busied herself with the knapsack. Did he have everything? His flute, his knife—wait, she had forgotten his raisins, and what about the book he had been reading? She scurried off to find it. Jesus waited, touched by her mothering but anxious to get started. Cocks were crowing, the sky was turning gray. He hoped to reach the first pasture while the dew was still wet on the grass; the sheep enjoyed it and it meant less watering. Yet it tore him to leave.

Mary followed him to the door. "Be careful. I won't hold you back, but I worry about you too, out there alone."

"Please don't," he said cheerfully. "I have many friends among the shepherds, as you know. I'm always welcome at their camps, the way those Bedouins once welcomed you."

"No wonder you feel at home with them, for you were with us." Mary smiled as she remembered, but her voice was urgent. "Yes, yes, take shelter with others whenever you can. Forgive me," she said quietly after a minute, "but I don't think I could go on living if anything should happen to you."

The sheep were now his succor and salvation. God surely had been leading him all these years, the chief shepherd training the lesser to lead the sheep. But now, this summer after Joseph's death, it was the sheep who seemed to be leading Jesus beside the still waters to restore his soul. And never before had his rod and his staff so comforted him. For as he watched over his flocks by day and night, it was as if his father and grandfather were beside him. This tough club of a rod for his protection. This sturdy staff. They had provided both, from the very beginning.

Mary's reminiscence about her own first proud little rod brought it all back. Again he walked excitedly into the brush beside Joachim to choose and dig a young sapling. Smelled again the damp earth and felt the roots with their clods of dirt clinging to his fingers. Heard the whack of his grandfather's hatchet cutting the root down to size. They carried it to the carpenter shop where Joseph carved and whittled it to exactly fit his hand. The thrill of that first small rod in his palm, and the clumsy zeal with which he hurled it when they took him onto a hillside to teach him.

Cleophas had gone along, for he was skilled in throwing, had even won contests with the Greeks. Cleo demonstrated first, then Joseph; it became a competition between them to see who could throw it farther. Jesus wanted to try his rod but was afraid to say so until Joachim stepped in. "Here, now, let the lad; I will show him." And clutching Jesus' wrist, he had pulled back and released the weapon with such force that lo, it flew so far and hard it broke a pitcher that was tipped against a tree.

"There, that's how you throw a rod!" Joachim had grinned in triumph over the younger men. . . .

One day, in a leafy glade beside a waterfall where the sheep were grazing, Jesus saw the girl.

He had been drowsing after his long struggle with a castdown sheep. He had missed the creature this morning when he first rose and checked the flock. Oh, no, not again! he thought. Affa, his fattest and strongest ewe with the heaviest wool, and heavier than ever in lamb. She was notorious for wandering toward greener pastures. Then when she had eaten her fill she would lie down, roll onto her side, and be unable to get up.

The sun was high before he finally found her under a

distant tree, feet still frantically flailing the air. She must have been struggling for hours; buzzards were already circling. Jesus ran to her, knowing there was no time to lose; gases were being built up in her rumen. Tenderly he rolled the big sheep on her side to relieve the pressure, and began massaging her belly. Poor foolish thing, when would she ever learn? He was close to tears. Fear that he might yet lose her gripped him, a sense of impotency and helplessness, for she seemed unable to budge, to lift herself.

At last he got the sheep up and held her erect, rubbing her legs to get the warm blood flowing. The afternoon wore on before the creature was finally able to walk, unsteadily with his support; twice it stumbled and would have fallen. But little by little its strength returned; by the time they reached the waterfall it trotted off and was soon chewing in peaceful rhythms with the others.

Exhausted, Jesus flung himself onto the grass. A sudden appalling discouragement assailed him. Words from the psalms began to chant in his head: *Why are you cast down, O my soul? And why are you disquieted within me?* . . . He heard again the desperate pleading of his mother: "Heal him, heal him, if you love your father—!" And his own feeble, terrible, "I can't."

How was it that he could save a mere overfat, overpadded, four-legged beast, while his father, his own father, lay stiff and lifeless in the cave? And Joachim, the dear grandfather from whom he had learned so much?

All the knowledge, the awareness, as if the whole world flowed in his blood and marched through his consciousness, the certainty, the sense of destiny, the moments of such rapport with all creation that he seemed himself one with the very Creator—all this had fled. Jesus felt as lost and bewildered and helpless as that flailing ewe with the buzzards circling overhead. What was he doing here, chasing after and propping up sheep? He was nearly thirty years old and he had accomplished nothing, as his brothers accused.

Who was he, to dare to think . . . to dream? What John had said to him in Jerusalem seemed preposterous now: mere boys, both of them, with lively imaginations and delu-

sions of grandeur. And his mother and even her own
mother, Hannah—the things they never discussed yet
seemed to believe, almost to take for granted. Didn't many
a Jewish woman fancy her son or grandson the Deliverer?
And himself—he writhed—the sense of authority and conviction when only twelve in the Temple. And since, his pri-
vate journeys of the soul ever since.

How many men fancied themselves Abraham or Moses
or Elijah returned, how many climbed their own secret
stairway of stars to wrestle with angels, or even the Nameless One himself? All Israel knew of them, those false or
tragically misled prophets and messiahs whose fate was
doomed, even as John's, now preaching in the desert, would
surely be. *Help me, help me, deliver me from this madness,*
he prayed, *or I too will be hanged upon the tree.*

He was tired and dirty and hungry, and once again he
beat the earth with his fists. "Tell me, Yahweh, tell me," he
cried out as he had so often, "what is it you would have of
me?"

Again there was no answer, only the muted pounding
of the waterfall at the cliff's edge, like the feet of dancers on
a threshing floor. In the grasses insects hummed and
clicked. He could hear the sheep bells ringing softly as the
flock moved about, their jaws making a silken music as they
pulled and chewed the foliage. . . .

Jesus slept.

Some time later he was awakened by a lamb nibbling
and nuzzling at his feet: a strange lamb, he saw at once,
with markings he did not recognize, like little copper coins
upon its brow, and a bleating that was unusually sweet. He
sat upright, astonished. Several unfamiliar sheep were grazing calmly among his own, while a number of goats, perhaps nine or ten, were greedily chewing the overhanging
mulberry leaves or gamboling about. Some shaggy, some
smooth, some black as Satan, others pied or tawny or purest
white. Their horns glistened in the falling sun; they tossed
their heads, emitting their wild goat cries, and he wondered for a moment if he had been transported to some
pagan frolic of horned gods.

Puzzled and rubbing his eyes, Jesus got to his feet. It

was then he saw the girl. She was bathing in the pool at the base of the waterfall, one of the falls he had enjoyed as a boy. The melting snows and the rains had been generous this year, spilling such torrents of water that it had formed this broad glistening pool. The girl was darting in and out of the spray, gamboling like one of her young kids, for surely the creatures were hers. Her charges must have wandered, come clambering up over the rocks to mingle like friends with his sheep.

Jesus stood transfixed. She had thrown off her outer garment. Only a little white shift covered her nakedness, but it was wet and clung to her body, and he saw that she was fair, very fair. Her limbs were small but lovely, and when she bent to free a pebble from her toes, he glimpsed the little brown apples of her breasts. And his heart beat faster, all the songs of Solomon seemed to burst in his throat. He wanted to fling himself into the tumbling water and clasp her there where it plunged, so joyously sparkling, and swim with her there in love.

Unaware of him, she gathered up her rough blue outer garment and began to dry her long, light brown hair. She wrapped the robe about herself then, took up her staff, and started to climb, nimble as the goats as she hopped from rock to rock. Her hair, still wet, was shining. She was humming softly to herself—until she saw him. Her song halted abruptly. She was startled. She gazed at him an instant, then turned, flustered, and began to run about barefoot, trying to round up her sheep and goats.

Without a word he sprang to the task of helping separate their flocks. Once they bumped into each other, with a little shock; their eyes met. An old ram of his was bunting one of her half-grown sheep. Yelling and brandishing his rod, he got it away. The dog dashed around, barking, helping. Soon the sheep were in line, but the goats were obstinate, mischievous, scampering away and then running back as if enjoying the game.

Finally, when the girl's animals were herded around her, she lifted her eyes an instant to thank him. He had never seen eyes that color, blue as the sky, with flecks of gold, and fringed with such long black lashes. Her skin was golden brown like the hair about her shoulders, but her cheeks were flushed. He realized that she was actually very shy, dismayed that he had seen her in the water. For she lowered her gaze at once, and crouching to pick up the lamb that had wakened him, she hurried off.

"Wait!" He ran anxiously after her. "You don't come here often?"

"Only today," she acknowledged in a low voice. "It is so hot, I followed the stream."

"Where do you live?"

The girl only shook her head and backed away.

"I'll still be here tomorrow," he called desperately. "Please come back! Please come this way again."

He scarcely slept all night, and when he did the girl filled his dreams. He was running frantically in search of her. She was in some danger, she was dancing in the waters, she was falling, drowning in the pool, and though he dived and dived he could not find her. . . . Then she was in his arms, limp and wet and sweetly cool; he must save her, he was kissing her lips to revive her, but then she slipped away. . . .

He awoke shaking and covered with sweat. He got up and walked about, trying to retrieve and yet recover from the dream. He went to the waterfall, wondering if the whole experience had been only a dream. It was still pounding and foaming under the stars. It was real. The girl was real. She must come back, he must see her again. Dear Father in heaven, send her back to me!

All morning he waited expectantly: watched and waited, several times walking in the direction where she had vanished among the trees, trying to will her into reality before him. His flock must be moved tomorrow. He would never see her again unless she came today.

In late afternoon, when he had almost given up hope, Ben began barking excitedly. Jesus sprang to his feet. Like a mirage in the distance he saw her approaching, followed by a much smaller flock than the day before. Her pet lamb trotted beside her, the one with the golden coins on its brow.

Almost beside himself, Jesus ran to greet her. "Peace

be with you!" he cried. "I was afraid I had lost you, and I didn't know where to look. This is the last day I will be here. My sheep have almost finished the grass."

"Oh, dear, then we shouldn't have come," she apologized softly. "I can't have mine robbing yours."

"No, no, there is still plenty for all. Especially since today you have brought so few. Where are the others? Where are the goats?"

"All but two have gone to be slaughtered. It is why I am so late. They did not want to go. We had to chase them; they tried to escape." Quickly she turned her head, and he heard the little choke in her throat. "I am comforted by the good romp they had here yesterday."

"I'm glad too," Jesus said. "I too grieve for your goats." He squeezed her hand. "But where are the rest of your sheep?"

"I was only tending them for a neighbor. These belong to my uncles."

"Come, then, sit with me while they graze. Let our flocks mingle, let them be our family, let us pretend they are our children."

He was so glad to see her he didn't know quite what he was saying. He regretted the words, for she sprang back, as easily startled as one of the sheep.

"Forgive me, you have nothing to fear. Come, I have something to show you." He led her to the place of last night's campfire, where he had spread his cloak. There was the acrid smell of the ashes and the pungent fragrance of earth and grasses as they sat down. They were both nervous, aware of the subtle excitement between them, that she had actually returned to him this day with her little flock.

Jesus dug into his knapsack for the beautiful stone. He had found it earlier and planned to carry it home for Mary, thinking perhaps Cleophas could have it set into a ring. But now the girl must have it, for it was the same incredible blue as her eyes.

The girl caught her breath and cupped it in her hand, then held it up to catch the light. "Where did you find it?"

"At the foot of the waterfall." He stopped short, for the

girl blushed, even as she continued to stare in wonder at the stone. "I want you to have it."

"But it's so beautiful! No one has ever given me such a gift before."

He was touched. It was only a little stone. "The water has already polished it, but I can polish its brightness even more in my father's carpenter shop."

"No, no, I like it as it is." She was clutching it protectively to her breast. "You mustn't take it from me."

He was astounded. "Do you honestly think I would not give it back to you? And more beautiful than before?"

"I don't know," she whispered, and looked up at him fully with those strange blue eyes.

He didn't know whether to laugh or cry. "Then keep it," he said. "Let it be as you wish."

Her pet lamb kneeled down beside them. Jesus stroked its head with the little bronze coins. "What is its name?"

"Gilda."

"And yours?"

"Tamara," she said, sitting very still under his frankly questing gaze.

For now the full impact of her beauty smote him. The light brown hair, dry now, like a shining cloud about her shoulders. The small fine-boned face, burned almost as bronze as the coins on her lamb's brow. She had a high innocent forehead and eager, fearful, yet at times almost impish eyes. The eyes, though intensely blue, were the shape of almonds, the brows above them very black. Her nose was straight and small, her mouth sweet. When she smiled, as she was smiling now, her whole face radiated.

"Why are you staring at me so?"

"Because I must feast on the sight of you. All the songs of Solomon are singing in my heart."

"Then sing me one."

"'How beautiful you are, my love,'" he chanted, half playfully. "'How beautiful you are! Your eyes, behind your veil, are doves; your hair is like a flock of goats frisking—'"

He broke off for she was laughing. Her own teeth flashed as she took up the song: "'Your teeth are like a flock of shorn ewes as they come up from the washing—' And we *did* come up from the washing, my sheep and my goats and I—up from the waterfall!"

"Praise heaven you did," he said, and joyfully persisted: "'Your lips are a scarlet thread and your words enchanting. Your cheeks, behind your veil, are halves of pomegranate—'"

"'Your neck is the tower of David built as a fortress,'" she retorted, "'hung round with a thousand bucklers—'"

It was no use, it was too absurd, they could not go on; still laughing, they wiped their eyes. Again they sat gazing at each other, both of them openly and honestly now. The sheep bells tinkled, the grasses hummed, white clouds drifted overhead.

Jesus leaned forward, spoke finally, though he hardly dared to ask. "Are you betrothed?"

She shook her head.

"But anyone so beautiful! Surely the fathers of all the young men must have beaten a path to your father's door."

Tamara's eyes narrowed. Thoughtfully she pulled a sprig of mint from the ground and bit it, staring into the distance. "I have no father," she told him. "I live with my uncles. They are in no hurry to find me a husband, since I am so useful to them, keeping their house and minding their stock."

"Doesn't this make you unhappy?"

"I am in no hurry to have a husband either. Our village is small, there are not many men. And I have seen no one among them whom I would have."

"But now?" Jesus was trembling. She was so little and beautiful and somehow—bereft. She was in many ways like his mother: her daintiness, her sweetness and humor; except for her bursts of shyness, she reminded him of Mary. He lifted her chin. "Have you not yet seen a man you might learn to love?"

"I don't know who you are," she protested. "You may have a wife and children!"

He threw back his curly head. How good it was to laugh again. He had never been so happy. "I am Jesus of Nazareth, without wife or children, much to my family's embarrassment, for I am old enough and past. But, like you, I have never seen the one I longed for. Until this day I had never seen a woman I felt I could love. Not until this day, Tamara—or yes, even the day before."

She gave a little cry and scrambled hastily to her feet. The color flooded her cheeks again, those golden cheeks; her face was like a sunset, he thought, amazed. "You saw me!" she wailed. "You saw me in the water. Oh, I am so ashamed."

"You were lovely in the water. Don't ever be ashamed with me, Tamara. I love you, do you hear me? I want you to learn to love me if you can."

He tried to clasp her wrists, but she wriggled away. "I must go now," she cried. "It's late, I shouldn't have come. You must think me wanton to come tramping across the fields after you like this!"

"No, no," he reminded her. "I begged you to come, and I beg you now, come back!" She wasn't listening, only running about to round up her flock. With his dog he set about helping her. "Come walk with me these next few days," he pleaded when the creatures were separated. "Bring your sheep, and we will find new pastures together. I must move my own tomorrow, but I will wait for you until noon. If you come later you will find us just over the second hill." He pointed. "Don't worry, we will not go far. Where is your village?"

"Near Cana."

"Then we will circle the pastures near it. Each day you can leave in time to reach your home before sunset. I don't want to get too far from Nazareth, either," he told her. "My father died a few weeks ago, I don't want to stay away from my mother too long. . . . Will you come to be with me?" he urged, as she hesitated.

"I will try," she promised, and pressed his hand. "I will come as often as I can."

All the next morning Jesus paced and prayed and scanned the valleys in vain. Finally, when it was long past noon, he knew he could hold the sheep no longer. Deeply disappointed, he set off to trudge the next weary miles alone. And when he reached the place he had chosen, the nose flies came swarming up out of the brush so vicious in their attack that some of the sheep went crazy. He spent half the night trying to calm them. He would have moved on had he dared, but he was tortured by the fear that Tamara might still come and not be able to find him.

When morning dawned, however, he knew he had no choice but to leave. Discouraged, he was stamping out his fire when Ben began his excited barking. Jesus' heart leaped, nearly exploded with joy, for here she came running, the beloved, along the dusty path. A white scarf bound her hair and she wore a tunic of blue and white stripes vivid as sky and clouds. The lamb Gilda trotted along beside her, and behind her the two remaining goats. Her cheeks were flushed; she was panting and again very bashful, apologizing. She couldn't come the day before because her uncles had other work for her to do. "And I dared not tell them why I wanted so much to leave!"

She looked about at the still restless flock. "Oh, your poor sheep. I could not sleep for thinking of them. This pasture—I should have remembered the brush and thorns. It is not a good place." She had brought a little flagon of her own remedy. She would help him ease them. But first she would lead them to a better place.

Surefooted, she hastened ahead of him along the path by which she had come, through a grove of silvery olive trees, past tumbled walls and gardens, up across weedy, rock-strewn fields. She was in a bright mood and as nimble as the goats, capricious, enchanting. Jesus was frustrated, for he must walk more leisurely with the sheep. Yet it delighted him to see her as she had been when he first saw her frolicking in the water. Her scarf had blown free in the brisk breeze here on the foothills north of Mount Tabor; her tawny hair tossed about her shoulders, and again she was singing. "Wait for me!" he called, brandishing his pipe. "I will play for you."

She paused, brushing back her tumbled hair. Eyes bright, smiling, she came to take his free hand now and walk demurely beside him into the flowering pasture. Behind them soared the mountain, below stretched the green valleys, and in the distance, sparkling as if paved with crushed blue sapphires, they could see the Sea of Galilee.

Knee-deep they stood among the blossoms, where so many butterflies were dipping it seemed the flowers were tossing their own petals into the air. Orange and white and gold, the butterflies danced to the incessant music of the bees. The sky was very blue, and so were most of the flowers here at summer's beginning: wild flax, grape hyacinths, blue and purple thistles—a fragrant sea of blue on which were spilled patches of yellow from the buttercups and golden broom, and starry drifts of daisies, and scarlet poppies scattered like drops of blood.

Jesus was surprised, quite lost—he thought he knew most of the grazing grounds between Nazareth and the lakeshore. "We're not far from Cana," she assured him, "and not really a long journey home. I will help you with the sheep, but then I must leave. I must be there when my uncles get home."

Here too a cold stream flowed. Cupping their hands, they knelt and drank beside the thirsty sheep. Then, as the flock began to eat, they washed and opened their knapsacks to share their bread and cheese and fruit. When they had finished she brought out her ointment for the sheep, a concoction of her own, smelling of sulphur and sage. "It will keep the pests away," she said proudly, "to torment them no more."

She insisted on doing the job herself. Sensing relief, the sheep were already crowding around. Jesus must be content to hold each head on her lap while she worked the stuff firmly into the woolly scalp, around the eyes, up into the nostrils. Her fingers seemed too small and dainty for the task, yet they were strong. As she worked she kept up a little crooning singsong of love and promise and comfort. From time to time she lifted her eyes to smile at him. She was like a mother with her children.

It took longer than they had planned. When they finished, the sun was so much farther over the mountains that Tamara sprang up, looking worried. "I must hurry. I must get home before my uncles!"

Jesus held her sticky hands. "But you will come back tomorrow?"

"If I can."

"You *must* come. I couldn't bear it without you. Tamara, tell me where you live. I must know where to find you if you shouldn't come again. Let me come to your house."

"No!"

"Why not?"

"My uncles wouldn't like it."

"You speak always of your uncles. Have you neither mother nor father?"

"She shook her head. "My mother died when I was born."

"And your father?"

"As I told you before, I have no father!" she said, and ran.

The next two days were hell, for she did not appear. The flowers had lost their sweetness; he could scarcely bear to look in the direction of the sparkling lake. He wandered around desolate until it was too late to hope for her any more. Then on the third morning, just as he was breaking camp, she came to him over the hills, tiny and fair, clad all in white, so innocent and eager in the rising sun she seemed like an angel flying. He cried out as at a vision, he raced to her and embraced her, if only to make sure she was real. He was close to tears.

"I had almost given up. I didn't think I would ever see you again!"

"I could stay away no longer," she told him. "I was so afraid you might leave."

"I am leaving," he said, "as you see, the sheep have ravished the fields. We must move on today, perhaps nearer the shore."

"I will go with you," she said softly. "I will lead you."

"Don't run from me," he pleaded as they set out. "Don't flee from me. There is so little time. In another day I must turn back, to spend the Sabbath with my mother."

"I will not run ahead of you today," she promised. "We

will walk together talking and singing. You don't mind if I sing?" she laughed, lifting her face.

"Sing to your heart's desire, and I will play my pipe that your songs may be lifted to the heavens."

They were both a little mad, intoxicated by the sunrise, the thrumming bees and the flowers. They moved on together ahead of their charges (she had brought only Gilda and the two white goats), in a trance. And he held her against him at times as they moved, and laced her small brown fingers into his own the seemed to him so much bigger and stronger this day. *Male and female created he them,* he thought, rejoicing, and could have wept.

And as they walked, or watered the flock, or rested on a grassy hillside, gazing into the mountains, she told him about herself, all the things she could not utter before.

"You asked me about my mother," Tamara said, quiet but determined. "I never knew her. Nor the man who is said to be my father. Now a prosperous man of Cana, I believe. He ravished her as she was leaving the well. She was younger than I am now." Tamara hesitated. "I am seventeen. As you know, that is quite old to be unmarried."

"Thank God you are *not* married."

"Her older brothers, my uncles, have never spoken my mother's name in my presence," she continued. "But it was also Tamara. All this I have learned from a distant cousin. The man begot twins by her, though one of them did not live. There was a terrible scandal, but he was already married. He was reprimanded severely by the elders, I understand, but that is all. While my mother, my poor little mother—!" Tamara's eyes were closed, she clenched her fists, fighting back tears.

"Oh, my darling, my precious darling—"

"Both my grandparents were dead. There was no one but my uncles to care for their little sister during this terrible time. And for me. For she died with the other twin."

Jesus tried to draw her to him, but Tamara twisted away.

"So you see why it is—perhaps you can see why it is. . . . You are a good man, faithful to God and the Law. I saw that in you from the beginning: the books you carry.

And there is a special shining in your eyes; there is about you a light of purity and goodness I have never seen in anyone before. That is why I must tell you, for you will ask." She was anxiously searching his face. "No, I do not go to the synagogue in Cana, for fear I might see him there. Even though I don't know who he is, I have a horror of encountering the man who might be my father.

"And my uncles . . . You must forgive them. They are rough men who do not wash as often as they should, and they too never go to the synagogue. But they are circumcised, we pray at meals, they are believers. It is just that they are bitter, and very protective of me. That is why, dear Jesus, you must understand. That is why I cannot risk coming to you often, and why I must hurry home lest they learn of you, for they will fear for my virtue, fear that something like that might happen to me."

"But I love you!" Jesus heard himself cry out. And the wonder of it smote him. All his life he had known that he was different; now suddenly a great radiance burst within him, he felt freed of some heavy burden. He was no longer different! He too was man and the son of man, knowing at last the greatest joy man could experience. The words were so beautiful he must say them again. "What you have told me doesn't matter. I *love* you! And how my father would love you, for you are so much like my mother. If only he were living. He would be so happy; he would go to your uncles with me to ask for your hand."

Again he tried to take her in his arms, but again she escaped. "Don't draw away from me, Tamara," he pleaded, dismayed. "I would never harm you. I want to marry you. I will go to your uncles and ask for you, myself."

"No!"

"But why?" He was gazing at her, astounded. "Is it that you don't love me? That you would not have me for your husband?"

"*Love* you?" A cry of anguish came from her. She had plunged her face into her hands. "That little blue stone you gave me—I kiss it over and over, I carry it day and night against my heart."

"Then you do love me. You can't deny it. I will have the stone made into your betrothal ring."

"No . . . no!" She had begun to sob, hopelessly. "You are right. I love you and want you as I never dreamed I could love a man." One hand groped out blindly to clutch his. "But don't you see what I am?" she demanded. "What we *are*?" Tamara caught her breath, and lifted her wet, shamed eyes. "There is—a name for such people as us. . . . A detestable name."

Am-ha-aretz. The realization struck Jesus with a little shock. The girl he loved must be one of the hated *am-ha-aretz*. People he had heard denounced since childhood by rabbis and doctors of the Law. Ignorant, dirty people, or so they were regarded; Jews unwilling to defend their faith, and so considered heretics and traitors, little better than the pagans.

"Don't say it, don't say it," Tamara warned fiercely. "It is an ugly name!"

Jesus gripped her hand tighter and pressed it against his breast. "Oh, my darling, do you think a *name* matters to me? It is only a word." He tipped back her chin and gazed into her stricken eyes. "And its meaning has been hatefully distorted. Do you know what *am-ha-aretz* really means? . . . No, no, don't shudder, let me tell you: People of the earth—that's the true meaning of the word—people of the land. And it applies to me too. It applies to my family. My uncles are farmers, so was my grandfather—people of the land."

"You're only trying to comfort me. You know that today it also means other things. . . . Dreadful things!"

"All right," he acknowledged, his heart aching for her, "but that's wrong. Very wrong. It's wicked and self-righteous to put such a label on anyone. People don't understand, they have no right to judge. Only the Father, who knows the secrets of all our hearts, can judge us rightly."

He held her close and stroked her hair—like silk to his fingers. He felt her warm little body against him—wiry, tough and strong from climbing the hills with her charges, yet her golden skin was soft as velvet to his touch. He drank in the dear sweet special scent of her—dainty, womanly, faintly spicy, fresh with wind and sun. He cupped her chin and gazed, newly marveling, at her face—so childlike in its innocent intensity, its beauty confirmed and enhanced by his love.

"Oh, Tamara, how beautiful you are! God sees how pure and beautiful you are, and that you and your uncles have been cruelly hurt."

They sat for a time in silence, her hand still upon his breast. Jesus' eyes were thoughtful, compassionate but troubled. He did not want to speak of this, but he knew he must. "My darling, I have something to ask of you. I know it will be hard, but I ask it only because I love you and want your happiness so much." Tamara tensed. She was regarding him, apprehensive. "You must forgive your father," he said. "I am asking you to pray for the man who hurt you so much."

She gasped. "I couldn't, not ever! That's impossible."

"And pray for your uncles, that they can forgive him too, and go back to the synagogue."

"No!" She thrust him away, appalled.

"Please," he urged. "If you love me, do this for my sake—and your own. And for their sake too, it will help them. Try to persuade them to be faithful to their religion."

"You don't know what you're asking! You don't know my uncles. They are very proud and stubborn men. They would never forgive, and they would never set foot in the synagogue again."

"Prayer can work miracles, Tamara. Try; at least tell me you will try. This is very important, my dearest, for whatever our differences, we are all Jews together in this land of Israel where we must live among the pagans. God has made a covenant with us, he wants us to worship him as one. He will bless us if we do."

"My uncles would be furious at the suggestion. They have been wronged and they don't want to forget it, or for me to forget it either—not ever. They would feel—robbed. Cheated of their outrage if we changed the way we live!"

"Darling—oh, my poor darling. But you are too fine and sweet to share those feelings and live that way. It is futile, destructive. Please, at least try. I love you so much, it would comfort me. Pray for this, my beloved. Forgiveness is the only way to banish such pain from your hearts."

He pulled her back to him and stroked her tear-streaked face. "And when we are married, we will go together to my synagogue in Nazareth, where you will sit in the balcony beside my mother, Mary. She too will love you," he assured her eagerly, "and you will love her. She will be the mother you never had." He produced a handkerchief from his girdle and wiped her eyes. "Come, smile at me again. We have been too serious for people in love on such a beautiful day. . . . You *do* love me, don't you?"

Tamara nodded, shaken. "More than life itself."

"Then give me the little blue stone you say you carry always next to your heart. It is unworthy of you, but all I can afford—these aren't even my sheep. But I will polish it with my own hands as I have promised, and have it made into a ring for you. It will be your betrothal ring."

The girl caught her breath, tempted—wildly tempted, but confused. She had never dared dream that love could come to her like this, love beyond all reasoning. She was frightened, her very ecstasy filled her with alarm. It was happening so fast; yet now that it had happened, dared she cast aside such happiness? Trembling, she reached into her breast for the stone. "Forgive me," she said nervously, "but my uncles—if I tell them about you, they will ask—what is your work, if these are not your sheep?"

"I'm a carpenter, and a good one too, for I was trained in my father's shop. I can work there again with my brothers. I will work my fingers to the bone for you, I will give you everything."

"And we would live in Nazareth?" she whispered.

"Yes. Yes, as long as God wills it."

He spoke the words fervently, joyously. A torrent of love songs was clamoring in his throat to be sung. He wanted to laugh and shout and sing, to hold her very close and kiss her. But something stopped him. . . . Puzzled, Jesus got to his feet, his eyes scanning the sky. . . . The day was bright and clear and cloudless. He saw only a crane, a brisk wheeling flight of swallows, yet it seemed to him that somewhere overhead an invisible cloud was gathering, hovering; soon it would be descending to surround him, envelop him.

Tamara felt a chill. She sat startled, bewildered at the look on his face. He seemed suddenly far from her, lost to her in some strange and threatening way.

"What is it? What are you thinking?"

Jesus gazed at her, wanting to share this with her, yet perturbed. He shook his head as if to clear it. "I too have something to tell you," he said carefully after a moment. "Something that is very hard to explain. I am—different in some ways from other men, Tamara. I have known it since childhood. Sometimes it is more certain than others, but it is always there: the knowledge, the certain knowledge that God has—a special mission for me. A very important destiny. I was sent to earth to serve him." He crouched beside her and gripped her hand. "Where all this will lead me I don't know yet. I only know that I love you, I need you. I want you beside me wherever I go, in whatever it is I must do."

"I love you too," she whispered, "of course I will go with you." But her face had paled. "It is getting late," she said anxiously, "I must start home."

"Tell me where that is, for I must leave early to lead the flock back to Nazareth tomorrow. And I may not bring them out again. Tell me how to find you," he insisted. "I have to know, so that I can get an older relative to come with me to ask for you."

"Wait, wait, I must think." Tamara was struggling to tie a scarf on her wind-tossed hair. Her hands were shaking so she could hardly form the knots. "I must think what to say to my uncles so they won't believe ill of you."

But at last, when they had hastily rounded up her goats and Gilda, she told him: Hiram was the name of her eldest uncle; their house was poor and small, near a grove of pines in the first village just north of Cana. Almost anyone there could direct him. "My uncles are known for their tempers." She laughed uneasily. "I must warn you—don't be surprised if people even try to discourage you."

"Oh, my darling, nothing could keep me from you. Expect me within the week!"

Chapter 12

*J*esus had meant to tell Mary at once. He could hardly wait to share his feast of memories. All the way back to Nazareth he had dwelt on the beloved, re-creating her over and over for himself as he fancied how he would describe Tamara to his mother. Her hair, how it seemed to float around her like a bright cloud, when she ran mischievously ahead of him: "Though she is really very shy," he would say. Her pet lamb: "It resembles her!" The realization came upon him suddenly and he laughed as he strode along. "For she too has tiny copper speckles on her nose. And she is so little, like you—my hands could span her waist."

This exultation, this wonder, how could he contain it? And who could better understand than Mary, who had herself known such perfect love?

Yet when he saw his mother's lamp in the window that Sabbath evening and ran eagerly up the steps, he heard the babble of voices and knew with only a twinge of disappointment that his news must wait. Most of the family were swarming about, so many they had spilled into the garden. They greeted him joyfully, telling him how wonderful he looked. "Never has the outdoors agreed with you more. You should ask Amos to sell you those sheep!"

"You don't even smell as bad as usual." Josey grinned, sniffing. Jesus laughed; he had had more reason to wash. His eyes were shining with his secret. Let it wait, it was too precious to share with anyone just yet. Let him hold it in his heart a while longer, let him have Tamara all to himself.

Bathing, he smiled to hear the familiar chatter beyond the doors. He had been afraid Mary might be lonely; it was good to find her surrounded by this lively circle of love. How the family comforted and sustained each other. One day Tamara would be among them, his little bride. How they would adore her—and she them.

He could not stop thinking of her even when he sat among them at table, praying, singing, and drinking the Sabbath wine. She was with him, a radiant music in his blood. He felt a hushed exaltation, everything looked new and exciting. He seemed to see them all through Tamara's shy-eager eyes: his rollicking uncles and brothers and in-laws; their wives and his sisters so fair. "Little Leah" was almost as tall and pretty as Ann now, with her pert nose and whimsical eyes; she too would soon be betrothed.

Even his grandmothers: Hannah comically scolding him for getting in her way as she tried to clear away the food; he took the platter from her and kissed her soundly; Timna nodding in the candlelight, holding her stick. She was still somehow stately, her hair a white halo. He knelt beside her and gently kissed her cheek as well, grieving for Tamara, who had never had even grandmothers to love. No mother and no grandmothers—it semed unbelievably pathetic. But now he would give her his! He could think of no finer gift.

Jesus looked around for Mary, wanting to convey this message if only with his smile, but she had disappeared again. She had been so busy with supper; beyond her first fervent greeting, she had had scarcely a moment for him. Well, there would be plenty of time later, after the others went home. How they would talk, how she would rejoice with him. Yet he longed to be near her right now, in his happiness.

He found Mary in the garden with the grandchildren, who were having one final shrieking race before they must leave. Mary was gathering them up, stooping to hug them or take them in her arms. How beautiful it was, the children so vigorous in their rosy innocence and determination, so robust and yet so delicately made. And their mothers, laughing and scolding, yet content, telling Mary good night. Pray heaven it was not too late for children of his own; in Jesus' mind he could see Mary with her arms around

Tamara as they were around Simon's wife now, holding their son even as she was holding Josey's little boy, who was clinging to her fiercely, crying about something there under the trees.

Mary became aware of Jesus as he halted beneath the willow to watch. She looked at him over the child's shoulder, a look that was long and searching. "Go now," she said, putting the child down. "Go to your mother."

Cleo was just arriving, with his lute. And Amos and Matthew, who had been detained; they too had brought instruments. It would be a merry evening for those who could stay. And this was good, Jesus realized, after his first minute or two of frustration. He sprawled on the grass, hands behind his head, listening blissfully to their music. Postponement of his revelation to Mary had actually heightened its sweetness. He would live with this wonder yet a little while, turning it over and over in his mind, even its troubling aspects. He would wait until the Sabbath was ended; only then were they likely to be alone.

Then he would tell her.

The Sabbath seemed interminable, beautiful as it had begun.

As he woke, he felt an aura of goodness about its very restrictions: that he might not spread up the bedding on which he had dreamed of Tamara, or tie but one knot in the sash of his robe; that these hands that had caressed her must carry nothing all day, not so much as a book, a stick, or an egg. Though Jesus was hungry, it pleased him that he and his family could not eat anything until after services at the synagogue.

There was an almost sensual purity about all this, an emptying of self to make room for the soul. The Sabbath, a token between Yahweh and his people. A day on which to rest and contemplate God's wonders . . . and the beloved.

Jesus walked in awe and reverence through the lovely morning, a trifle lightheaded from love and lack of food. The synagogue was a rose-stone building set on the highest hill, facing toward Jerusalem. To it all the people were flowing, clad in their colorful robes: blue and white, lavender, gold, and rose; they were like the field of flowers into which he and Tamara had gone running ahead of their flocks. The women's perfumes brought back the stirring fragrance of the blossoms.

Inside, though he was not called forth this day to read the Scriptures, he could hear his own voice joyful in the singing. How glorious the Sabbath music; mankind's first song, it was said, was that of Adam on the seventh day, thanking God for his forgiveness. Even the Red Sea had parted on the Sabbath to let the people of Israel pass. And each week did not Yahweh himself celebrate his own creation by resting?

If only Tamara could know and share this joy of discipline and submission. Again it struck him how much she had been deprived. Anxiety mingled with his tenderness. Even now she might be performing some forbidden task. Now and then Jesus glanced up at the women's gallery, trying to visualize Tamara there with his mother and sisters and aunts. Usually Mary, gazing down, was quick to return his smile. But today her face was vacant and still; she didn't seem to see him. Was she thinking of Joseph? he wondered. Or just overtired from last night's feast?

As the day wore on, Jesus' mood plunged. That sense of wonder and excitement, as of some delicious tryst with life, was gone. He became restless after the midday meal. He missed the sheep; he would have liked to walk to the farm to check on them, especially one lamb that had shown signs of scab; it had been rubbing heads with one of Tamara's charges that he feared might be infected. Yet such a long walk was forbidden, nor could he lift a hand to help the creature unless its life was in danger. Rigid followers of the Law argued that even this was a violation, and some, even saving the life of a man. Over the years the rabbis in their zeal had worked out a code prohibiting thirty kinds of activities to steal the happiness from the day.

No games could be played, nor instruments put to the mouth or strummed. He yearned to write to the beloved; it would comfort him to put his thoughts down—one day he would read them to her, one day he would teach *her* to read, as he had taught his mother. But as Jesus went to the cupboard to find his tablet and stylus, Mary came swiftly into the room and frowned. She had always insisted that her children keep a strict Sabbath; strangely far more so than Joseph, who would light a fire, if the house was cold, or occasionally even pick a flower or a piece of fruit. Jesus had often wondered that his mother, who was so merry and casual about many things, should be so stern when it came to the excessive rules that could turn this day of rest and celebration into such a prison.

He thought of going back to the synagogue, where the rabbis and a few doctors of the Law might be found to discuss theological questions, but this too seemed dreary. Finally he lay down on the couch and covered his eyes. The day must simply be endured until the hour when he could pour out his heart to Mary.

Toward late afternoon Leah called him for the evening meal. The sky was still light, birds chirping. His heart began to pound; the Sabbath would soon be over. Tonight the table was smaller, with only Grandmother Timna and Ann and her husband as guests. He prayed the guests would leave early and his sister and brothers go early to bed. Jesus smiled hopefully at his mother, trying to tell her how much he wanted to be alone with her. A curious apprehension was beginning to temper his soaring spirits. To his relief Mary smiled back at him just as the shofar blew, signaling that this day, begun with such delight yet somehow so dismal, was ended. They said the final prayer, finished the final washing of their hands, and it was just as Jesus had wished: Ann and Naboth must go; they would guide their grandmother down the steps.

"Then I will go with you a little way," Jesus found himself saying. Cheerfully they walked together under the stars, down to the carpenter shop and through the passage that led to Timna's quarters. Ann lighted the lamps for her, and Jesus sat awhile with her after the two had gone, listening to her tales of the grandfather he had never known. "How you must have loved each other," he said.

"Yes, oh, yes. We were like your mother and father." She lifted her gracious, wrinkled, kind old face. "Some day, Jesus, I hope you will find that kind of love."

His eyes brightened. He had been holding her hand; now he pressed it to his lips. "Dear Grandmother Timna," he confided, "I have!"

Jesus told her nothing more; he did not want to diminish the importance of first sharing this news with Mary. But to his surprise, he found the house dark when he returned, the roof and garden deserted. He stood for a moment puzzled and troubled, yet somehow relieved. His first bright anticipation was gone; for some reason the ardent word pictures he had so eagerly rehearsed had fled. Tomorrow would probably be better anyway, after Mary had rested. His mother must indeed be very tired to have already slipped off to bed.

It was midmorning the next day when Jesus got back from the farm, where he had gone to see about the sheep. He had risen early and left before anyone else was awake. He could hear the grating sound of the mill just outside the garden door where Mary was grinding barley. There was a haze of chaff in the air, when he strode out to find her, and a toasty smell from the grain in her large earthen bowl.

"Here, let me carry it inside for you," he said. "Let me watch while you work." Fondly he plucked a stray tuft from her hair and bent to kiss her. "I have something important to tell you."

Mary rose, brushing the dust from her hands. "I know." She managed to smile, despite her obvious concern. "I saw it in your face the minute you walked in on Sabbath eve. You have been bursting with it ever since."

"Then why have you fled from me?" he scolded as she followed him into the house. "Why have you given me scarcely a moment to be alone with you?"

Mary drew a deep breath. "I—had to have time to think," she told him after a minute. "I have been trying to prepare myself for—this thing that you have to tell me."

"Then you have already guessed!"

Mary looked up from the small bowl of water where she was crumbling a handful of fermented dough, saved for the bread's rising. "A mother can always sense when a child of hers is in love," she said. "Especially a son." To keep busy, she thought. It helped to keep busy. "I have been afraid of this for a long time, Jesus."

"Afraid?" he gasped, and studied her, bewildered. "But it would have pleased Father so much that I find a wife!" He pulled a stool up to the table. "If only it could have happened while he was alive." He sat watching, dismayed, as she only went on mixing the meal. "You loved my father so much. I should think for his sake you would be glad."

Mary bit her lip. "No," she said in a low pained voice when she had finished her stirring. "Not even for Joseph's sake can I be glad."

Jesus was stunned. Then he wondered why he had not realized this sooner—and prepared for it. Their closeness. Mothers often clung to their firstborn sons. And between him and Mary the closeness was even more than that. It went back, no doubt, to that time of exile and danger when the three of them were alone together—and even after their return to Nazareth, before the others were born. It was no secret in the family, however Mary tried to hide it, that he was special to her in a way no other child could be.

And now that Joseph was gone . . .

"This will not come between us, Mother," he assured her anxiously. "You must live with us. Or, if you wish, we will live with you." He reached out to squeeze her wrist. "How you will love her, and she will love you. You are alike in many ways. Never until I saw her did I think the earth contained anyone as beautiful as you. It is why I have waited so long. My love for Tamara is a tribute to you!"

Mary had gotten out her wooden trough and was vigorously kneading the dough. She looked up, astonished and distressed. "Oh, my darling," she protested, "surely you don't think that I'm worried about myself? Oh, no, no, no, surely you realize *that* has nothing to do with it!"

"Why, then, why?"

Again Mary drew a long difficult breath. "It is simply that this girl can never bring you happiness."

"But she already has," Jesus cried. "Never have I known such happiness!" He made an expansive, beseeching gesture as he rushed on, trying to say all the things he had planned, to convey to her somehow the enchantment and

joy that had swept into his life. But it was futile; his most
eloquent attempts did not sound right. And his mother did
not respond, only continued bending to her task. Still he
must complete the picture, all of it, even that which he
dreaded most. "There is one problem," he admitted finally,
getting up to stride about. "Tamara has not had the oppor-
tunities we have. She—has not been trained to practice her
religion the way you and my father trained us."

Mary glanced up quickly. "Surely she is Hebrew? She
is not a pagan?"

"No, of course not. But life has dealt harshly with her.
She has no parents. She lives with very humble people."

Mary went on with her kneading. "*Am-ha-aretz?*" She
uttered the word calmly, without derision.

"I'm afraid so, Mother. But she is truly devout. She
knows many of the songs and Scriptures. And we can teach
her more. She is so good, so willing—" Jesus halted at the
expression on his mother's face. Not shocked, as he had expected, but akin to the expression she had always worn
whenever he brought her some poor injured creature to be
tended. A look of absolute loving compassion. Her hands
had gone quite still.

"Don't you see, it doesn't matter *who* she is," Mary
said gently, "an *am-ha-aretz* or the daughter of a priest.
Since you love her, I too would love her. I would take her
into my heart and love her as my own daughter, just as I
have loved the women chosen by your brothers. *But you
must not have her, Jesus.*" With the back of one sticky hand,
Mary brushed a lock of hair from her forehead. "You must
not do this to her, my son . . . or to yourself."

"Why?" he pleaded. "In the name of heaven, tell me
why."

"Wait, I must set the bread to rise. Stir the coals for
me."

The fire had almost gone out, he must blow on it. He
added a few dried olive roots. Mary smoothed the mound of
dough in its heavy crock and covered it with a napkin. Holding it against her apron, she carried it to the little bench
beside the oven. Then she washed her hands once more
and rejoined him at the table.

They sat for a time in silence, sipping the mugs of milk she had brought. Carts rattled by on the street below; from the carpenter shop came the familiar droning of saws. Through the open doorway a butterfly drifted to land on the sill, waving its delicate black and gold fans.

"Mother, why?" Jesus demanded. "Why should I not know the joys of love like other men?"

"Because of who you are." Mary was scanning his anguished face. "Surely you know," she echoed the words of John. She sounded incredulous. "You must have always known. I felt there was no need to tell you, since God himself would have put it in your heart. And the words you said when we found you in the Temple—"

Jesus gave a short sardonic laugh. "Many men have believed themselves to be the Messiah, Mother. Yes, and boys, mere boys." He sat for a moment, groping. "True, I felt sure of it then. You know Cousin John, how persuasive he is—John had just declared it in no uncertain terms. But I was only twelve years old," he reminded her, "and more easily impressed. It was my first trip to the Holy City."

Jesus stopped abruptly. The words did not ring true.

"I was dazzled," he reasoned. "Horrified by all the butchery of the sacrifices—and the greed, the waste—but dazzled. And enjoying the attention the scribes and Pharisees were giving me. . . . No, no, it was more than that." Jesus was perspiring; he drew a hand across his wet flushed brow. "It had to be more than that. There were other things. Sensations I have had since childhood. For a long time I thought everyone had them." He was frowning.

"What kind of experiences?"

"Experiences of the mind and soul. That I had lived it all before. Everything that ever happened."

Mary was bent forward, studying him anxiously. "And Bethlehem? Did you have such feelings about Bethlehem?"

"Yes. But you have often told me I was born there, in a cave. I can see it all vividly, the beasts and the fire and the star that shone so brilliantly. And the shepherds who came that night, and later the men on camels—the sages."

"I have never told you these things."

"Then someone—perhaps someone else. It doesn't

matter, they are a part of my memory, but only that. Many people have such feelings: the prophets, the magicians, those very sages. They mean nothing. And the feelings I had in Jerusalem—that I had been there many times before, lived there—I seemed to recognize every street and alley, every court and passage of the Temple. And the things John prophesied for me—" Jesus wiped his brow again. "All this was when I was still a boy. Before I became a man and realized my limitations. I am almost thirty years old," he blurted suddenly, "and I have accomplished nothing! I have no special gifts. I have no power to heal, as you believed. I could not even help my own father when he lay dying."

"You will have that power," Mary said quietly. "And soon. When you yourself are ready, as you said even then."

"But I am *human*, Mother. I am torn, I am tempted!" Jesus plunged his face into his hands. "I love Tamara. I want to lie with her and love her and give her a son."

No, oh, *no*! Mary's heart moaned softly, even as it broke for him. Her composure was shattered. She felt limp, almost ill. In her distraction she noticed details of the room: the fire that was beginning to smoke—it should be stirred; the bread—one of the loaves was lopsided; the butterfly hovering over some honey she had spilled on the table— she must wipe it up. . . . Yet she seemed unable to move, such desolation threatened to overwhelm her.

Had it, then, been all in vain? Or only some cruel joke, some mental aberration on her part? The voice she had heard so clearly, the unutterable presence summoning her, assuring her . . . She thought of all the scandal, the suffering, the waiting—but shining through it all, every moment of sacrifice, was the promise, and the honor: that whatever its terrible cost, out of all Israel he, her son, was to be the One!

Then she was ashamed. Father, forgive me for thinking of myself. I don't matter. Only help me to make him understand. All that really matters is that I make him understand.

"I cannot believe this is the will of God who sent you," she said. "You are to have a different destiny from other men."

"Our rabbis marry," Jesus argued, just as Joseph had.

"Our priests marry. In fact, they must. There is nothing in the covenant God made with Israel that says those who lead us spiritually should be deprived of a woman's love."

"Yes, but you were not born to be merely a leader. You cannot live comfortably as a priest or even a rabbi. Like John, you will have to go forth to proclaim the news. John is preaching it by the Jordan even now, that the Messiah is coming, the kingdom of heaven is at hand."

"John is eccentric. He may very well be mad."

"John is a miracle child and so are you. God does not perform miracles only to produce madmen. It is you John is talking about!"

"How do you know this?" Jesus demanded grimly. His eyes were burning. "Tell me why you are so sure."

Mary returned his gaze, heart racing. Except for Joseph and Elizabeth, she had never spoken of this to anyone, not once in all the years since it began. She wondered if she had the strength or the words to try now.

"Because I bore you out of wedlock," she told him, unflinching, "though I was a virgin betrothed." Mary paused, then plunged on. "A voice spoke to me—it was in that shed at your grandfather's where the ass and the ox are kept. An angel, a presence—something—appeared to me there and a voice out of heaven spoke to me, telling me that I, a virgin, was to bear a son. The very son of God! . . . I was terrified," she said. "I couldn't understand. How could this be? I kept asking, for I had known no man. Not even Joseph."

Jesus was staring at her, astounded.

"How could I explain this to my parents? How could I make them realize Joseph and I had not sinned?" Mary caught her breath, shaken by the memory. The butterfly had landed on her wrist; its wings were folded. She moved a finger carefully to touch their golden arch. "As you began to grow beneath my heart, how could I explain my state to Joseph, my betrothed, who loved me so much?" Mary lifted her eyes to Jesus. "At first even he could not believe my story. Joseph, who raised you as his own son."

For a moment Jesus was too stunned to speak. "What are you saying?" he protested then. "That Joseph was not really my father?" It was as if he had been stabbed. It was as if he must suffer his father's death all over again. Yet another part of him stood watching with acceptance and understanding. "Oh, Mother, why have you withheld this knowledge from me so long?"

"I thought you knew," she said simply. "I thought you must somehow have known. Out of your own deep wisdom. Because of some of the things you have since told me—even today."

Yes, yes, he must have known. A part of him must always have known. Had he not sensed and enacted his own destiny from the beginning of time? Had he not declared this himself with innocent certainty that day on the Temple steps? Where had that blinding clarity gone? Why these contradictions? Why should this hurt so much?

Unashamed, Jesus put his head down and wept.

"Please forgive me." Mary came swiftly around the table to comfort him. "Please don't grieve for your father," she pleaded. "He *was* your father, Jesus, chosen by God himself to love and care for us both. He stood by me through all the gossip and pain, he brought you into the world with his own hands. He protected us on the flight into Egypt and worked for us there—worked so hard for us every day he lived. And he loved you, how he loved you! In some ways he loved you more than the children of his own flesh."

"It is not only my father I grieve for," Jesus said, "but for you too." He reached back across his shoulder to grip her hand. "Both of you—all you must have gone through for my sake."

"We had no choice but to serve God," Mary said. "But the Lord gave us strength, as he will give you strength."

Absently, Mary began wiping up the honey. Gathering courage. The butterfly had vanished. When she finally spoke, her voice was gentle but determined. "You must not marry, Jesus. You were created for a greater love. To serve that love you must go forth alone. You are not as other men."

"Oh, but I am! The One who sent me did not make me a graven image, Mother, would that he had!" Jesus sprang up and strode to the door. He stood looking out upon the garden: Its worn paths. His parents' favorite bench beside the old stone wall. Its patches of vegetables drinking up the sun; its bushes and trees and flowers. "God gave me a body the same as my brothers," he said desperately. "The same as the husband who loved you so much. If I have been given senses like other men—if I can taste that honey or see the beauty of that sky—!" He made a broad gesture and wheeled. "If I can smell the roses out there, or your fresh warm bread rising by the oven—if I can love you, Mother, and weep for my father, why is it strange that I should see the beauty in a woman and want a mate like other men?" His throat was taut; his fists were clenched at his side. "I am not made of wood or stone, I am flesh and blood, I hurt, I long, I yearn!"

Mary couldn't bear it. She ran to him and held him against her breast, tall as he was. "Oh, my darling, I cannot help you. If only I could! I can only try to spare you—yes, and Tamara too."

"We love each other," he said. "I need her and she needs me. Like you, she is innocent, but she too has suffered terribly, Mother, she too has been the victim of pain and shame."

"Then you must not bring more upon her. If you love her you will spare her. It would not be fair to her, Jesus, not fair to any woman to have a husband who could not stay with her, provide a home for her and her children."

Mary's eyes were tragic, fixed upon his face. She spoke in the stern and awful voice of prophecy while tears rolled down her cheeks. "You will be homeless, Jesus. You will have no wife to comfort you, no children, no sons. You will be a wanderer, sometimes hungry, thirsty, and in need. There will be times when you will have no place to lay your head. You will have followers, yes, but in the end you will be rejected and denied."

"Tamara loves me," Jesus cried brokenly. "She would never reject me."

"Don't put her through it, Jesus. Spare her. Don't let the sword plunge through her heart, as I know it will plunge through mine."

Chapter 13

*J*esus was gone when Mary awoke the next morning.

She was not surprised and she tried not to worry, even when James, who volunteered to go to the farm, brought back word from Amos that he was not with the sheep. But when he did not return that night or the following day, she was beset with concern. She knew that her words had created great turmoil within him and she remembered them in fear and anguish, wishing they had been better said. Yet she had no choice but to speak them, since she had put them off for so long. And that too filled her with remorse; if only she had told him sooner, warned him of his fate . . . God, forgive me if I have failed you in this thing. Forgive us, help us—oh, dear Lord, take care of him.

She prayed too for the girl, Tamara, who would be cruelly hurt. She will hate me, she will never understand. Surely Jesus would not have gone off to her without a word. That prospect was too painful to contemplate. No, no, she must not punish herself like this; was it not all in God's hands? She must go on about her work, cooking, washing, mending, trying as best she could to hide her trepidation from the others.

Toward evening of the third day, just as the family was finishing supper, Jesus came wearily up the steps. James spied him first and ran out to confront him. James was still the peacemaker, very sensitive, with a slight, intense, hopeful, affectionate young face. "Oh, my brother, it is so good to see you," he exclaimed as they kissed. "But where have you been? We have all been concerned for your safety."

Jude, the short, brisk, often fractious youngest son, was just behind. "You could have left some message! Our mother has been worried sick."

Jesus regarded them with haggard eyes. He had not eaten or slept. "I thought I had," he said. "On a piece of pottery—at the moment it was all I could find. She must have failed to see it."

It was discovered that their sister, not recognizing what it was, had thrown it out. To compensate, Leah gracefully carried the basin and towels for his washing. Mary stirred the coals to reheat his food.

"You must eat."

"Please, only some bread and a little soup. I can't stay long." Mary was staring at him, stricken. "Forgive me, Mother, but I have been up in the hills. Praying," he told her. "Praying and thinking. Now I must go to her. I must see her again."

"Tonight?" Mary gasped.

"Yes. This cannot wait."

"And what will you tell her?"

"I don't know yet," he said.

Jesus emerged, bathed and shaved, his black curls oiled and shining. He was wearing his best robe. He ate quickly, to the consternation of his brothers, especially Josey and Simon, who had just dropped in, hearing he was home. Josey's strong square aggressive face was furious. "You can't leave again," he demanded through set teeth. He jerked his head in the direction of Mary, dishing up the food. "It's not fair to our mother, going off the way you do so soon after our father's death."

Though less adamant, Simon too was angry. "He's right. Sometimes it seems like you don't care about any of us!"

"As the eldest you should show more responsibility." Josey stormed on, though still trying to keep his voice low. "What kind of example are you setting for the rest of us?"

Despite their caution, Mary had overheard. Carrying more soup, she came to join them. "Leave him alone," she ordered sharply. "He must do what he must do."

She tried to replenish his bowl, but Jesus pushed it

aside and rose. Mary followed him to the door, as usual, carrying his cloak. "Wear this, for the night will be cold. And a lantern," she said anxiously, "you will need a lantern."

He pulled the cloak gratefully around his shoulders but refused the lantern. "The stars are bright and the moon will be out."

"Please ride the donkey, it's a long walk to Cana," she pleaded.

"No, no, it's not far," he said as he kissed her. He held her hard for a moment, as if to draw from her strength. "Pray for me, Mother."

James broke away from a heated debate with his brothers. He had not joined in their berating, and it hurt him to see Jesus setting off so late alone. It must be urgent. For some reason, though Ben was barking frantically, Jesus wasn't even taking his dog. "Wait!" James called, and ran anxiously after him down the steps. "Let me go with you."

Jesus was shaking his head.

"Whatever is troubling you," he offered hopefully, "maybe I could help."

"No, James, this is something I must do by myself."

"But if it is a girl whose hand you seek—" The idea struck James with a pleasant shock. He was right! He could sense it instantly from Jesus' reaction. "Oh, I am so happy for you!" he cried, eyes twinkling. "And even though I'm younger—perhaps, since our father is dead, I could speak for you, I could help persuade her father."

Jesus laughed softly and pressed his arm. "It would not help, not in this case, but I will never forget that you offered."

"Then take Benjy. Listen to him; he wants to go along."

"Ben's tired, he's already walked miles today. And I'm afraid it would not look good to appear on such a mission accompanied by a dog."

"Then it *is* a girl!" James exclaimed triumphantly.

"Yes," Jesus said. "It concerns a girl."

It took longer than Jesus had thought. Though he strode swiftly along the starlit road, the streets of Cana were

deserted when he arrived, only a few scattered lights burning. Her village was a couple of miles to the north, Tamara
had said, a mere settlement along the road to the lake. He
trudged on, wishing he had brought Benjamin, after all.
The road was dark and silent, except for the chorus of insects, clacking and singing. A half-moon had risen and lay
beaming on its back, yet the mountains and thick groves
blocked most of its light.

He was suddenly exhausted; he felt weak and foolish
and uncertain. Yet he must find her. . . . At last he came to
a cluster of houses perched on a bald hillside. All the houses
were dark, although here the moon shone with stark brilliance. Her house would be set apart some distance, she
had told him, in a grove of pines. But he was not sure which
direction. Whom could he ask? To his relief, he heard the
muted clopping of a donkey's hooves approaching and
hailed its fat rider.

"I am looking for the house of a man named Hiram. He
lives with several brothers, I believe."

"And a beautiful niece?" The fat man grinned, showing
broken teeth.

Jesus nodded.

The man twisted about on his beast and pointed. "You
still have a way to go. Turn toward the lake at the second
bend in the road." He was still wearing his dubious grin.
He leaned forward, spoke in confidential tones. "If you're
sure you want to go there?"

"Very sure," Jesus said.

"Well then, good luck. But you'd best carry a stout
stick!" Kicking the donkey, the man trotted off.

Jesus pressed on, determined, and finally knew that he
was near. For from among the ticking, gently swaying pines
that sheltered the small poor house, drifted a fragrance so
poignant and familiar he was shaken. Cassia. The pungent,
faintly spicy scent that sometimes clung to Tamara herself;
she had mentioned that a few of the valuable aromatic trees
also grew there. To his surprise, several lamps still glowed
in the windows. Jesus stood for a moment, trying to quiet
his pounding heart. Then he strode forward, breathing
hard, and knocked on the door.

He had an impression of footsteps within, but no one answered. Jesus waited and knocked again, began to pound. At last the thick drapery was jerked back. A heavy, hairy Goliath of a man peered out, a man so huge he had to crouch. Pale eyes glared suspiciously from under shaggy brows. "Who are you," he growled, "and what do you want?"

Jesus regarded him steadily. "I am Jesus, a carpenter and shepherd from Nazareth," he said. "I have come to see you about your niece."

"She is not here," the man claimed. "She has run away."

For an instant Jesus was alarmed, though he knew better. "That is not true. Please let me come in. I must speak to her. And speak to you about her."

"She is ill!" the man bellowed. "She has swallowed something. I don't know what, but she is dying. Get out of my sight!"

Again he felt the piercing chill of fear. Yet he knew the man was lying. "I don't believe you," Jesus said grimly. "Let me in. Let me see her."

"You have already seen her and touched her as the devil once touched her mother. It is *you* who have made her ill!"

Jesus braced himself; controlling his outrage, he spoke in a voice of authority. "I command you, in the name of the God who created her, bring your niece Tamara to me."

She appeared then behind the enormous man, even smaller than Jesus remembered, in the soft white garment she was wearing, enshrined by the cloud of her hair. "I am here," she said quietly and simply in her low musical voice. "I am not dying, or even ill. Let me pass, my uncle, for this is the friend I have spoken of. I would walk and speak with him a while."

"Your friend?" the man scoffed, and launched into a thunderous tirade. "The man you've been meeting in the hills like a common slut! Beating on the door in the middle of the night—"

"*Stop*," Jesus ordered quietly through the storm of insults. "Don't ever utter such words again."

"He doesn't mean them," Tamara said. "It is only his way." To Jesus' surprise, she stood on tiptoe and kissed her uncle, who seemed to melt under her touch. He was panting, perspiring; now he calmed and wiped his brow. He was like some huge animal whose roar has suddenly failed him.

"Be careful," he pleaded, patting Tamara's arm. "Don't be long." He lifted big mournful eyes to Jesus; the whites were very prominent in his jowled face. "Forgive me—she is very precious to us."

"And to me," Jesus said. "Give us only a little while. I assure you she will come to no harm."

The drapery fell, shutting out the light. They groped for each other's hand. Silent, they walked together a little way down the rustling path to a place where a cassia tree had fallen. They could smell the faintly cinnamon tang of its bark when they sat upon it. Beyond, through the tangle of leaves, they could glimpse the lake sparkling. The moon was higher now, the leaves glistened. There was the steady orchestra of insects and the insistent, throaty calls of mating frogs.

Jesus trembled; it seemed to him incredible that she should actually be here beside him, she who had possessed his dreams for days. It seemed to him an eternity since he had beheld her. He lifted her face in awe and gazed into it a long time. She sat motionless under his touch, eyes closed, as if unable to move. Then she bent to brush her lips across his hand.

"I knew you would come!" she said, with a childlike exultation. "Each night, I bathed and dressed and waited. And no matter how late, I kept the lamps burning. I had to tell them, of course. I had to prepare them. I knew they would take it hard, especially Hiram. I feared he would rage and shout as he did when you came to the door. But I knew you would understand. Thank you for taking it so well." She drew back suddenly, and now it was she who was studying him. "You've changed," she cried softly, puzzled. "You are—different. There is something new about you."

"I love you," he told her with emotion. "I will love you forever. That has not changed." He reached unsteadily into his girdle and brought forth her gift. The poor little stone sparkled like sapphire in the moonlight; he had polished it well and taken it to Cleo to be fashioned. "See, I have kept my promise, I have brought you your ring."

She caught her breath, a little sound of wonder. "My betrothal ring!" Then her face fell. "Oh, but Jesus, I cannot accept it—not yet. Not until you have spoken to my uncles and the arrangements have been made."

"The arrangements? Tamara, my dearest—wait—"

She wasn't listening. He could only sit stricken, as she raced on. "They will not demand much money, for I have nothing to bring. That is not what I worry about—it is the rabbi, the synagogue. I doubt if they would be willing to announce our betrothal in the synagogue."

She halted at Jesus' expression. He looked grave; there were tears in his eyes. "My darling, oh, my darling, you must take the ring now," he urged. "If you cannot wear it on your finger, at least wear it against your heart. For this is only a ring of love"—he bit his lip fiercely; he had to say it— "not a betrothal ring."

"But you said—you declared—you told me—!" Her face had gone pale, bewildered; she was breathing hard. "What are you trying to tell me now?"

"That I cannot marry you, Tamara. Though I love you as I love the God who made us both and gave us this precious time together—I cannot ask you to share what I am destined to endure. I cannot put you through that agony."

"I will live with you anywhere," she said plaintively. "I won't mind being poor, if only we can be together."

"Oh, my love, my one and only love, that is why we can't marry. Because I must go where no woman could follow. Certainly not a wife and children. I will be scorned and spat upon," he warned her. "I will have enemies, I will be shamed. You have been hurt enough. I cannot put you through further hurt and shame."

"Are you crazy?" she gasped. "Are you ill? What are you talking about? Where have you been that you should talk like this? What have you been doing?"

"I have fasted," he said. "I have been in the mountains fasting and praying. Begging for guidance."

"And what has that God of yours told you?" she taunted

in her heartbreak. "That you must not sully yourself with a mere *am-ha-aretz*? A girl who does not march dutifully into the synagogue every week like your mother and sisters, to sit alone in the gallery because nobody will come near her? No, no, I break the Sabbath laws, I feed my uncles meat that has not been properly bled, I don't know all the prayers to worship this God of yours as I should—I am unclean!"

"My darling, he is your God too, who loves you; you must not blaspheme."

She raced on. "A bastard child born out of wedlock, is that it?"

"Tamara, Tamara, please, my little one, listen to me." He held her and caressed her and quieted her against his breast. Then once again he lifted her chin. "Look into my eyes," he pleaded, "and tell me what you see."

"I see Jesus of Nazareth," she sobbed. "I see the one I love."

"You see Jesus of Nazareth, another bastard," he said, "or so the world would call it. You see a man born out of wedlock, though my mother, like yours, was pure."

"Then why?" Tamara begged. "We need each other more than ever. We belong together, we can comfort each other, help each other."

"No. No." Gently he disengaged his arms and rose to stand with his back to her, gazing toward the sea. "I can't, I can't," he said in quiet desperation. "For I am not destined to live as other men. I have known this—it seems I must have always known this, from the time I was a child."

"Then why have you let me love you?"

"Because I have feelings like other men! Because when I saw you every desire in me was awakened. I wanted you. Heaven help me, I wanted you as I never thought I would want a woman." He shuddered. "Then I was made to realize—only these past three days have I realized for sure—it cannot be. Yahweh himself has finally revealed himself to me, that I am the one who must give up his own desires for the world. He himself has sent me for this purpose. It is why I was born to my mother, a virgin, as the prophets predicted."

She was staring at him appalled. Yet awed. Her whole

body went limp. "The *Messiah?*" Her lips formed the words almost without sound. "The Messiah!" She clapped one hand over her mouth, sat gazing at him for a time, shocked and bewildered. "Yes, yes, yes, you are a great and holy man," she marveled at last. "I should have realized. I saw it in your eyes from the beginning. There is a spirit of mystery and goodness in your eyes. It is like—almost as it might be to look into the eyes of God! . . . But, Jesus, if this is true, then it is a great honor," she cried. "I am not worthy to be your wife—no, no, not if this be true. But oh, what an honor: the Savior of Israel!"

"It will be no honor in the end," he told her. "I will be hunted down like a criminal. I will be betrayed, I will be denied, I will die a horrible death." Trembling, he turned back to her.

"I would never be ashamed of you," she cried, "I would never deny you."

But as he reached out for her, she drew quickly away. She was still gazing at him, transfixed. "No, no, I am not worthy, I am afraid of you, you are not the man I thought you were! You are sent from God, you are special, you will reign over all the world, no matter what you say; you will touch people and they will be healed, you will have special powers—"

"Right now I am only a man," he broke in. "Give me just one moment as a man. Kiss me, Tamara. Let me taste at least one moment as a man."

"I love you," she kept sobbing over and over as they kissed. "I love you, I love you!" And suddenly she could not stand it. She was no longer in awe of him or afraid of him, she was possessed only by the terrible fear of losing him. She was wrong about him, he was no god, he was flesh and blood alive with longing, like herself.

"Don't leave me," she heard herself begging, in panic. "Please don't leave me, Jesus, give this up!" She was almost hysterical; she began beating at his breast. "I can't go on without you. I will die without you! Please ask God to spare you, to let you live as my husband. Give this up, whatever it is," she wailed. "Please don't put me away!"

"Put you *away?*" he cried in agony. "You will be a part

of me forever." But she had broken from him. He stood helpless, impotent before her violent sobbing. He could not remember ever seeing anyone cry so wildly as this, not even his mother at the death of Joseph. He could not remember ever hurting anyone like this. And now, with ironic insistence, it began again, the phrase that had come to him on the mountain and given him no peace since: *Heal the hurting. Heal the hurting. You must go forth to help the people who are hurting.*

And his own pain seemed intolerable, the price he must pay to do that work of love too monstrous: that he must first strike this savage blow to hurt his own beloved.

Yet he had no choice. Despite all his protests to Mary, had he ever had a choice? Had not the decision been made for him long ago?

He pulled Tamara to her feet. "Come, your uncles will be angry. We must face them. I must tell them—"

"Tell them what?" She pleaded, trying to stop the tears that still streamed down her face. "What will we tell them?"

It was a time before Jesus could bring himself to answer. The wind rippled the trees—and her hair. He could hear the pine needles dropping, smell the moist fragrance of the earth, and the heady scent of the cassia bark. "That you must marry," he said firmly at last, gripping her arms. "They must find a good husband for you. A man who will love you and care for you the way you deserve. . . . Don't let them keep you from this, my darling. It is your right as a woman. Marry, have children, raise them to love God, train them to keep the commandments. This is best even for your uncles; your life can be an example for them."

Tamara nodded bleakly. Arms about each other, they stumbled back up the path toward the house. Only one lamp burned in the window now. They stood a moment in its shadow, wordless, drained.

The heavy curtain stirred. A voice growled from the doorway, "Tamara, it is late. You have lingered too long."

Tamara caught her throat, choking back any betraying sounds of grief. "In a minute, Uncle Hiram," she called out bravely. She turned blindly back to Jesus. "He's right, it's late—much too late. We must part here."

Jesus dropped his hands, stepped back, fighting tears of his own. "Goodbye, my beloved."

"Jesus!" She held out her arms again and they clung to each other fiercely one last moment.

Jesus lingered, torn, after she had fled inside. What if she needed him? He would go to her yet, speak to her uncles even yet, if she needed him. But only a few sounds came from the house—of voices murmuring, footsteps, a door closed. Then all was silent. And presently the final light in the window went out.

It was quite dark as he started his long walk back to Nazareth.

Chapter 14

It was a bright cool day of spring. John strode into the river rejoicing, shouting as he went, "Repent, repent!"

A raucous flock of crows, disturbed by the noise, thrummed swiftly up from the trees, cawing rudely back. "Repent, repent!" they retorted—or so it seemed. John threw back his shaggy head and laughed. Beautiful things, the crows, their black throats shimmering green and purple in the sun. His first audience of the day, for it was still early; the banks of the Jordan would be crowded by noon.

Right now he was testing the water, seeing how deep and strong the current was here near Bethany after the winter rains. Once last year when he was preaching farther up, a repentant sinner had been swept out of his arms and almost drowned. John, an excellent swimmer, had had to dive for the man and haul him, still panicky and kicking, onto shore. A narrow escape, yet it did not stop the people; it only seemed to heighten their fervor for the vigorous baptist, who could insult them so brashly, and yet was determined to save them.

The trees were mirrored on the water, striping it with their trunks, kissing their own lacy reflections, so green and lovely with little new leaves. The rushes swayed. The water, cold and sparkling, felt marvelous to John's tough hard limbs. He would have hurled himself into it, if he had time, and enjoyed it. He always missed it during the winter months he spent with the Essenes, those stern but wonderful monks who lived at Qumran, a place south of here on the banks of the Dead Sea.

At first they had been skeptical of him, that the son of a

high priest—however sunburned and shaggy after a summer in the wilderness—should come pounding at their door. For theirs was a priestly sect that had years ago rebelled at the excesses of their own priesthood in the Temple, and fled back to the desert. They set themselves apart, took no interest in politics, did not mingle with men, lived solely for the coming of the Messiah. Yet John had overcome them with his wild young enthusiasm and dedication. Literally he had hurled himself at their feet, begging them to take him in. He would wash and cook and clean for them, if only they would let him share their simple life and learn.

He swore total obedience, gave the Community, as they called it, everything he owned: his bracelets and gold rings, the fine linens he had worn to please his mother whenever he returned to Jerusalem. What a joy it was to be unburdened. No more Temple ceremonies, no more polite charming of his mother's friends. Just to pray and fast and study and serve them, these Sons of Light.

They were his kind of people; they ate no meat and would have nothing to do with blood sacrifice; their offerings were fruit, or the freshly ground flour of the golden wheat. When he had finished his period of probation they gave him work in the monastery library, carefully copying the sacred books and manuals. . . . Outside the rain beat down, streaking the walls from a leaky roof; the winds howled, tormenting the Dead Sea and dashing sand against the sills. John's back ached from bending over the scrolls, yet he loved it—the sound of his pen scratching away through the storm, and his rising excitement as he approached the places that must be left blank for the Holy Name. Later another scribe, made pure by ritual ablutions, would be found worthy to inscribe it.

John had never been so happy. A kind of rhythmic bliss supplanted his usual restlessness. His natural ebullience and loquacity were tamed. Here he walked and spoke softly, pacing his cell with his hands behind him in the manner of the monks. He had trimmed his beard and his wild yellow mane. After the sweat and grime of living alone in the wilderness, there was something sublime about being so clean; several times a day he bathed as they did, every inch of his tough hairy flesh, even between his toes.

Yet after three years thus, when the rains stopped and spring burst across the hills in all its sweetness, when birds sang and flowers exploded even on the desert, something burst in John as well. He awoke one night in a cold sweat. He was like a caged animal. He knew his time had come to depart.

The next morning he rushed to tell the abbot, a man with a long skeletal face and that sweet, blank, yet loving look common to those who have lived apart from the world for a long time. The abbot was very disappointed but not surprised. He had sensed John's intense and special qualities from the moment he first arrived, known that one day all John's vigor and passion must again be released.

"What is it that would drive you from us, my son?" he asked.

"The words of Isaiah," John told him, striding excitedly around the narrow room in the old way. "The same words that are heard so often within these walls: 'The voice of one crying in the wilderness, Prepare the way of the Lord, make his paths straight.' I am that voice, Father. I can keep silent no longer. I have to go out now and proclaim the coming of the Lord!"

The abbot stared at him, heart suddenly pounding. He rose abruptly and came to place his bony hands on John's shoulders, fixing him with his pale blue eyes. Was it for this then that John had been sent to their door? *The son of a priest.* "Are you——?" he whispered, his dry lips scarcely able to form the words. "John, tell me, can it be you? Are you the One we have all expected so long?"

"No!" John gasped, shocked. "How can you suggest such a thing?"

"But you are of the line of Aaron. We know our priest is coming—the Messiah, the final and perfect priest."

"Yes, yes, the Messiah is coming. But he will be so much better than I am——" for once John groped for words—"I am not fit to take off his shoes. But he will be no priest."

"No priest? Then who? Why are you so sure?"

John drew a deep breath, thrust out his chin. "Because

he is my cousin," he announced with proud conviction.
"Jesus, of Nazareth!"

"Nazareth?" The old man looked startled, almost
amused. "Why, nobody of any importance ever came from
Nazareth."

"My cousin was born in Bethlehem, as the prophets
predicted. I haven't seen him for several years, yet his message has been burning in my heart—ever since we first met
when both of us were boys. Jesus will soon be thirty, the age
when at last a man's word means something in Israel. He
will soon be ready to reveal himself. I must go out and warn
the multitudes; I must prepare the way."

The abbot had released him reluctantly, for John had
been like a bright breeze blowing through the monastery.
And though it was against their rules and they thought John
mistaken, they had not only welcomed him back to Qumran
each winter, but sometimes on summer nights when,
hoarse and exhausted from his preaching, he came limping
in.

And now, this spring, how good it was to hear his own
voice shouting once again, and to see the crowds beginning
to gather. Word of his preaching had spread. His outrageous
insults, his zeal and fire and incredible charm. This was his
third summer to storm up and down the riverbanks while
the people stood astounded but enthralled. At first only a
trickle of farmers, shepherds, laborers from neighboring
villages. But the ranks quickly swelled to include bankers,
merchants, Sadducees and Pharisees, tax collectors, soldiers. From all over the land they were flocking now, attracted by this wild-eyed man dressed like Elijah, in a
garment of camel's hair, with a leather girdle about his
waist. Listen to him, come see and hear him for yourself—
only a true prophet would dare speak to us like this!

He exulted at his audience, for he was a born actor, like
the Greeks most alive when commanding a stage. But not
for himself all this attention, no, no, only his passion to
warn them of the wrath and the blessing to come. "You scor-
pions, you brood of vipers! Why are you such hypocrites,
you Pharisees? Why do you cheat the windows and steal
bread from the mouths of their children? And you scum,

you tax collectors—!" Though some stalked away in anger, even many of those he condemned so savagely stood shaken and humbled before his scathing attacks.

And when he had scolded and exhorted them for hours, when at last, wearied yet exalted by his own words, he only wanted to hurl himself into the water and swim away, they poured down the banks just as they were, fully dressed, arms outstretched to where he stood, clad only in his loincloth now, his legs tough and hairy, with the Jordan kissing his knees. And he held them with all his fierce young strength, loving them with passion and speaking to them tenderly as he plunged them into the water to be cleansed and forgiven.

Thus had it gone for the past two days. But now, today, John sensed something fresh and new among the people beginning to assemble upon the grassy banks. There was laughter among them, an eagerness he had not sensed before. A number came up to embrace him, followers, disciples, people he had already baptized. There was adoration in their eyes.

"Tell us who you really are," they began to plead. "Come now, admit it, don't be so modest. Surely you are the promised Son of David. You are the Christ!"

"No, no, no," John declared impatiently, half laughing. "How many times do I have to tell you? I am not the son of David you mean. Though he is coming soon to lead you, yes, and to judge you." He shooed them back to their places and began again his energetic march along the water's edge, kicking up little explosions of sand and water as he went. "You idiots, how many times must I repeat? The one who is coming is so much better than I am I'm not fit to touch his shoes!"

"Then who *are* you?" a voice demanded, a burly man perched on a rock. "If you are not the Christ, who are you? Elijah, a prophet?"

"That's right," another voice joined in, a man named Zerah, a tax collector, baptized only yesterday. He sounded dismayed. "Why then do you baptize us?"

"To make you fit to receive him!" John yelled. "To tell you what you must do to be saved. For his winnowing fork will be in his hand to clean the threshing floor; he will gather the wheat into the granary, but the chaff he will burn with unquenchable fire. You, Zerah, take no more than is due you according to the Law. You soldiers out there, rob no one by violence or false accusations, stop intimidating people and complaining about your wages, be thankful with your lot.

"And all of you—I speak to all of you now—if you have two coats, take off one and give it to somebody who has none. And if you have food, share it with those who are hungry. Treat other people the way you want them to treat you. Those are some of the things that the king who is coming will ask of you." John bent over, scooped up some water, and flung it into the air. "*I* baptize you with water," he cried, "but the mightier one who is coming will baptize you with the Holy Spirit and with fire!"

John stopped short, the words suddenly frozen in his throat. His heart had begun to pound. Now it was he who stood transfixed, eyes riveted on the white figure that had appeared among the trees and was making its way through the thickets that led down to the river. That beard, that black curly hair! And the shock of seeing Jesus thus approaching after so long was too much; John put a hand over his eyes as if to shield them from a great light, his knees sagged, he felt faint.

Two young followers rushed up, concerned. "Master, are you all right?"

John nodded and uncovered his eyes. "He has come!" he told them hoarsely, pointing. "See? Over there."

Again John crouched and scooped up handfuls of water, which he hurled joyfully over his face. "I am only the voice crying in the wilderness," he shouted once more, exultant. "Make straight the way of the Lord! As I have said, I can only baptize you like this, with water, but behold the Lamb of God. For he is standing among you even now, the one I have been talking about. Even he, the one whose sandal thongs I am not worthy to untie!"

With that he strode toward Jesus, holding out his arms. "Cousin, oh my cousin," he wept as they embraced. "Why have you come? Why are you here?"

"To be baptized of you," Jesus said simply.

"Baptized of *me*?" John gasped. He drew back, appalled. "No, no, no, I am not fit to touch you. You are the pure and holy one, it is you who should baptize me."

"It must be done." Jesus' face was grave. "I must go down into the water and share the fate of other men."

"But you have no sins to be forgiven!"

"How do you know the secret torments of my heart?" Jesus asked quietly. "How do you know my doubts and my desires? All this must be washed away, John. It will give me strength for what lies ahead, it will give me courage. It must be done," he said. "It is fitting that I fulfill all righteousness." And, as John continued to hesitate, "Let it be now."

So while the crowd watched, astonished, John took his hand and led Jesus into the river; and when they had prayed, John pressed him deep into the cold sparkling water, and pulled him up, gasping like all the others, his white garment clinging to his back, his black curls drenched and dripping. And when together they came up out of the water, the two young disciples of John raced up with towels to help dry him, as they always dried the rest. And from the crowd another young man named Andrew came running, bearing a cloak, for he had taken John's words to heart. "Here, take it, keep it," he urged, his voice choked with emotion. "I don't need it."

And even as the cloak was wrapped about Jesus, the sun broke through a cloud, intensifying his radiance. And a white dove fluttered down to light on his shoulder, while a voice spoke clearly to the little group of men gathered there, though they turned their heads and looked about in bewilderment, trying to see from where it came: "This is my beloved Son, with whom I am well pleased!"

The dove flew ahead of him into the barren mountains, into the rocky wilderness, leading, leading, and he must follow, wet and cold and barefoot though he was.

John had begged him not to go. "I'll dismiss the crowds, they can come back tomorrow. Come to the monastery with me; we can make it by nightfall if we set out now.

Please," he urged, "I want the abbot to meet you, I have told him about you, I want him to see you for himself."

But Jesus was watching the dove that kept circling above him, crooning softly yet on a note of urgency. "Forgive me, John, but it is very important that I go away. I must go into the mountains and be alone for a time."

Jesus turned to him then, and with a shock John saw the deep pain in his eyes. "What is it?" John pleaded. "You must have been hurt, terribly hurt," he whispered. "Come with me, we will rest and eat and talk." John clutched his arm. "Jesus, my cousin, I love you so much, let me help you."

"There is only One who can help me," Jesus said. "I need to fast and pray until I am released."

On the dove flew, up and up, higher over the gorges and canyons and rocks that crouched and reared in grotesque shapes as far as the eye could see. The landscape shimmered in the heat, its tan flanks rising and falling as if all these bizarre creatures were gasping for breath. Eons ago, raked and clawed by some master hand, this earth too had squirmed, erupted, given birth to these monsters that reared up from some nether world. Castled cities . . . faces leering . . . tawny hips heaving . . . giants suckling at fat bursting breasts of sand. . . . This mad and ugly beauty! *Adonai, Adonai, why are you bringing me here?*

His feet were bruised and bleeding, he hungered and thirsted, longed to lie down and rest, and yet on he went, on and on, blindly following the bird whose little white tail flirted and twinkled before him. Was it not enough that he had overcome, walked away from the woman forever, and set out to find the prophet many people believed to be Elijah, who was shouting the way of salvation along the banks of the Jordan? Although Jesus has known from the beginning that it was John.

Was it not enough that John had received him, weeping, and buried him too in the cold bittersweet waters, to wash away his fears and doubts and surely, pray heaven, all desire for the one he could not, must not, have? *Help me, Father, I have submitted; now raise me up equal to fulfilling John's faith in me—and my mother's—and your own!*

He began to shiver, for after one glorious conflagration of scarlet and gold, the sun sank, night was upon him. He came to himself, out of his blind daze, and found he had climbed halfway up a steep mountain. He could no longer see the dove, and he felt suddenly abandoned and desperately alone. He called out to it, making little bird sounds, pleading, hoping to lure it back, but there was no answer, no returning whir of wings. And he realized that this was as it should be. Lord, lead it safely back to its nest to be cuddled against its mate. Suddenly such loneliness beset him as he had never dreamed. Not like this, oh, never had it been like this, not in all those years he had wandered by himself or lain alone under the stars, watching the sheep.

Not until Tamara. . . .

But he must not think of her. He had come here to pray and dedicate his life afresh—but now, right now, he could go no farther, he must lie down and rest. He found a place where a few bushes had burst out of the barren rock. He stretched out, pulling the young man's cloak over him, blessing the youth, for it was soon very cold. The stars were beginning to claim the sky, at first a jeweled scattering, then constellations drenching it with brilliance, while among them bloomed the planets—always huge here in the desert—burning like enormous flowers of fire on the canyon's rim.

The wild things had begun their rhythmic screeching, baying, and howling; two bats sliced overhead, chasing each other with a gritting sound of teeth and black leathery wings. The long glistening body of a snake slithered across his ankles, then another glided after, following it into the rocks. Shuddering, Jesus rolled over, one fist beating the sand, for he sensed their writhing embrace. *Help me, oh, Father, forgive and help me—even the snakes—!*

He reached up to pull a branch down across his face, breathing in the familiar, almost intolerable fragrance of its cold damp leaves. Willing her into existence here, now, as she had been on that last night among the cassias; feeling she must somehow emerge out of the shadows and speak to him, hold him as she had then. Wanting her, driven a little bit mad by the dream of her, the children he might have had from her; the comfort of her food waiting for him in the evening and her love day after day when he was jubilant with his strength, the thrill of his achievements, or distraught and weary with the poor results of his striving. Above all, the comfort, the dear warmth of her lying close against him in the night. Even the bittersweet waters of his baptism could not wash these things away.

Yet as he lay suffering, he thanked God that he had tasted love, if only briefly: sweetly, terribly, as men have tasted love from the beginning of time. For he knew now how desperately men are tempted—need to be tempted, yes, and to yield and be fulfilled, that the race of men and women might go on.

And he knew too, with a tearing and rending of his whole being, that he had no choice but to turn his back upon her and walk away from her, the beloved who had plunged crying into her uncles' house. Not coldly or uncaring, for his heart was torn asunder, but driven by something beyond his comprehension, a force, a power, a compassion for even more than the wailing woman: for the whole world, who seemed to be crying at his feet. The crippled, given pain and humiliation instead of wholeness and pride. The men, given defeat and despair and poverty instead of success. And the children, above all the children, given snakes instead of bread.

That little boy in a house not far from Bethany where he had stopped for a drink of water on this very trip. A humble hut made of tan, bread-colored, loaf-shaped stones that blended deceptively with the snakes that crept inside sometimes, coiling there for warmth. And the child toddled about, whimpering that he was hungry; and the father, reaching for a loaf, had accidentally picked up the reptile instead. The child had screamed; Jesus would hear it forever, that piercing wail, frightening the creature as much as the boy. And the father's anguished, "I wanted to find you a loaf, my son, and I have handed you a snake!"

These scenes riddled his heart that first night in the wilderness after his baptism. He lay in anguish for them, all the confused bungling fathers and the pathetic children hungry for a mouthful of bread. And for all the people so hungry for love. He must help them, he must heal them. He must make them understand that God, the true and loving Father, wants only to feed their every need.

Father, forgive me when I too am hungry. Forgive me if there are times when I too scream.

Forty days he fasted and wandered and prayed and became one with the will of God. No longer lonely, for everything around him became his companions and his friends. Lizards and bats and vultures, the lions that prowled by night, the cougars, the jackals, the hyenas. One by one they crept near to lie down and watch over him, or they appeared, to hover above his head—butterflies, birds, and stars; even the small white dove came circling, followed by her mate and several little ones. Jesus smiled to see them, reached out to touch and caress them before they drifted gently away or simply vanished in a puff of wind.

His lips were parched and cracked, his nose burned scarlet, his empty stomach began to swell. His feet were tough as leather boots, though gouged by thorns. At times he walked without touching the earth, felt himself borne upward on a cloud. The face of Yahweh smiled upon him and murmured over and over, "This is my beloved Son."

Then late one afternoon when he sat weak but blissful, though dreading the night, he was startled to see far below him a spiral of dust rising, and to hear the faint but distinct sound of hoofbeats. Breathless and disbelieving, Jesus realized that a horse and rider were approaching, ascending the steep face of the mountain.

His heart raced. Who but Cleophas could possibly have dared to follow him here?

Jesus sprang up. "Cleo!" he called out in great excitement as horse and rider drew nearer.

"Who?" The rider laughed. With a great rearing and neighing and rattle of stones, the huge jet-black stallion was pulled to a stop.

"I'm sorry, I thought you were someone else!" Jesus said, rubbing his eyes. For this was a much younger and even more handsome man, tall, whip-slim, and very graceful, leaping down from his jeweled saddle. He wore a tight-fitting suit of creamy white silk, embroidered with scarlet and gold. There was a musical chink of golden bracelets from his ankles and his wrists. His blue eyes sparkled, his white teeth flashed, his cheeks were pink as a girl's. A mop of wavy golden hair swept back from his brow to fall glistening about his shoulders. Never had Jesus seen anyone so dazzling. Certainly never a man.

"Forgive me," Jesus gasped, "but what are you doing here?"

"I followed you," the stranger beamed. He was very charming, his voice rich and sweet. He extended a slender hand that blazed with rings. "My name is Lumini. I was in the crowd; I saw you baptized in the Jordan. I don't mind telling you it was the most beautiful, inspiring sight I've ever seen. I didn't want to intrude on your privacy for a time, but I knew I had to find you. And so—here I am!"

"Welcome," Jesus said, almost overcome with surprise and sudden joy. "Though I fear I have nothing to offer you." He looked about, concerned. "There is no food here."

"Don't worry about it. I know, I have brought my own. I have more than enough for us both." He gestured to the bulging saddlebags that were likewise elaborately adorned. "Wine, bread, all that we need. You must join me for supper."

Jesus swallowed, but shook his head. "That's very nice of you, but I'm afraid I can't. I am not yet ready to break my fast."

"I certainly understand. How admirable. Well, if you'll forgive me, I'm very hungry. Would you mind if I brought out my own humble repast and ate?"

"No, no, not at all," Jesus said, though he trembled as he watched his new friend unpack and spread out his feast on a white linen cloth. Bread that looked crusty and newly baked, glossy boiled eggs, crisp brown fish, succulent breasts of chicken, delicate pink slices of lamb, silver dishes of vegetables and sauces, ripe fruit, figs, nuts, sweet cakes, a cruet of red wine. All of it smelling so delicious Jesus' mouth watered, his stomach clenched.

"As you see, I had really hoped you would be my

guest." Lumini smiled regretfully, shaking out his napkin. "Are you sure you won't change your mind?"

Again Jesus shook his head.

"Well, then, I'll proceed. Fortunately—" he chuckled boyishly—"I have a big appetite!"

Perched on a silken cushion, the beautiful youth ate joyfully, although somewhat apologetically, glancing sweetly at Jesus from time to time. "I hope this isn't bothering you," he said, lifting his glass in salute. He gazed at Jesus with anxious affection. "If it is, I will put it away. I can't tell you how much I admire you. I wouldn't want to hurt you or tempt you in any way."

"No, no," said Jesus. "Go ahead."

"When I finish, I will leave if you wish."

"Don't go, you must stay, now that you've come so far!"

"Well, yes, it is a long way back down the mountain, and it will soon be dark." Lumini kicked aside his cushion and sprang up to look across the hills, already in purple shadow.

"It would be foolish, it would be dangerous!" Jesus agreed. "It's much too far to travel after dark." He was trembling, no longer from hunger, but from the awful dread of loneliness that had returned. "You must stay with me."

Lumini tossed back his shining hair. "That's just what I hoped you'd say!" he admitted in mischievous triumph. Gathering up the white linen cloth with all its food and silver dishes, he strode gaily to the ravine and pitched the whole thing over the side. Then, obviously delighted that Jesus was shocked, he ran gaily to the saddlebags and returned with two pallets over his arm. "I came prepared for that too. See, I even brought beds for both of us." He surveyed the rocky ground. "Where do you sleep?"

"Wherever I am," Jesus said. His heart was hammering. He felt curiously uneasy and yet elated. Surely God had sent him this dazzling companion to reward him.

"Amazing!" Lumini looked incredulous but amused. "Well, Jesus, dear friend—if I may call you that?—I'll be happy wherever you are. How about over there? That looks like a good enough place, over by those cassia shrubs."

"Not there," Jesus protested. "Any place but there."

"I'm so sorry," Lumini said softly. "The fragrance? The smell of cassia brings back memories? Love memories?"

"It's something I can't talk about."

"I understand. I know from experience. Certain odors do rouse the emotions. I wish you'd tell me—" He pressed Jesus' arm. "You'd find it helps to share this pain with someone."

"It is something I can never share with anyone," Jesus said grimly. "Not as long as I live."

"Whatever you wish. Look, there is a nice cleft between those overhanging rocks; it's like a cave. Let's go over there."

Jesus followed him, he didn't realize how weak he was; he let Lumini spread out the pallets, a few feet apart, and lay down gratefully. The soft padding was like heaven to his limbs after these weeks on the hard ground. He drowsed almost at once, though the man lay talking half the night, it seemed, about places he had visited: the palaces, the dancing girls, the bazaars. . . .

Beyond the opening the stars danced in the sky, the beasts began their plaintive howling and calling. Several crept to the doorway as if to find him, then slunk swiftly away. Jesus was only vaguely aware of where he was, he only knew he was no longer alone. And later, gradually later, he became aware of a hand holding his. Lumini lay fast asleep. He looked like an angel lying there with the moonlight shining on his face.

When Jesus awoke the next morning he could smell the tang of a crackling fire. His new friend was crouched over its bright blaze, stirring a little pod of gruel. He looked up, beaming. "Sleep well? What a glorious morning! Would you care to share this barley? I've seasoned it with cinnamon and honey, and I have peeled a pomegranate for you."

"Oh, dear, again forgive me," Lumini apologized. "I quite forgot your fasting. I wouldn't want to tempt you, I really admire your willpower. But then I've heard that you are a very special person. I wanted to see you for myself, it's why I came."

He chattered merrily on, so innocent and refreshing in

the sunrise. What an engaging personality he was, and devout as well as considerate. Lumini had been up for hours, he said, and had already washed and prayed. "Go ahead with your worship, it's so important, nothing in life is more important, don't let me interfere."

It troubled Jesus somewhat that again he blithely threw away the remainder of his meal. Yet there was something dashing and grand about even that—to see him standing so boldly on the canyon's rim, with his bright hair blowing, as he watched the small fortune disappear.

"Don't worry." He grinned at Jesus' expression. "The birds won't let it go to waste."

"But the cloth, the dishes!"

"There's plenty more where I come from. It's worse to waste time, life! This glorious scenery. Come on, let's explore it together."

Jesus was enchanted to have such company. Never had he found anyone so joyfully aware of his surroundings, even here. He was proud to lead him about the mountainside, pausing to point, to marvel at the magnificent grotesquery. They laughed, too, for Lumini bubbled over with quips and songs and stories. A spell of sheer foolishness came upon them; they felt young and free, like boys again, dangling their feet from jutting boulders, balancing themselves precariously on the edges of cliffs where a misstep would pitch them to certain death in the wadi below.

Lumini spread his arms like wings, prancing about with a capricious grin. Dimples flashed in his delightful face. "Fly, fly, let us fly!" he cried.

Jesus laughed painfully. "Stop, you'll fall, this is ridiculous!"

"No, it isn't, I'll try it if you will. Don't be afraid, nothing can happen; I hear you're such a favorite in heaven God would send his own angels to bear you up on their hands!"

A strange euphoria had come upon Jesus. His eyes were fixed in fascination on the threat below, his heart was beating fast. Had he not already winged lightly over the rocks these past days, sipped the wind for wine, and drunk the chill elusive milk of the stars? He felt suddenly powerful, immortal, and almost overwhelmed by the urge to prove it. Why not indeed spread out his arms and step forth into the clear blue space above the canyon? Already he seemed to hear a legion of angels gathering, ready to descend, to support him.

He caught himself in time, gave a choked little cry. "It is written, 'You shall not make trial of the Lord, your God!'" he shouted. "Be careful, come back lest you fall yourself." Jesus retreated to a safer place, mopping his brow. "Who ever told you such a thing?"

Laughing, Lumini followed him farther back from the ledge and flung himself down. "It is John's claim," he said. "John the baptizer is telling people incredible things about you. I have heard him. And they believe him; the people themselves are repeating them, beginning to proclaim your wonders."

Jesus regarded him steadily. "Are you a disciple of John's?"

"The man intrigues me. I began to follow him only when I got word of these sayings about you."

"What sayings? What wonders?"

"That you have magical powers." Still twinkling, Lumini's faintly green eyes locked with his own. "I'm not sure if I believe them, although I'd like to. It's why I came. To become your friend. And we are friends now, aren't we? Surely you will give me a demonstration." He inched closer, smiling, eyes still sparkling; his voice was eager. "Show me, right now. I have eaten or thrown away all my bread, I'm hungry, and I know you must be starving. These rocks—" Lumini stroked one with long slender fingers—"see, they look like loaves. Prove that I haven't come in vain—turn them into bread!"

Suddenly Jesus recovered; he threw back his head and laughed. "Man does not live by bread alone, but by love. The love of God and the love of woman and man. Listen," he said, "I have already been tempted beyond your poor powers to tempt me. Do you think I would turn my back on the One who sent me here for *food*?"

"All right then, love. More love than you ever dreamed. Since you put it so bluntly, yes, I've been testing you, because I really adore you, Jesus. And if you're all they claim, it's you I want to follow." Lumini moved even closer, his shining eyes intense. "I don't mind telling you I'm a rich and powerful man. We could do great things together, you and I. Come with me right now! Just as you are. Get on my horse and ride with me to Jerusalem. Never mind how you look," he said, as Jesus shrank back. "We can stop at one of my inns. I'll have my servants bathe you in a golden tub and dress you."

Lumini paused, surveying Jesus critically from head to foot: gaunt, unshaven, and in tatters. With merry, half-mocking affection he yanked at the ragged tunic. "Don't be embarrassed—though frankly I can't understand why anyone as beautiful as you are could let himself get into such a state even to please his God! But never mind, it's time we cleaned you up. I've got an elegant wardrobe that will fit you. Then I'll take you to the Sanhedrin, the high priest, the king himself. Even Herod listens to me; he'll adore you too. He won't try to kill you, or chase you out of Israel, the way his father did."

Jesus gasped. "How do you know about that?"

"It's common knowledge; all the Herods have wanted to destroy any threat to their throne. As, I warn you, if we're not careful, this one will want to kill John too because of you! That's why we've got to win him over. I tell you he'll be crazy about you, he'll shower you with riches. You can give your poor mother anything she wants."

Jesus felt weak and shaken; his head was spinning. He thought of Mary, who had done without so much—if only he could make it up to her, shower her with gifts at last. And John! Dared he endanger John?

"Why do you promise such things? Why should I trust you?"

"Because I have already proved my love for you: by coming to this godforsaken place to keep you company when you were lonely, by offering to share my banquet when you were weak and hungry. By offering right now to share all that I have with you: power, riches and power. And passion! Never mind Jerusalem, look out there—see, beyond this desert lie all the kingdoms of the world. I have been there in the palaces, I know the crowned heads. Sultans, princes, kings, they have given me gifts." He made a flourishing gesture with his jeweled hands. "They have shared their daughters with me, yes, and their sons; they have brought their concubines to my bed, and the loveliest of their wives."

There was a charged silence between them. Both of them were breathing hard. "Such things mean nothing to me," said Jesus then. "For I have known love."

The man before him flinched. *"Love!"* Lumini sneered, no longer the delightful young companion with the merry voice and laughter, the dancing eyes. His face was suddenly beginning to change: the eyes were narrowing, thin and cold as a serpent's; the mouth went down in a cunning half smile. He was gripping Jesus' hand so fiercely the rings bit into his flesh.

"Why do you promise me all this?" Jesus demanded again.

"Because it is mine to give. I will bestow it all on you myself, power, authority, riches, passion—and punish severely any who do not do your bidding."

"And what do you ask in return?"

"Loyalty, that's all. That's not much, is it? The whole world can be yours, I tell you, if you'll just prove you love me in return. That you're willing to serve me."

"Serve you?"

"Fall down and worship me," the man said softly. He was grinning boldly now, unmasked, the last vestige of his beauty gone, his whole countenance revolting and cruel. For several minutes a strange odor, barely detectable, had been coming from him; now suddenly it was strong and ugly, so foul it was almost overpowering.

And Jesus recognized him at last and rose up in rage. "Get you hence, Satan!" he ordered in a loud voice. "For it is written, 'You shall worship the Lord your God, and him only shall you serve!'"

For the first time all morning, Jesus became aware of the horse. It reared up, pawing and screaming, and, with a great thunder of hooves that echoed throughout the canyon, came charging toward the hideous figure before him. With it came a cloud of thick black smoke, which enveloped them both. It hung there for a moment, hot and choking . . . then they were gone. Though the terrible stench lingered.

In another moment a cool wind rose and blew it away. The air was clean and clear once more.

Jesus stood trembling, sweat running down his face. But the spell was broken, he had come to, he was awake and aware now, fully himself once more. He no longer felt even weak or dizzy, but strong with a strength he had never known. And he realized his time of temptation was over. He was ready now to begin his ministry, to call all men to the Father by his own example, all he himself had experienced, and overcome. It was for this he had been preparing, all the days of his growing up and maturing. He must lead them, he must help and heal them, not only their sick and broken bodies but their tormented souls. He must show them that the kingdom of heaven exists right here on earth, if we simply love the Father enough to love each other, and to live by the Father's rules.

Above all, he must save them from the tempter. Through love he must save them. And he must start soon!

Throwing Andrew's cloak over his arm, Jesus started back down the mountain. As he walked he began to sing, for the power of the Spirit filled him, he heard the voice of the Father commending him, and he knew the angels were watching over him.

He knew that his first disciple would be waiting there with John.

ABOUT THE AUTHOR

MARJORIE HOLMES is the author of the highly successful *I've Got to Talk to Somebody, God*; *Lord, Let Me Love*; and a host of other books, novels, and magazine articles. The *New York Times* described her as "an American phenomenon," and the *Washington Post* as "the housewives' patron saint." For twenty-five years her column LOVE AND LAUGHTER was a popular feature of the *Washington Star*. She also wrote the column A WOMAN'S CONVERSATIONS WITH GOD for *Woman's Day* magazine. She has taught writing courses at the University of Maryland, Catholic University, and Georgetown—all in the area of Washington, D.C. Marjorie Holmes was born in Storm Lake, Iowa, where she attended Buena Vista College, before graduating from Iowa's Cornell College. She has traveled widely, visiting Israel a number of times to do research for her novels. She is the mother of four grown children. After the death of her first husband she married Dr. George Schmieler, a physician from suburban Pittsburgh, where she now lives.

Romantic Favorites

Eugenia Price

☐ 24480	MARGARET'S STORY	$3.95
☐ 25618	BELOVED INVADER	$3.95
☐ 26362	MARIA	$4.50
☐ 25017	NEW MOON RISING	$3.95
☐ 24137	LIGHTHOUSE	$3.95

Grace Livingston Hill

☐ 24736	AN UNWILLING GUEST	$2.50
☐ 24799	GIRL FROM MONTANA	$2.50
☐ 26364	A DAILY RATE	$2.75
☐ 24981	THE STORY OF A WHIM	$2.50
☐ 26389	ACCORDING TO THE PATTERN	$2.75
☐ 25253	IN THE WAY	$2.95
☐ 25806	LO, MICHAEL	$2.95
☐ 25930	THE WITNESS	$2.95
☐ 26104	THE CITY OF FIRE	$2.95

Buy these books at your local bookstore or use this handy coupon for ordering:

Bantam Books, Inc., Dept. PL, 414 East Golf Road, Des Plaines, Ill. 60016

Please send me the books I have checked above. I am enclosing $_____ (please add $1.50 to cover postage and handling.) Send check or money order—no cash or C.O.D.s please.

Mr/Ms _____

Address _____

City/State _____ Zip _____

PL—12/86

Please allow four to six weeks for delivery. This offer expires 5/87. Prices and availability subject to change without notice.

HEARTWARMING BOOKS
OF
FAITH AND INSPIRATION

Charles Swindoll

☐ 25923	STRENGTHENING YOUR GRIP	$3.50
☐ 23615	HAND ME ANOTHER BRICK	$2.95
☐ 25394	THREE STEPS FORWARD TWO STEPS BACK	$3.50
☐ 24570	YOU AND YOUR CHILD	$2.95

Robert Schuller

☐ 25093	POSITIVE PRAYERS FOR POWER-FILLED LIVING	$3.50
☐ 25222	REACH OUT FOR NEW LIFE	$3.50
☐ 24704	TOUGH-MINDED FAITH FOR TENDER-HEARTED PEOPLE	$3.95
☐ 24245	TOUGH TIMES NEVER LAST BUT TOUGH PEOPLE DO!	$3.95

Og Mandino

☐ 24139	CHRIST COMMISSION	$3.50
☐ 23559	GIFT OF ACABAR	$2.95
☐ 23479	THE GREATEST MIRACLE IN THE WORLD	$2.95
☐ 23472	THE GREATEST SALESMAN IN THE WORLD	$2.95
☐ 26545	THE GREATEST SECRET IN THE WORLD	$3.50
☐ 24220	GREATEST SUCCESS IN THE WORLD	$2.95

By the year 2000, 2 out of 3 Americans could be illiterate.

It's true.

Today, 75 million adults... about one American in three, can't read adequately. And by the year 2000, U.S. News & World Report envisions an America with a literacy rate of only 30%.

Before that America comes to be, you can stop it... by joining the fight against illiteracy today.

Call the Coalition for Literacy at toll-free **1-800-228-8813** and volunteer.

Volunteer Against Illiteracy. The only degree you need is a degree of caring.

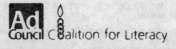